REACHING FOR THE BEAUFORT SEA

. . . .

AN AUTOBIOGRAPHY

Al Purdy

Edited by Alex Widen

HARBOUR PUBLISHING
Madeira Park, British Columbia

HARBOUR PUBLISHING
P.O. Box 219
Madeira Park, BC Canada V0N 2H0

Cover photograph by Richard Harrington
All photographs pages 281–290 are from the author's own collection.
Epigraph from ''Northwest Passage'' © Estate of Stan Rogers. Used with permission.

Canadian Cataloguing in Publication Data

Purdy, Al, 1918–
   Reaching for the Beaufort Sea

ISBN 1-55017-088-0

   1. Purdy, Al, 1918– —Biography.   2. Poets, Canadian (English) —20th century—Biography.*
I. Title.
PS8531.U73Z53 1993   C811'.54   C93-091643-3
PR9199.3.P87Z475 1993

ACKNOWLEDGEMENTS

Books in Canada
Poetry Canada Review
The Second MacMillan Anthology
Quarry Magazine

Special thanks to Avie Bennett of McClelland & Stewart for permission to include the poems.

Printed in Canada

To the memory of Stan Rogers

Ah, for just one time, I would take the Northwest Passage,
To find the hand of Franklin reaching for the Beaufort Sea,
Tracing one warm line through a land so wide and savage
And make a Northwest Passage to the sea.

STAN ROGERS

Contents

CHAPTER ONE

. . . .

MORNING AND IT'S SUMMER

The unborn child of Mrs. Eleanor Louisa Purdy rested comfortably inside his mother, in timeless calm and measureless peace—then all hell broke loose. People scurried back and forth frantically, the noise a little muffled by insulation. There was a kind of electric hum of tension pervading things outside. Loud noises; breaking glass; men shouting and women screaming.

It was all very puzzling. The child had no idea what all the fuss was about. And handicapped by ignorance of a strange language, surrounded by tubes and valves and pumps, he had no way of finding out. It must have been very frustrating.

The British Chemical Company's munitions plant, just north of Trenton, had exploded, then exploded again and again. Wave after wave of explosions buffeted the air, continuing through the night following Thanksgiving Day in October, 1918. During a grey, smoke-filled morning, fire ravaged what was left of the factory. Every window in the nearby town was shattered; many people fled in terror for their lives—on foot and by horse and automobile.

On December 30, two-and-a-half months later, the child was born. Me, of course. The explosions no doubt accounting for any oddity and eccentricity in my character.

. . . . .

Trenton in the 1920s was a town of about six thousand people, east and west divided by the Trent River, united again by the downtown bridge.

Settled by United Empire Loyalists at the beginning of the nineteenth century, it has few claims to distinction. An over-sized molehill in the north-west is called Mount Pelion. The "mountain" boasts an ancient cannon at its crest, said to have been used to fight Indians in the early days. And, of course, the river. Not "painted a deep-sea blue or sea-shore green," but tar black. With marvellous floating rainbows on the surface sometimes, legacy of the creosote works upriver. Also a children's playground, especially in sleighbell winter.

Think back to that time and wonder: how has time changed things? Sixty years ago, down the wrong end of memory's telescope through which I'm peering myopically, how was Trenton different then from any other town today? I mean apart from automobiles, pumpmakers and blacksmiths. A black and white, almost colourless town, in which dark male clothing made them seem shadowy, and women only marginally brighter. Store signs painted, not neon. Time passing with such slowness I thought I would never grow. It's like the difference between horehound candy and Coca Cola; and spicy horehound candy is unknown today.

. . . . .

When electricity came to our street in Trenton, around 1921 or '22, I was three or four years old. In late evening when the lights flashed on for the first time, people rushed outside to see what the streetlights looked like, each with an aureole of moths and flying insects. And there was a feeling of foaming lakes and rivers coming from far away, while the overhead wires hummed urgently.

Some people left their house lights burning all night, just for the novelty, and being so pleased at not having to use messy oil lamps and candles any longer. And the birds on our street kept on singing, probably thinking this new kind of daylight would never end, feeling hoarse and exasperated. Of course I was too young to remember all this, only a little; but my mother told me the rest.

When my father died and we moved from the Wooler farm into the red brick house in Trenton in 1921, it was already more than a hundred years old. The floors were sagging upstairs and down, as if the house was tired from all those years and couldn't stand properly upright any longer. Some of the doors wouldn't open or close without a struggle. At night, when I was awake and listening, small noises came from everywhere: the sound of old floor joists, boards and square-headed nails talking together.

The wooden barn was red as well, a cobwebby place of shadows that filled most of our backyard. There was still hay in dusty corners, and iron rings on walls where horses once had their stalls. In fact, our house and barn were probably part of an old farm. When you closed your eyes and made all the surrounding houses disappear, there was nothing left in your mind but green grass and flowering buckwheat, and a hum of bees filled the air.

McLean's pump works stood just across the street from the house. The rusty tin-covered building was too small to be called a factory, but too large for a workshop. Old McLean, sandy-haired, sour-faced and bad-tempered, made wooden pumps for farmer's wells. The pump-works hummed with belts and pulleys, whirring lathes in pine-scented gloom, shavings piled deep on the floor, small boys crowding the doorway, deeply interested in yellow-bearded McLean and the small men he made from wood.

That's what they looked like, small men. When chisels and lathes had done their work, and black metal bands encircled their four-foot bodies to prevent splitting, with an iron mouth and long wooden pump handle attached, then by an act of magic a small man was created. Other men might be doctors and lawyers and storekeepers, but the men McLean brought to life spent their days lifting water up into the sunlight. It was cold and sweet. It tasted of deep springs and wells and rivers under the earth.

. . . . .

I was about three years old. And still retain this almost mythical memory of an incident that happened then. I used the toilet, then called for my mother to button me up again, since the flaps and buttons were a complete mystery. She wasn't there. I wandered downstairs and out onto Front street with short pants dangling around my knees, calling "Mother, Mother, Mo-ther!" She wasn't there either.

A farmer and his wife were passing by in their horse-drawn wagon, on the way to market with a load of farm produce. They heard me bawling, stopped, and tried to find my mother. But she wasn't in sight or sound.

Speculating that my mother might have gone to market herself, they took me onto their wagon. We clopped off to market while the farm-wife tried to comfort me with soothing words. But I was not to be comforted so easily.

The market was jammed with people. Farm wagons piled with bright orange pumpkins, yellow onions and brown potatoes were backed up at the market square. Puppies in cages awaited buyers. Chickens squawked in other cages. Some were dead and stripped clean of feathers, wearing bloody bandages where their heads had been. A big blue policeman with shining buttons strolled through the mob of townspeople: the Trenton market square also housed the police station.

It was terrifying. I squirmed out of the farm-wife's grasp, dashing into a clotted mixture of vegetables and people, calling "Mother, Mother!"

All I could see was legs legs legs, the bottom halves of people without any heads. Maybe they had no heads, which might have been cut off like the dead naked chickens. I screamed and ran.

Then I was surrounded, in the middle of a circle. People with potato heads and potato eyes were looking down at me. People with pumpkin heads and pumpkin eyes, onion heads and onion eyes. The live chickens squawked, the dead ones swayed where they hung on cords by their feet. A tremendous wind roared through my own head, a sound like the end of the world.

I didn't, couldn't think. But I knew. I was all my other selves. For the first of many future times, you're in a situation which you don't know how is going to end. Whatever action you take might make it better—or worse. The temptation is to stand perfectly still, close your eyes, don't even think, because an unknown something might notice the flashing lights inside your mind. If you moved. If you talked. If you didn't close the shutters in your head, while the alarm bells somewhere rang and rang. Which is sheer terror.

That is the memory, simple enough to explain and rationalize as you grow older. How my mother appeared and I was comforted. How the noises stopped. And so did terror. It was ended. But the memory doesn't end. It stays at the beginning of memory, hovering on the edge of consciousness, where the beasts with onion heads may still be waiting.

. . . . .

At the bakery a block away , I hung around to smell the bread baking, and played with the little girl who lived there. The B.W. Powers coal sheds filled nearly a whole block on the river side of our street. I watched great teams of dray horses struggling out of the sheds, their wagons loaded with canvas bags of coal, delivered by black-faced sweating men to the town stoves and furnaces.

On Saturday market days the "leaners" leaned against the Gilbert Hotel, watching people go by on the street. Their faces are now only a vague blur in my mind. But even as a child they provided me with an heroic example of uselessness, and they are still dear to my heart.

REACHING FOR THE BEAUFORT SEA

BOOKS BY AL PURDY

Poetry:

The Enchanted Echo (1944)
Pressed on Sand (1955)
Emu, Remember! (1956)
The Crafte So Long to Lerne (1959)
The Blur in Between: Poems 1960–61 (1962)
Poems for All the Annettes (1962)
The Cariboo Horses (1965)
North of Summer: Poems from Baffin Island (1967)
Wild Grape Wine (1968)
Love in a Burning Building (1970)
The Quest for Ouzo (1971)
Hiroshima Poems (1972)
Selected Poems (1972)
On the Bearpaw Sea (1973)
Sex and Death (1973)
In Search of Owen Roblin (1974)
The Poems of Al Purdy: A New Canadian Library Selection (1976)
Sundance at Dusk (1976)
A Handful of Earth (1977)
At Marsport Drugstore (1977)
Moths in the Iron Curtain (1977)
No Second Spring (1977)
Being Alive: Poems 1958–78 (1978)
The Stone Bird (1981)
Birdwatching at the Equator: The Galapagos Islands (1982)
Bursting into Song: An Al Purdy Ominibus (1982)
Piling Blood (1984)
The Collected Poems of Al Purdy (1986)
The Woman on the Shore (1990)

Editor:

The New Romans: Candid Canadian Opinions of the US (1968)
Fifteen Winds: A Selection of Modern Canadian Poems (1969)
Milton Acorn, *I've Tasted My Blood: Poems of 1956–1968* (1969)
Storm Warning: The New Canadian Poets (1971)
Storm Warning 2: The New Canadian Poets (1976)
Wood Mountain Poems (1976)

Other:

No Other Country (prose, 1977)
The Bukowski / Purdy Letters 1964–1974: A Decade of Dialogue (with Charles Bukowski, 1983)
Morning and It's Summer: A Memoir (1983)
The George Woodcock–Al Purdy Letters (edited by George Galt, 1987)
A Splinter in the Heart (novel, 1990)
Cougar Hunter (essay on Roderick Haig-Brown, 1993)
Margaret Laurence–Al Purdy: A Friendship in Letters (1993)

At Simmon's Drug Store, at the corner of Front and Dundas, the town's two main streets, bottles of red, blue and green coloured water with lights behind them shone from the store windows. When I owned a nickel or rare dime, I bought horehound candy and gazed longingly at the big red *Chums* books from England displayed there before Christmas every year.

Reddick's Sash & Door factory across Front Street overlooked the Trent River. Lumber and heavy planks were piled in sheds where thick-bodied willows leaned over the water, their red roots waving under the surface like a drowned girl's hair. I went there to be alone, sitting on the sweet-smelling lumber, trying to get used to being alive. At that early time of my life, five, six and seven years old, I still had the feeling of belonging somewhere else, having lately arrived without any explanations given. Even the colours of things, that later became so familiar, gave rise to questions in my mind. Aware of it for the first time, red was a phenomena. As also green, blue, yellow and orange. I wondered: are black and white things dead? And only coloured things alive?

I was a stranger in that world. Other people acted in such a way as would allow them to be comfortable and at ease while getting used to human existence. Some learned very quickly, others haven't even now. Some part of me still remains a child: sitting on a pile of lumber behind Reddick's Sash & Door factory in 1924, trying to explain to myself how I got here and what I'm going to do about it .

Overhead, a bird goes "Wow-ee! Wow-ee!" among willow leaves that gleam and gleam, having trapped the sun a million times in three-inch strips of green. Then another bird, one that sounds like a medieval musical instrument which I've never heard played. It is enough to hear them for this moment, to feel the mind stop thinking and join the mindlessness of red willow roots and mud of the blue-black river.

Later, days later or only hours, lying on my back in deep grass, watching clouds drifting towards the world's edge. And adjust their shapes slightly with my mind, so that they became altered into fat faces, thin faces, or the body of someone you know. Grandfather, for instance, called "Ol Rid" by his friends.

"Old Nick" my mother would probably have called him, since he had lived with us shortly after we moved to Trenton from the farm. Grandfather chewed tobacco, drank whiskey, was personally careless and untidy of dress, used a few cusswords at judicious moments, and played cards with other ancients (he was about eighty in 1920) at a floating poker game in downtown Trenton. "Floating" meaning that the location of the game shifted whenever public or private criticism became strong enough to make them change the venue.

Grandfather's unregenerate character, and my mother's religious one, forced him out of the house shortly after his arrival. He rented a long narrow room, resembling a bowling alley, over a drygoods store downtown, where poker flourished and chewing tobacco decorated the greasy floors whenever it missed the spittoons.

I visited him there as often as I could, with the feeling of being slightly wicked. My mother permitted these visits, but I think she felt suspicious that he was corrupting me somehow. And I listened to his stories when he wanted to tell them, which wasn't very often, for he was a taciturn old man with cold, watery blue eyes and a look of calm ferocity.

Grandfather was slightly over six feet tall. He weighed 260 pounds. His nose was a parrot's beak; his face had the look of youth, or remnant of youth—not of young and carefree days in the past, but the bullmoose time of being a lumberjack and backwoods wrestler, barnraiser and don't-give-a-damn-about-anything stud and hellraiser. He was.

Grandfather tolerated me. And all the time something smoldered and burned inside him which I felt too, something out of the far-distant past. He was eighty years back of me in time, and seemed less a relative than a queer aging animal from the forests where other animals had avoided him. My father had been fifty-eight when I was born, and my mother had been forty. My own connection with these people seemed many generations distant. All the world was old, this very world that was closest to me.

That ferocity, that smoldering and burning self, concealed or half-concealed in rotting flesh! His talk about wrestling the woods bully: and no doubt he was a bully himself, although that never occurred to me. Barn-raising and booze, and "I wanted to get into her pants." Nothing softened or euphemized for me, he said what he thought and felt. Death was "I'll turn up my toes," and "You don't dast stop—" Or everything would fall down.

I pictured (later, of course) those 260 pounds of gaseous body and fatty muscles back at Canadian Confederation in 1867, when it was trim and sleek as a wolf, when it was young, but always having foretraces of being an old man living over a drygoods store in Trenton. The stench of stale food around him, dirty dishes in the sink, most of his friends dead: yet he exhaled power. And I am not mistaken.

I couldn't imagine him ever being defeated, physically humbled, despite his age. When I walked with him to Tripp's Pool Room, holding onto his hand at age five, his great flat feet beating onto the concrete sidewalk towards earth beneath, I felt a thrill of pride. And partook of that power just by being with him. Myself a child, so weak and fearful of the dark, but joined to this strength extending back in time.

Ol Rid, in his late eighties, with a heavy walking stick: the scarcely waning strength and huge body carried with it all the weight and majesty of the darkness I feared so much. Not just a fading physical power either. It was an aura, a feeling, even a rightness. I felt it like mental calories, infused through all my senses. And grew stronger inside this casual gift of knowing. And it was a casual gift from him, for it never occurred to him that he was giving. Perhaps I was too. While my mother worried.

> Not now boy not now
> some other time I'll tell ya
> what it was like
> the way it was
> without no streets
> or names of places here
> nothin but moonlight boy
> nothin but woods
>
> Why ain't there woods no more?
> I lived in the trees an
> how far was anywhere was
> as far as the trees went
> ceptin cities
>   an I never went
>
> They put a road there
> where the trees was
> an a girl on the road
> in a blue dress
> an given a place to go
> from I went
> into the woods with her

it bein the best way
to go an never get there

Walk in the woods and not get lost
wherever the woods go
a house in the way
a wall in the way
a stone in the way
that got there quick as hell
an a man shouting Stop
but you don't dast stop
or everything would fall down
You low it's time boy
when you can't tell anyone
when there ain't none to tell
about whatever it was I was sayin
what I was talkin about
what I was thinkin of—?

—*My Grandfather Talking—30 Years Ago* (1965)

Campbell's Tombstone Works was just next door, with dozens of red, black and green granite tombstones, crated and uncrated, arriving there from all over the world. Every day but Sunday chisels pounded at stone. The names and dates of dead men and dead women were carved in granite, or those of living people anticipating their own demise. Later on, compressed air powered the chisels, and later still, sandblasting operations were installed. With that last innovation, choking clouds of stone dust floated inside and outside the building, "a pillar of cloud by day."

In moonlight, the tombstones next door were like a small cemetery; granite and marble seemed to attract a silver light around them. But I was never afraid for some reason, despite being terrified of darkness. Perhaps it was the familiarity of the headstones. And there were no human bodies buried beneath, no ghosts of the dead haunting our neighbourhood. It may have been that the noise of steel chisels and the roar of sandblasting kept them away. No ghost could stand such noise.

Bernard Campbell was my own age, and we played together, along with Jack Clegg, a distant cousin. My mother and Mrs. Campbell visited back and forth. At age five or thereabouts, I owned a little wooden wagon with rubber wheels, and pedalled it along the sidewalks. Model A Fords were becoming plentiful at the time; the Campbells owned one. Scattered around in their garage were miscellaneous tools and junk that accumulates in such places. Also six or eight sparkplugs. When I wandered into the garage, I knew that sparkplugs had something to do with making Ford cars travel the roads, but not exactly how. And if they did that for automobiles, why not for my wagon? I installed them along the wagon railing, thinking that I now possessed something the grown-ups had, something to astonish everyone with the additional speed I could achieve.

Of course the sparkplugs didn't add any speed to my wagon whatever. I left them in the wagon that night. Next day they were gone. I was slightly indignant and went to look for them again in the Campbell garage. Sure enough, my sparkplugs sat on the window ledge in a shining row. Maybe I hadn't installed them correctly. The little gleaming bits of porcelain and steel must have a secret, some magical power that would make things go fast, faster and fastest. I intended to find out what it was. Maybe if I put them under my pillow when I went to bed at night, like you did with a tooth when you lost one, then made a wish . . .

Something dark came into the garage from outside. The red-faced Campbell called Arnold loomed over me. "You little thief!," he said. "You little thief!" He picked me up with one arm, so that I swung upside down and dangled there. He carried me in front of the tombstone works next to the street, tied me with thick hempen ropes to the block and tackle hook, used to lift tombstones from one place to another.

I bawled and caterwauled for my mother. As it happened, the ropes were tied loosely enough for me to have slipped out of them, but some part of my mind knew that escape would solve nothing. All the Campbells came out of their shop and house to look at me accusingly. "Thief," they said. "Thief!" My mother heard the racket after a few minutes, and came over to secure my release. "Don't you think he should be punished for being a thief?" the Campbells asked her. "Yes," she said, "and I should have the opportunity to punish my own son." I agreed with her, of course.

When grade school age arrived, and secondary school later, Bernard Campbell turned out to be the smartest kid for blocks around. Perhaps in the whole town of Trenton. His marks were often the highest in his class, my class, any class. Eventually, a scholarship to university was mentioned. And for all those years, Mrs. Campbell arrived to inform my mother of her son's triumphs. These visits occurred fairly often, and sometimes I would listen behind curtains or door.

"Bernard topped his class again this week," said Mrs. Campbell. "Isn't that nice?" My mother agreed that it was nice, after which ensued a long silence from Mrs. Campbell. A silence that might be construed to mean: *Why isn't your son as smart as Bernard? In fact, your son is just plain stupid.* There was no possible answer to these thoughtful statements, since they were unspoken. But there was a faint sizzling in the air at times.

· · · · ·

The calendar moves forward then backwards. I have a memory so frail that any additional effort to add details might break a thread to the past. Two small boys are standing, looking at each other, both are seven years old. Both feel terrible, with tears not far away. The other kid's name is Jack Corson. He has been accused of stealing at school, and is unable to defend his innocence to the satisfaction of the school authorities. In fact, he may be guilty. That doesn't matter. The important thing is that we both feel so badly. The Corson family is disgraced. Now they intend to move to another town.

It was like dying. We loved each other. Both felt what the other felt. All of human existence had narrowed down to two boys feeling an inexpressible sorrow for which there was no outlet, no beginning or end. Time, of course, covers everything with a cynical or sentimental overlay, but time had stopped for us at this exact moment.

We never did see each other again.

· · · · ·

From the age of two until perhaps ten or twelve, I was always conscious of living in a land of giants. The child me was anywhere from two to four feet tall during those ages, and being confronted continually with enigmatic doorknobs high over my head and difficult to open, kitchen and bathroom sinks made for towering monsters, winter snow piled into great chalk cliffs making mountain climbing equipment necessary to scale them. And always, when you talked to an adult, or were talked at, you'd be gazing just above or below a belt buckle, somebody's waistline, either fat or thin.

Adults talking to children don't address them directly very often, acting as if they were some kind of object about to be disposed of. Ada Kemp, my mother's old girlhood friend, used to look at my mother and say: "Alfred, (I hated that first name), I think you should be helping your mother, doing more things around the house." And her bony face convulsed a little as if she had a bad stomach ache , but controlled it heroically. My mother would make a mild rejoinder, for she was a mild person despite the wildfire of religion raging in her veins. Sometimes she made me acutely uncomfortable, as if she wanted something from me, and yet took my response for granted. But I lived on different levels from hers.

If you were climbing a tree or hiding from the calling giants, small size was a positive advantage. The big chestnut tree in our driveway provided a leafy perch for hours; climbing to the slender topmost branches among flowery spring lanterns was as close to the sun as I could reach. Sometimes shaking the tree vigorously, sending a shower of prickly chestnut burrs tumbling down on the heads of the people beneath. That was very helpful for my Lilliputian complex.

. . . . .

The darkness was worst of all. It was peopled with ghosts, goblins and dead men with their throats cut and blood pouring from wounds. All these were-creatures of horror had once been living, some had their blood drained out by vampires, whether animal or human. They often had gruesome physical deformities, hunch backs, black flattened nostrils, twisted faces, insane minds. Children talked about these beings and their habits with hushed voices, collecting a pool of information about them. Whatever you knew about horror might be useful for protective purposes. All these discussions secretive and unknown to adults. In fact, adults were sometimes even listed in the catalogue of demons.

Sometime around 1925, an officer of the Trenton police force had died violently, from what reason I can't remember. He was a young man named Brown. On the night his body was laid out in a coffin on Division Street two blocks away, Jack Clegg and I had managed to evade the bedtime-calling voices, and were still playing in the streets.

It was a warm summer evening. We wandered to the death house, which had a funeral wreath hanging from the door that was slightly ajar. We could see the shape of a coffin through the curtains of the dimly lighted front room. One of us said, "You go in, I'll wait here and keep watch." One of us said, "I dare you!" And the other said, "No you don't, I double dare *you!*" Unwilling to back down, both of us sneaked through the open door, but cautiously, ready to run if the corpse made any movement.

The coffin and waxen face of Constable Brown dominated the room, which was piled with flowers. They gave off a sick smell, advance notice of their own decay. The dead man's face had no expression, bore no marks of the violence that had killed him; the body lay there in a kind of unnatural repose, hands folded across the breast, in full policeman's uniform with glittering metal buttons.

It was quite different from finding the body of a dead cat or dog in the bushes where someone had thrown it. And brought to mind a fear that death might even visit someone I was close to, my mother, Uncle Wilfred, or even Grandfather. For this dead man was a symbol of authority and strength, who ought to have been safe from that other presence which was also inside the room.

We were uneasy and left quickly. There was no fear of the body itself, only from a fresh personal experience with something that had only been talked about among children before. Confirmed in that pale face there was something that walked abroad on the streets and roads, had no heartbeat nor specific shape, and yet possessed a form of reality, was in being, was a thing. It was there in that room with the body of Constable Brown, and is not certainly absent among these words which I am writing now.

. . . . .

Living a block away on our street, another boy. At Merker's Junkyard, where trucks loaded with scrap iron, old newspapers and magazines rumbled onto a weigh scale, their cargoes joining jagged mountains of junk. His name: Jacob Merker. And Jacob was a terrible liar. Bernard Campbell, Jack Clegg and I gathered around him in a semicircle, all three of us spellbound and listening. Jacob told the story of his adventures out west among the Indians, when he was a cowboy working on a cattle ranch. His face dark, clenched into a grimace, with flashing hypnotic eyes, about eight years old. When he crawled through the grass on hands and knees, in Indian country, stripped to the waist and wearing buckskin britches, I was with him too, moving when he did and stopping when he stopped, my nerves tingling, adrenalin bubbling.

This was a truth of life. I crawled through prairie grass on hands and knees, knife gritted and sour between my teeth, cutting my tongue just enough for me to taste my own blood. That little string of sound whispering in my brain? Was that Jacob, or my own thoughts telling me that Black Eagle was waiting? Black Eagle, most formidable warrior of the Cree nation, he of the livid forehead scar who killed enemies with his teeth or slashed up their guts—that man was waiting for me beyond this grassy hummock.

I sprang to my feet, unwilling to die in this disgraceful prone position. We confronted each other. Black Eagle raised his right hand with palm toward me in token of greeting and respect. For was I not Tall Man, most famous of all the white scouts? I stretched out my right hand in identical salutation, for were we not brothers even though our nations remained enemies?

With my knife in my left hand and a twist of rawhide in my right, we circled each other warily, respectfully. Black Eagle leaped, lunging sideways then forward, swiftly as his carnivorous namesake. His knife slashed at my side. Pain, sharp and sickening . . . I touched the blood with numb fingers. And Black Eagle's face wavered back into the face of Jacob Merker, feathered head-dress changing to sunlight in his curly black hair. The brown prairie grass transformed into walls of junk on either side of us.

"I don't believe it! I don't believe it!" Bernard Campbell shouted. "You were never a cowboy. Your father buys junk and old rags and things and sells them. How could you be a cowboy? How could you—"

"Of course he was a cowboy," I said, springing to Jacob's defence. "What do you know about cowboys? You've never even been outside Trenton, living with those old tombstones. Tombstone Campbell!" I chanted. "Tombstone Campbell!"

We stood breast to breast, Bernard and I, faces red with anger, in much the same positions that Black Eagle and Tall Man had occupied a few moments before. Yes, Jacob Merker was an awful liar. But he was a cowboy too.

. . . . .

I learned to read in a flash of understanding, sitting on a beautiful girl's lap. That was the reason for my precocity, no doubt at all. She so stimulated me at the age of six or seven, Viola Valleau did, that verbs and nouns danced in my head. From that time on I devoured a book a day, sometimes as many as a dozen a week, from the Trenton Public Library. The words capered into my head like swarms of silent wasps. *The Wizard of Oz*, *Doctor Doolittle*, Peter Rabbit, Tom Swift and Horatio Alger. *The Warlord of Mars* and *The Gods of Mars* by Edgar Rice Burroughs, when I was older. The big red *Chums* books with their school stories from England. Books by Zane Grey, Frank Packard, heroic tales of Bulldog Drummond and Raffles, the gentleman crook. Pulp magazines, *Black Mask*, *Argosy*, *The Shadow*, *Doc Savage*, the whole Street & Smith series of pulps, sport, adventure, western, science fiction and love. I didn't care for the love stuff much, but I read that too when there was nothing else.

The pulps were exciting reading, much more exciting than the library could provide. One Sunday, sneaking into Merker's junkyard from the river side on a hunch, I noticed that among the newspapers, jammed into huge wirebound bundles by the screw press, were many scattered copies of my favourite reading matter. The pulps. On Sundays and holidays when no one was working, I'd slip into the junkyard from the unfenced river side, climbing over wrecked automobile bodies and battered fenders twisted together in dangerous grating mountains of steel and iron.

The magazines were not easy either to locate or extract from their compressed six-foot bales. But I'd worry and work away at them, twist back and forth patiently until the bright covers of *Doc Savage* and *The Shadow* were freed from bondage. Always nervous that I might be caught. And one day I was.

Mr. Merker must have noticed that his bales of wastepaper were looking a little anemic from my magazine extractions, and perhaps sometimes the bundles would even fall apart. If they did, it meant a great deal of extra work, pressing and baling them all over again. Therefore, he patrolled the junkyard at unexpected times. And I was caught with the evidence in hand.

Mr. Merker's face was terrible, skull-like and black with anger. He was Isaiah the prophet, he was Jeremiah about to pronounce doom. My head shrank back down into my shoulder bones when he grabbed me by the ear and collar, frog-marching me to the yard's front entrance.

But that was all. Surprisingly, he didn't inform my mother. I wasn't thrown into jail to languish for days on bread and water as I had feared. I was free, but much too scared ever to return to Merker's junkyard. Reading can be dangerous.

. . . . .

Weller's Theatre was the Mecca and passionate goal of every kid I knew, and some I didn't, on Saturday afternoons. The movies were silent, but the place rocked with noise. An audience of several hundred kids screamed, booed, exploded brown paper bags, chewed gum and ate candy, cheering their heroes to a degree that must have shaken the Egyptian pyramids.

Tom Mix and his white horse rode the shadow range, punishing evil-doers. But Tom never kissed the heroine. He seemed very much in love with his horse. Hoot Gibson and Ken Maynard also rode the range, likewise seeing that justice was administered to the bad guys. Good guys and bad guys were our identification labels, the latter generally sporting evil-looking droopy moustaches and a week's beard. Good guys were mostly well-dressed, clean-shaven, wore Stetson hats, and silver spurs that jingled soundlessly. The bad guys were shabby and dirty, except for bankers who told them what to do. The bankers were evil: they masterminded foreclosures of mortgages on poor but virtuous ranchers with beautiful daughters. The slimy well-dressed bankers and their nasty henchmen always lost out in the end; Tom Mix, Hoot Gibson and Ken Maynard always triumphed.

The serials were best of all. Every instalment ended with the hero or heroine in mortal danger. My breathing stopped while the heroine was about to be divided into bloody halves by an enormous whirling circular saw. Or tumble off a cliff that appeared suddenly at her feet when it was too late to stop the horse or speeding car. Or else the train on which the heroine was a passenger seemed about to be wrecked and disappear forever down a rocky canyon. (I swallowed my gum and nearly strangled.) The kids either roared and hooted their disdain or cheered and applauded wildly: it was bedlam, it was the Christians and the lions, it was the supreme innocence of childhood.

When the next installment began a week later, miracles happened. The good guys escaped by happenstance or their own quick thinking. And all these hair-raising adventures continued for twelve or fifteen weeks of suspense and vicarious terror.

Since much of childhood is unrelieved boredom waiting to grow up, the nickels I spent for the privilege of experiencing this spasmodic excitement were very precious. Harold Lloyd clambered around window ledges of tall buildings, clung to railings or drainpipes by his fingertips, glasses making him look like an acrobatic owl. Richard Dix exhaled quiet menace, gangsters threatening him to no avail, his double-breasted suits always immaculate.

One day I found a whole roll of tickets for Weller's Theatre in the alley outside the building. Someone had been careless with Aladdin's Lamp. I doled them out, sparingly, to my friends, Jack Corson, Bernard Campbell and Jack Clegg. I was very popular, for about a week or two.

Whatever happened to those tickets? Did I really dispense them to all the kids I knew, or did the theatre management become suspicious at all the freebies and take them away from me? I can't remember. But the feeling of supernal joy and exaltation when I found them—as if a candle had lighted in my head—has been with me ever since.

· · · · ·

There was a god in my world. He hung around in unexpected places, backyards and street corners. He knew everything, saw everything, and was not responsible. At King Street United Church, He was presumed to be always in residence. Especially when the preacher invoked Him with a chorus of Thee's and Thou's like stinging bees and cawing crows. Not a god of clover fields and yellow dandelions, but a god of nettles and thistles who would sting you badly if you didn't watch out.

I was a prisoner of religion, sitting on the hardwood church benches from which my behind ached, listening to Thee's and Thou's, hellfire and damnation, from which my head ached. He was a shape-changer who sometimes looked like McLean the pump maker and sometimes like my Uncle Lou. When I was in bed before falling asleep, He looked under the blankets to see what I was doing to myself. And He strongly resembled Mr. Sherbert, ex-German, teacher at Dufferin Public School, about to crack my knuckles with a ruler. God was Fear, and I was scared to death of Him.

But I read the Bible. Jeremiah begat, Joseph begat, everybody begat somebody, and I knew enough about words that begat signified something dirty. That was forbidden, that was attractive. Begat really meant fuck, at least it did among the naive and innocent children of my acquaintance. So I read the Bible from cover to cover, Genesis to the New Testament. And didn't actually know what either of those words meant, begat or fuck. But I looked for what I thought were the dirty parts. And my mother approved.

Job and all those boils, punished for something he didn't do. Joshua and his magic lanterns, tromping around the walls of Jericho until vibrations toppled the mud-brick battlements. Was it Jael or Judith who drove a nail into Holofernes' head and was praised for murder? And "Thy breasts are like unto two young roes"—or something similar. I liked that bit. Samson pulling down the temple walls in blind rage; David and his slingshot, popping a Philistine giant in the noggin.

My own slingshot was fairly easy to manufacture with a forked branch and some rubber bands cut from an old inner tube. Windows beyond our neighbourhood suffered. Strange kids bigger than me approached at their peril. I didn't believe that "Jesus wants me for a sunbeam" stuff. Both Jesus and the Old Man wanted to grill me over a hot fire about my good or bad behaviour. They were completely beyond my comprehension, evil shadows that haunted childhood.

I think now: if I could have had my own God then, something to hold tightly in my childhood darkness, He would have been a deity of soft spring rains, a God of mud puddles and little earthen dams you made on water running downhill, getting your feet wet and being late for supper. A God of bread baking, of rainbow minnows in river shallows, of those long ago evening voices that lulled children to sleep when the world went pouff like a snuffed candle, a God who re-invented the world every morning. A Grandfather God, an Uncle Wilfred you could talk to, who hit the spittoon fifty years ago with a plopping brown sound from the other end of eternity. And I said to Him, "Jack Corson didn't really do what they said he did?" And God said, "Of course not." And I fell asleep.

· · · · ·

Stanley Steamers, Auburns, Stars, Willys, and Durants, and McLaughlins out of Oshawa. Despite those names, horses were still masters of the roads in the 1920s. And the road, incidentally, was not paved, just a dirt track meandering into Trenton from the north. The horses were thick-bodied creatures with ruffs of hair on their legs, Percherons or Clydesdales. But the buggies in summer and the little sleighs of winter jingled into your mind like music, were music and the sound of bells. The dainty small prancers with graceful curved necks were at least counts and barons of equine aristocracy.

I'd wake up early on a winter Saturday morning and hear the sounds of summer: jingle-jingle, and bees buzzed in the hollyhocks, morning glories leaped open, pansies sighed demurely; jingle-jingle and death dates on tombstones next door erased themselves, leaving only birth-dates; clocks whirred swiftly backwards into spring and summer.

Many times Gyp would lick me awake in the morning. Gyp was my dog, and forbidden in the house. But, hiding behind furniture, he would often escape notice until the lights were out. Of untraceable antecedents, he was loved and tormented and chased and jumped on and never even growled or protested semi-slightly. A stoic pooch, lovable cur, philosophic hound, resembling the Gilbert House leaners but much more articulate. His midnight howlings for love or a fight invaded the sleep of the just and the unjust.

Gyp's customary attitude toward the world was very calm, approaching doggy strangers with mouth-open wariness of greeting. He made up his mind swiftly, never doubting instinct. He received the stranger pooch with studied indifference; or else turned swiftly into a brown-bronze warrior of such fearful aspect and ju jitsu teeth that he was never seriously challenged. 134 Front Street remained comparatively clear of mooching mutts and pan-handling curs. An open space, a no-dog's land. At least, none but Gyp's.

Wake up. It's summer. And very early morning. Slip into black stockings, short pants and blouse, then quietly downstairs to the screen door, careful not to slam it. Gyp is waiting outside (another little light glowed in his doggy brain to match yours the instant you woke up). We cross the deserted road to Bronson's dock and the river.

Make no noise. (Someone would be bound to object if they knew you were happy.) Covered with floating mist, the river is. Silvered over the black water, its farther shore a foreign land, the country of strangers. Willow leaves sigh and tremble; Reddick's lumber yard smells of pine and cedar; so does McLean's pump works. The sun is a red glow inside the orbit of the outer planets. The dog, half Airedale and half mongrel but wholly human, presses against your leg. We are silent together.

Haunter of all the chicken runs for miles around was Gyp. A tail-wagging all-day-long snoozer beneath the shed was Gyp. And my friend. Hauled into canine court for chicken murder, he put up no defence, had no lawyers but me. I had tears, very many of them, which had always been effective before. Not this time. Gyp was "put away," in the euphemistic term that means killed painlessly but which I am sure is a lie. I never owned a dog again, not until I suddenly became an adult—and that is a very different thing.

. . . . .

Uncle Wilfred was my non-uncle uncle—he was really a fifty-sixth cousin or thereabouts. But I didn't know that until much later, long after drinking milk and eating cookies in his living room as a child. "How are you, boy?" and "How's your mother?" I'd say fine. It was not exactly a brilliant conversation.

Uncle Wilfred was about seventy. He wore a faded yellow and brown moustache of the soup-strainer type that made moustache cups necessary. Sometimes he smoked a pipe, sitting with elbows akimbo in a rocking chair and gesturing with the pipe stem. And sometimes he chewed tobacco. It seemed a peculiar combination of the same vice.

His wife had died many years before, but Uncle Wilfred had adjusted well to living alone. At the same time, he was a domesticated man, and would have been most comfortable yoked in the married state. Evidence of this was the orderly condition of the house, clean floors and well-dusted furniture. And probably he was lonely. Why else put up with weekly visits from a small boy whose company was certainly not very stimulating. The mystery to me was: why did I go there myself?

Uncle Wilfred's house was a quiet and secure place, restful if you like. But why did I need a rest? Such curiosities as the silver-and gold-coloured spittoons strategically placed so they wouldn't get kicked over and yet still be available for expectoration—these were commonplace. For this was the age of the tobacco-spitters. Some of these could even extinguish a lighted match from a distance of ten feet or more. And narrowly miss a pair of fashionable white shoes with a casual spu-utt of brown poison. Most public and private buildings had spittoons, unless in the latter instance some religious lady had impressed her husband with the evils of tobacco. Uncle Wilfred hadn't lived the colourful life of my Grandfather, and wasn't given much to talking about it anyway. But I liked to visit him.

When I was eight or nine, he gave me a copy of Tennyson's poems. I read a couple of poems aloud to him. He showed no evidence of appreciation. I was probably a very bad reader. The Tennyson must have belonged to his wife, but there were no sentimental associations attached to it on that account.

He was a kind man. He spoke well of other people, which was partly courtly manners but also a genuine humanity. And just being there in the dim rooms of the past with someone who seemed not to belong anywhere, beyond turbulence and perhaps even beyond caring about the faded quality of his life—well, in the smoke of his tobacco was a misty grey-coloured peace. In fact, I think Uncle Wilfred's life was over, the times when he cared deeply about being alive were over, and now he was waiting for death. Blowing smoke rings, rocking and puffing on his pipe. While outside the window, lilacs were in bloom.

. . . . .

Joe Barr was the town idiot. Chased by children, and sometimes even stoned, he would turn, unshaven lantern jaw wagging and going "Aw-aw-aw" in futile defiance. He lived in a shack made of flattened tin cans and broken boards, somewhere near the town garbage dump, finding food wherever he could, wandering the wastes of smoking garbage, looking for something valuable—valuable only to him.

I have seen him, when he wasn't aware of being watched, with an odd gentle look on his face, as if he were thinking of something he couldn't say, for which he couldn't find words. Or did I read that nowhere and notime expression into him when it wasn't there? Of course he knew there was something wrong with him, but never found out why the world was such a cruel place.

> I could have learned from Joe myself
> but I never did
> not even when gangs of children
> followed him down the street

chanting "aw-aw-aw" in mockery
children have for idiots
In a town that looked like a hole
torn in blue clouds
where I made-believe myself
into a moonlit grasshopper
and leaped the shadowed boundaries
that bore my mind's feet lightly
forty years ago
In the grey town of memory
the garbage dump is a prison
where people stand like stones
the birds are stuffed and mounted
a motionless sun still hangs there
where Joe is a scrap of crimson
when the sun at last goes down

—from *Joe Barr* (1968)

When they made a movie in Trenton during the 1920s, called *Carry On Sergeant*, Joe hung around doing odd jobs for the movie makers. Young men wearing World War I uniforms, puttees, khaki shorts and shirts walked the streets and wore the uniforms home at night. It puzzled me greatly, for I didn't know anything about wars.

I questioned my Grandfather about it when we went fishing on the Trent River in a borrowed rowboat. He said, "There's always fighting." That didn't help much either. I rowed the boat as near to the rapids below the hydroelectric dam as my muscles would take us, while Grandfather trolled for pickerel. We didn't catch any. I ached when we got home.

. . . . .

My mother inherited the farm near Wooler, with a big apple orchard, when my father died in 1920. She was trying to sell it, had been trying for a couple of years. In the meantime it had to be looked after, the trees sprayed, marauding crows chased off, all the necessary things done. A courageous but rather helpless sort of woman, my mother was. She needed assistance; but those who didn't help her were trying to cheat her. And which was which?

My father had been an educated farmer, having attended Guelph Agricultural College years before. Either for this reason, or because of his own shrewdness, he was a reasonably successful man. Called "Fred" by those who knew him, he owned a Ford Model A, dressed like a businessman sometimes, and owned other property besides the farm. He died of cancer.

In yellowing snapshots, selecting a bunch of grapes from arbours in his vineyard, sitting stiffly upright at the wheel of his new Ford car with my mother and me, his face looked stern and guarded. There were only two years between the time of my birth and his death. When those snapshots were taken, behind that unyielding face he was probably already aware of the cancer that killed him.

Or perhaps he was only a very serious man, but one who could laugh sometimes, on social occasions. The answers to such questions are lost. I can't remember him at all. But it occurs to me that in the best moments of my own life, when I have seemed to myself to live joyously and well, there may be some small recompense for him in ways that neither of us could understand.

But the springtime apple blossoms! As if the sky had fallen, with immense fleecy pink and white clouds blanketing earth between trees for miles. Seen for the first time in your life, it was breathtaking and breathgiving, for waves and waves of perfume seemed vividly percept-ible to all the senses. Everything small and of little importance: the apple blossoms, three black snakes under a fallen door, Grandfather and myself, a few trivial moments in the 1920s, they were gathered together at exactly the right time for memory to hold them—in a synchronization of little separate etchings and images beyond time.

Grandfather owned a great double-barrelled shotgun, a weapon that appeared only slightly smaller than the Crimean War cannon atop Trenton mountain. When he fired at crows in the magical pink and white orchard, echoes boomed and bounced from the nearby Murray Hills with echoes echoing echoes. A cascade of petals fluttered from the apple trees, with the following silence containing the faint ringing of bells. Fairyland was profaned by gunpowder. Grandfather grinned. "Gotcha," he said.

As night was falling, Grandfather and I wandered to a swampy area near the farm. While I clutched his hand tightly, feeling the big calluses in his palm that signified hickory axe handles long ago, and meant safety for me in the darkness. Perhaps several acres of watery landscape, with thousands of frogs singing that loud song which seems to surround and encompass all nearby objects. The plink-plunk din multiplied several score for each frog, adding up to a tympany of millions, tinkling into the ears like water music.

Then frog terror. The sound of death. A snake—what else could it be?—had seized one of the singers, and was swallowing him whole. My hand clenched in Grandfather's hand, thinking of those flailing legs protruding from a snake's distended jaws. The little green body being urged forward head-first into a scarlet cavern, swallowed alive.

The night quiet. The singers had all plunged beneath water, leaves or stones, into deep mud. They knew. Every sound ended. Then, maybe one little green imp couldn't stand the silence any longer, forgetting fear, forgetting everything but the need to say this is me this is me for as long as I am. Everyone joined in, thousands and thousands, the sounds entering my ears as one sound that had joined together and set up a corresponding tremble in the bones.

All around us, little frog faces pointed upward out of mud toward the sky, as if they were trying to make their souls reach the sky. And up there, maybe a hundred yards or so, all the green sounds hovered and stopped, couldn't climb any higher. A coloured blanket above the swamp. In imagination, my ears left my body, travelled up a quarter mile high, and then I couldn't hear them any more. Back on earth though, they didn't stop. They couldn't stop. And I have heard them and their friends and relatives continuing the song many times since.

In September and October of those years, our backyard at Trenton was crowded with apples to prevent them being stolen. But many barrels were stolen anyway, both from our backyard and the farm—trucked away in wagons and pickups. The golden Russets, pale green Tolman Sweets, red-streaked Snows, flaming Northern Spies, the fruits of summer. I sold them from door to door in six-quart baskets and bushels, for nickels and dimes and quarters, transporting them in my wooden wagon, without motivating spark plugs, across the streets of Trenton.

. . . . .

Trenton had been a lumbering town in the days before dams were built on the river, when sprawling log booms floated downstream and coal oil lamps lighted the houses. In my Grandfather's era, the Gilmour Lumber Company supplied much of the town's prosperity. Potash, lumber and squared timber were shipped outward by sailing ship from the rivermouth harbour in the nineteenth century—in fact were shipped from all the half dozen or so Bay of Quinte harbour towns. Exported to the United States, Britain, and European countries.

—and the wind-high ships
that sailed from Rednersville
to the sunrise ports of Europe
are delayed somewhere
in a toddling breeze—

—from *Roblin's Mills [II]* (1968)

Beyond the limestone gothic post office in Trenton, there was a shipyard and dry-dock—when I was six and eight years old. And a cooperage mill. When I went swimming from the railway bridge near Merker's junkyard, the creosote works upriver rainbowed the water. Tugs and barges of the Weddell Towing Company had sunk in shallow water below the downtown bridge, their brass fittings dull, shining whistles and bells silent. I fished for mudcats from their slanting decks, peering into dark, rancid holds: fearful of seeing the bloated greenish bodies of drowned sailors drifting in slime.

Below the town bridge, the river widened and became the Bay of Quinte. In winter, when I owned my first pair of skates and kept falling down repeatedly, we chased an old tin can or lump of coal on the frozen river, batting at it with a broken board, or an old hockey stick if we were lucky. When the river was clear of snow, the game sometimes took on wider dimensions. A fast skater might stick-handle clear of the small boy ruck, making for the bridge and under it to the bay, with a coloured, screaming rabble of children pursuing him onto Quinte.

And far out there on the black river, in really cold weather the ice would rumble and crack with the sound of eternity. I'd stand there shivering, alone, knowing there were monsters waiting, looking at me under the ice. See their shadows wavering back and forth behind the ice barrier, hungry. And notice also another boy watching me, red-nosed from the cold, lifting his hand when I lifted my hand, uncannily like myself but not myself, reflected on the ice.

Farther north on the river road, Mayhew's Mill. The mill pond covered several acres, fed by many shallow streams that froze quickly in winter. At night, girls and boys of the town lit torches of bulrushes dipped in coal oil or gasoline, skating away and waving them over their heads, into the hinterland of creeks and winding little streams. As if the moonlit world had many doorways. Or they built fires at the pond edges, toasting marshmallows and hot-dogs, or sitting in blankets while the daylight world vanished.

In winter, the sleighbell time, also came Christmas. With the usual bunting and scarlet ribbons stretched across streets, as they still are everywhere. And Santa Claus. While being very dubious as to the actual existence of that distributor of children's largesse—and trying to trap the non-existent visitor with cunningly concealed threads looped across doorways it was necessary for him to pass—I was still greedy for the good things I knew, or hoped, would be left for me under the Christmas tree.

Red *Chums* books from England, windup trains, tinker toys (a collection of small sticks and perforated wooden spindles with which you could fashion skeletal skyscrapers), horehound candy, knitted sweaters and mitts my mother made for me, things I was eager to receive but which were seldom very surprising.

And every second year, the advent of my Uncle Lou Ross, Aunt Edith and their three children, Jean, Claire and Don. Uncle Lou was my mother's brother, a craggy man with a Roman nose, his dominating character quite the opposite of hers. He owned a farm near Wellington. After my father's farm was finally sold, Uncle Lou generally brought a barrel of apples for Christmas, often my favourite Northern Spies. As years went by, the barrels became bushels and finally six quart baskets.

They were hearty people, all of them, exuding Christmas cheer like skunk perfume. I disliked them cordially. Aunt Edith always felt she had to kiss the small town boy, cornering me between stairways banister and front door, obviously enjoying my discomfort. Uncle Lou was hearty, Aunt Edith was hearty, Jean, Claire and Don would obviously be hearty when they grew older. We exchanged presents, me hoping to get the best of the deal, but never doing so. My dog Gyp, when he was alive, always disappeared beneath the woodshed on such occasions, disliking so much heartiness.

More than that, they were beautiful people, physically beautiful, and they got along well socially with everyone they met. Other people liked them. That was intolerable to me, a solitary pale child who was obviously a dreaming mother's pet as far as they were concerned. I envied them, these beautiful people. They were profoundly adjusted to the world they lived in, or so it seemed. Whereas I made discoveries, was elated or depressed sometimes, I suspected things and tried to read people's minds, and I acted the way I thought other people wanted me to act. And was wrong more often than not.

They didn't suspect or discover, they knew. Sure they did. Why it rained or snowed, where milk came from, how babies were born, the reasons for springtime and winter, how it was that flowers blossomed or birds sang—and made it all seem ordinary by knowing. They were well acquainted and friendly with a great big terrifying god somewhere in the sky who knew everything I did and didn't approve.

We ate Christmas dinner together, after Uncle Lou said a prayer, mentioning things "for which we are truly thankful." All of us. Uncle Lou carved the turkey, and did we want light meat or dark meat? I could hardly ever make up my mind under interrogation.

Jean and Claire were well-behaved and quiet at table. They would obviously be even more beautiful as they grew older. Don was not quite so well-behaved, and kept nudging me under the table with his foot. We would giggle, and Uncle Lou would frown. He reminded me of the Hebrew prophet Isaiah sculptured in stone by Jehovah, or Moses maybe, delivering legal tablets from the burning mountain. At meal's end Don and I would shift and wriggle in our chairs, and beg to leave the table. The gastric dictatorship was ended. Gyp waited near the woodshed, tail wriggling.

．　．　．　．　．

Drift in your sleep to those lands in the night, when all directions are possible. A wind from far places stirs and riffles through the past times. A voice in your mind asks, "Is this the way it was, or is this the way you wanted it to be?" And you will say, "This is the way it was, when nothing moved or changed." Where the high sun hangs motionless: it is always morning, it is always evening, it is always noon.

Joe Barr stays where he was forever; the leaners against the Gilbert House nodding wisely, continue to lean; when Grandfather's flat feet went slap-slap so hard that earthworms under the sidewalk heard and wriggled in terror. Uncle Wilfred waited for death in his dark house, and his dead wife waited for him in that place *"from whose bourne no traveller returns . . ."*

There is perhaps something to be said for the idea that the best parts of life are the exaltations, those rare occasions when something happens which so moves one emotionally that everything else is driven into the far background of the mind.

The best parts of life—maybe even the tremendous grief one feels at six or seven years old, in sympathy for a corresponding grief and shame in the mind of Jack Corson when he was accused of stealing. A sympathy that must be so akin to the original feeling that it becomes one of the absolutes, like hate, terror and love. For we are partial beings in what we feel much of the time, seldom carried away or captured by one of the unadulterated emotions, the absolutes, merely nibbled at by terror, hate and love. It's likely, of course, that the human psyche is too frail, too cobweb fragile to survive the full strength of a complete obsession. Fever would rage through our bodies, fire would spring from our mouths and eyes.

With very small effort of the mind, I reconstitute those faces. Even from a long time and distance, I can transport them back into here and now. I can see those faces in my mind, their features, characteristic stance and telltale gestures. As if they were pictures in my own brain, as if they are real now as they were real then. And I know they are true people, because when I compare a photograph that may exist of their faces and bodies with the one in my mind, then the photograph is nearly identical. Of course, some would say that I am remembering the photograph, not the person. But even if there is no photograph or snapshot in existence, the dead and living faces can exist in my mind. It is a flash only. Then disappears.

Perhaps a gift, since other people have told me they cannot see these faces from the past, their mental effort will not conjure that moving flash for even a brief instant. Then I suppose, for those people, such images from the past must come accidentally, or in dreams, since I am sure that all of us, in some parts of our minds, must have this gift of seeing. And seeing not in any supernatural sense, but simply as one of the attributes of being human. It is a similar attribute to that of reading a poem silently on the page, but hearing it lift aurally from the page: so that instead of just black squiggles on paper you may hear a living sound.

It is probably one of the illusions that accompany growing older that you keep seeing faces that you think you know. Faces of people who form part of your own past life. And for a moment, you think you are living backwards, the uncanny reel of time reverses, you have retrieved something that was not valuable when it happened, but is valuable now. Then disappointment, for the face you thought you knew is only a simulacrum, maybe a genetic palimpsest, at any rate not the person you thought it was.

Walking the street of my hometown, Trenton. The hundred-and-some-years-old house I lived in is still there, its tired red brick and creaking timbers squatting in time. McLean's pump works across the street is a ghost building, although I can still visualize its tin-covered walls and McLean's tobacco-stained yellow beard. Trenton Creamery is gone; so are the B.W. Powers coal sheds.

The leaners against the Gilbert House have vanished, and so has the building they leaned against. I watch them for an instant, their faces vague but absolutely precise, then allow them to disappear. Weller's

Theatre where Tom Mix and Hoot Gibson rode the range is gone. So are all the other cowboys who played such havoc with childish emotions; but they were silvery ghosts even when I first saw their shadows. And those half-century-old films are probably dust as well.

And you say, what does it matter? But it does matter, for they are your life, all these things.

At the corner of Front Street and Dundas, where there is now a traffic light, I see an old man, his monstrous flat feet going clomp-clomp-clomp on concrete, searching for real earth underneath. It's Ol Rid, my Grandfather! Wait, I say, wait! Of course it isn't him, I knew it wouldn't be. Even so, the veritable flesh and bone of my Grandfather rises from the dust, flashes in my mind, lives again inside the flesh and bone that is myself.

And so does Ada Kemp, my mother's old kitchen gossip friend. I'd know that thin, mean, admitting-nothing bony profile anywhere. And say, "Do you remember me? I was that small child you scolded, now grown six foot three and almost as old as you. Do you remember?" And hurriedly, "No, I don't want to borrow money, I don't want anything from you at all. Your old age is safe from me and everyone else alive, money to buy your coffin is safe; stay warm, stay comfortable, stay dead, good-bye."

My mother, too. She will not be very happy immured in cold ground, because she was never warm enough above earth except in August heat. Who was so religious and wanted love so much, she made me uncomfortable. Always. The fussing over me, the loving me that spoiled me—whatever spoiling is. Her hopeless yearning toward the little brat, myself, that primal savage who took so long to change into a human being and may never make it.

There is no excuse for me that I didn't respond to her requests, importunities and demands for love, even if they were unspoken. I should have faked it, even as a child. That would have meant I had some idea of the torture, pain and ecstasy of people who can actually love. I should have faked it, leaned my head against the bony decaying skullface of love and pretended to be human.

And now, walking west on Dundas, near the ghost yard of the Gilbert House, which is an empty lot, someone I don't know stops me and says excitedly, "Why, aren't you—?"

No, I'm not. Whoever you're looking for is much younger than me, and is probably much smaller as well. But then, come to think of it, maybe I am. And say so. "Yes, I am." I am still.

CHAPTER TWO

· · · · · · · ·

SCHOOLDAYS

When did you know you were a writer?" "How did you know?" The young always ask you the same questions you asked yourself years ago, and for a long time there was no response possible. There were no writers. All across the streets of my home town there was silence. Everyone sold groceries, or they sold drygoods and hardware, they sold coal and lumber. Their words were about buying and selling and making money; and sometimes, when they were young, love. But writers? There were none.

· · · · ·

In school we had to memorize poems, some of them the most awful stuff one could imagine. My memory still clings to "The Private of the Buffs," by someone called Hastings Doyle, and I use it for an example of the worst poem ever written. It's so bad it emerges on the other side of badness, to achieve a peculiar malodourous merit. But writing poems began for me at age thirteen, when I read Bliss Carman:

> Arnoldous Villanova
> Six hundred years ago
> Said peonies have magic
> And I believe it so.

Terrible, but I didn't know it then. So I wrote my own poem, even worse than Carman's. Blessedly, I didn't know that either.

. . . . .

Around this time (I was twelve or thirteen) our neighbours, the Shaws, moved away from their house behind ours. Mrs. Shaw must have liked me, and presented me with a parting gift of a hundred or so copies of Frank Merriwell books by Burt L. Standish. While attending Dufferin Public School, there was no possibility of being able to read that many books and still keep up my schoolwork. The problem was baffling. How would Doc Savage, the Man of Bronze, have solved it? What bold stratagem could he have devised in order to deceive my mother's watchful eye?

I became suddenly ill. My stomach was upset, my legs ached. My mother realized the seriousness of it quickly. She put me to bed—with stacks of Frank Merriwell books piled high on chairs and tables around the bed. And perhaps ice cream would be good for me? Presto, the ice cream appeared. Comfort me with oranges and apples? Open Sesame! The chest of drawers blazed with oranges and apples. But still I languished.

And read Frank Merriwell. He went to Yale University, Frank did, in New Haven, wherever that was. His loyal girl friend was Inza Burriage. She was very beautiful. Of course. And Frank Merriwell played games: baseball, hockey, track and field, football, basketball, everything. He was good at games, scoring the winning run or goal or basket, generally at the last moment when the outcome seemed still in doubt. If, by some underhanded finagling, Frank's enemy, the evil Bart Hodge, he of the black brows and dubious morals, should disrupt the course of virtue, such disruption was brief. Frank's baseball doubleshoot when pitching struck out the most dangerous opposing batters; playing football, he was as elusive in the open field as an eel on roller-skates.

It was borne in upon me fairly soon that Frank Merriwell was an American, and that Americans always won. While a band, hidden somewhere in the bleachers, played "The Star-Spangled Banner." Or if they didn't win, skullduggery was afoot and at hand.

However, justice always prevailed, given enough pages for the blind goddess to see "what evil lurks in the hearts of men." It was also impressed upon me that winning was very important, while I nursed some doubts that I would ever personally achieve such invariable triumphs. I was lousy at games—in fact, it was hard to find anything at which I really excelled: perhaps a rather good disappearing act when work or bedtime was mentioned.

Doctor Johnson called at our house. He examined me carefully with stethoscope and finger thumpings of my anatomy, questioned my mother about diet and bowel movements. After lucubration, cogitation and colloquy with her, Doctor Johnson agreed that my illness was serious. But he had difficulty with the diagnosis. It was decided that I should remain in bed somewhat longer. My mother continued the ice cream treatment. I finished reading all the Frank Merriwell books, rose from my bed after a month or so, went back to school. And Jack Clegg said to me, "Where were you?" And I said, "Catching up on my reading." And he said, "Yah, I just bet!"

· · · · ·

My school years were boring and frustrating and unpleasant. I was a timid youngster, and while physically large for my age, lived in fear of other people. Oh, not all the time; I didn't think of my fear constantly. But there are inevitable confrontations when you're young, a school boy; of course when you're older as well. At this time—oh, say around 1933–35, I was often afraid. And perhaps others sense that fear, and take advantage of it; or is it mostly in your own mind? In any event, one day I walked up to one of the people who'd been taunting me after school and punched him on the jaw. He went down with a surprised expression. There was no aftermath; it seemed to end there.

That was an exorcism of sorts. I was able to think outwards instead of nearly always inwards. Is that understandable? I don't think any of us escape fear entirely, nor should we be able to escape it, since it's a survival device, and personal extinction is the last of a whole series of dangerous inevitabilities. And besides, I think a certain limited amount of fear makes life more interesting.

At Albert College, a private boarding school in Belleville where my mother sent me when she thought I'd never graduate from public school, there was fear as well. I hadn't learned to deal with it then, however. I was dominated mentally by smaller and older kids, one especially. This youngster was three or four grades ahead of me in classes; his name was Godspeed. I think he'd been reading English public school stories, and gotten the idea from them that I should be his "fag." (In Canadian terms, for "fag" read unpaid schoolboy servant.) Godspeed had me pretty well under his thumb, and I've always remembered one thing he said when he wanted me to do something menial for him: "I won't make it compulsory." The whole master/slave relationship is wrapped up in that one line.

It was not exactly the inequalities
of schoolboy against bullying teacher
or later the fear of fitting into
a strange conformity at a boarding school
or how cruelly alien boys were
—for at the time I searched out chinks
of reality in the high walls around
me and found perilous escape in books with
night flights west and sky causeways—

—from *What It Was*— (1965)

· · · · ·

Trenton High School was a culture shock that bewildered me; I felt lost in its thronging desert of people. At age fourteen, I had shot up to a gawky six feet tall, while still retaining the insecurities of a much younger kid. Among the people I knew, Bernard Campbell was a year ahead of me at THS, Jack Clegg was a year or two behind. Harold Wannamaker, who became a friend that year, was my own age. Despite all of them, I sank into a mental quagmire.

Latin, French and algebra! I hated them all with a wild and hopeless hatred, which included a kind of lazy despair. My grades became disgraceful, both to me and to my mother. I failed and failed again, sinking into such depths of pimply depression that nothing could rouse me from it. Nothing but a girl.

I fell in love. The even tenor of my ways became hoarse and gravelly. Life was glorious and awful. Her name was Jean. She floated above, rather than prosaically sat on, the wooden seat on my right, while I watched her stealthily, aware of every movement. And undoubtedly, I made her very uneasy.

Jean was a shy and reticent girl, her hair a pale yellow, face so white it was cloud-like. She conveyed to me a delicate feeling, as if she were too sensitive to live on earth, the princess feeling a hard pea through a thickness of forty mattresses. And tall, but not imperiously tall, blue-eyed, ethereal and plain lovely. I was scared of these strange creatures called female, and this one terrified me.

A great churning and turmoil took over my insides. I forgot my own name once or twice, then remembered someone else's and thought it mine. Secrets of the universe were revealed to me, but I was unable to explain them to teachers. My grades continued to decline. But I found out where she lived, and hung around the street corner nearby: holding onto a telephone pole, I swayed back and forth moaning in moony passion like Heathcliff on the moors.

· · · · ·

Harold Wannamaker was everything I was not. An athlete, popular (seemingly anyway), supremely confident of himself, adequate in his studies, at ease with other people. And a rather good-looking youngster, as well. I went out of my way to seek his friendship, probably hoping that Harold's social graces would rub off on me.

Of course they didn't. I was a miserable kid, unhappy, self-conscious and ill at ease, bad at schoolwork, despite one year when I did well at English.(The next year my new teacher knew her stuff, and I failed).

Nor was Harold the "shining example" of what I wanted to be, not exactly anyway. But I felt ambiguous: I did think he was somewhat admirable, and wanted in some ways to be like him, but was slightly repelled by his personality. Most of all, I wanted friendship; I needed to break out of my aloneness. Was there anyone else in the entire world who understood what it was like to be me, the me of a one-person universe?

Harold played high school football; he was the star player and had dazzling speed. I was conscripted for the football team as well—because of size, not athletic co-ordination. (I weighed 180–185 pounds.) And yes, it was fun. My position was centre, the guy who snapped the ball to the quarterback. I was Horatius at the Bridge, barrier of flesh to enemy players, and I don't remember very many line plunges ever getting past me: they may have gotten around me, but not through me.

You braggart, I say to myself. I may well have been extremely ordinary as a football player. But I enjoyed it. Boom went the bodies, meeting at the line of scrimmage: you stood there a moment, reeling, dizzy from the impact, forgetting all about the scanty crowd on the sidelines, forgetting yourself even. Once we played Belleville, on a field that had been much rained upon shortly before the game. Because of the wetness, my feet picked up ten or twenty pounds of sticky goo every time I took a step. Another time: the opposing halfback aimed himself at me directly: I'd meet him at the line of scrimmage, the impact of our coming together stopping both of us exactly where we stood, unable to fall for a moment, unable to take a step forward or backward. This happened two or three times in the game, and might have been more often. Oddly enough, our meetings felt momentous, as if a great deal depended on each of us. Later on, I was told the other kid had been drinking; it must have been powerful stuff. I felt like a hero playing football, and didn't even think to laugh at myself then. Yes, it was fun.

. . . . .

I was writing poems at that time, and getting them published in the school magazine, called the *Spotlight*. They were pretty bad poems, but I didn't know that, which was just as well. The magazine paid a dollar each for poems. Enthralled with Bliss Carman's stuff, I began to write at a furious rate, filling notebooks with them. Copying the poems on a neighbour's typewriter, I bound them into little leather-covered stapled books. These books contained some fairly long effusions, an epic on Robin Hood, another on the Norse myths, Thor and Odin, etc. Our neighbour, Harry Moore, was editor of the local newspaper, the *Courier Advocate*. He printed several of my verses in his paper, along with a short article about me. I suppose I found all this intoxicating, but it's so long ago, the fumes have completely dissipated.

In the mid-thirties, Wilson Macdonald, a fairly well-known poet, visited our school to give a reading. I was ushered into his presence and introduced as "the school poet." And I didn't even have the grace to do more than wriggle slightly at the description. Macdonald was a gaunt, middle-aged man, with a big nose and dark hair combed sideways across his bare skull. He looked at me solemnly—I could think of nothing to say. He couldn't either, although he used more words to do it. And I departed the august presence.

But I still remember his reading, which featured a poem about tugs on English Bay, another called "Whist-a-Wee" or similar to that, and "Song of the Ski." The last named went like this:

> Norse am I when the first snow falls
> Norse till the ice departs,
> The fare for which my spirit calls
> Is blood of a thousand Viking hearts—

Now that was more like it, the same sort of heroic drivel I was writing myself with Robin Hood and the Norse myths. Many years later, reading Stan Dragland's *Wilson Macdonald's Western Tour*, I chuckled over the bit where Macdonald locks the doors of his reading hall so that the audience couldn't escape when he sold his books.

. . . . .

It was around this time I got interested in hockey. The Toronto Maple Leafs were next to gods in the minds of Trenton youngsters. The dream of the local hotshot being discovered by a big league scout, and going on to fame and fortune with the Leafs, was rampant in teenagers. And me. I picked over the town garbage dump looking for Beehive Golden Corn Syrup labels, in exchange for which you would receive the photograph of a big league hockey player *in veritas* by return mail, or nearly. Primeau, Jackson and Conacher (the "Kid Line") were in their heyday; so were King Clancy, Hap Day and Red Horner, the latter a dispenser of thunderous body checks. I tried to imitate Horner and thump every body that came near me in pickup hockey games at the town rink. Alas, only rarely did I ever connect. And there was a peculiarity about my skating abilities: I could skate straight ahead like an express train, almost running on my skates: but I couldn't turn or stop. Crashing into the end boards, I was an extreme peril to anyone in my vicinity.

At Albert College I had learned to swim in the college swimming pool, accomplishing this by standing in as deep water as I could, then making for the shallow end with furious thrashing. On return to Trenton, the river became my second home.

Jack Corson once dared me to dive off the town bridge. I remember being perched atop the bridge's steel framework, a flat place where two girders joined: sixty or seventy feet above the river, maybe more. The boardwalk for pedestrians was directly below. To avoid crashing down on that boardwalk and breaking my neck, I'd have to leap outwards at least six feet.

Sitting there above the bridge, sweating, afraid, waiting for something to take the decision to jump or not to jump out of my hands. And below me, the bridge traffic—autos, horses and wagons—flowed by sedately. No one even looked up. All the other boys had gone home, sure I wouldn't jump. As I was sure.

But the other boys' "I dare you!" had soaked into my mind. The unendurable thought of being a coward! I jumped.

The leap outward was perfect, arms and legs clamped close to body. The river felt thick as I entered it, neither liquid or solid. There was no lapse of time. I went down like a slow bullet, then kicked vigorously back to the surface, to traffic sounds and voices.

Clambering ashore, I felt a terrible pain in my groin, and remembered that I'd forgotten to keep my testicles tucked between my legs to protect them from the water's impact. My balls ached like twin coals of fire. Hopping up and down in agony, feeling a little silly and a little proud, I resolved never to do such a stupid thing again.

That summer I built a crude sort of row-boat, robbing the backyard barn of some vital components, to my mother's consternation. A year later, I secured plans for a small sail boat, and spent all summer putting it together.

The completed boat had a single flaw, but a serious one. It wouldn't tack into the wind worth a damn. I didn't like centre-boards, with their steel plates for keels, which dropped into the water through an envelope in the boat's bottom. Therefore, I fashioned what I thought was a proper keel, shaped like a half moon and screwed onto the boat from below. This keel was made of three-inch-thick planks, and supported by metal shelf brackets. The resulting contraption was so heavy it took several people to carry, although only about eleven feet long. I had traded an expensive tent to someone for a sail (again to my mother's extreme displeasure), and the expanse of canvas was much too large. My sailboat turned over one day near the town bridge, in only a moderate wind. I had to be hauled back to shore ignominiously by a power boat.

My schoolwork had again deteriorated. I failed to pass from Grade Nine to Ten, but remained at school another year to play football. There was something mindlessly attractive about standing there in your heavy pads, snapping the ball and blocking the line of scrimmage, waiting to be hit and believing you couldn't be hurt. That last is an illusion, of course, but I was never injured. Being larger than most of the other kids, that was a help. So I just stood there, in a kind of bewildered euphoria, waiting for opposing players to come to me, then stopping them in their tracks. But pretty soon they caught on: if they couldn't go through me they'd go around, scampering past on either side like frenzied rabbits.

. . . . .

During my schoolday summers, and after I quit school, there were odd jobs—picking apples, making boxes for apples, farm work, almost anything. When the Bata Shoe Company built their Frankford factory, they took me on as a machine operator. I was a terrible workman and never did learn how to make shoes. I left after only five or six weeks.

Of course, my mother worried. Her opinion of my capabilities was never high; by this time it had sunk to just about nil. She loved me and spoiled me, though; but I'm not sure if her love was greater for me or her Redeemer.

Then everything speeded up. The eternity of summer, endless Arctic winter, hours of lying in tall grass staring upward at human shapes of clouds, these things ended. One day I was fifteen, the next day sixteen. Instinctively, I knew that something valuable was over.

And life grew boring. At seventeen, I still seemed to myself to be afraid of everything, but I had even grown bored with my own fears.

And also of seeing the same face every morning in the bathroom mirror. To escape it and the ever-present awareness of the boy-next-door's scholastic excellence, I rode the freight trains west to Vancouver.

· · · · ·

And what does all this surface description tell about me, enlighten even me about what kind of kid I was? And I'm embarrassed to confess— very little. Most of it is conjecture anyway. Certainly my mental processes were dim and slow. I was not a social being, despite football and pickup hockey, still shy and awkward around people. Day-dreaming was a nearly constant occupation, and I suppose that's a clue to myself: I wanted to be a hero, and never realized that other ordinary people were much like me, with the same hopes and desires and frustrations. To be a hockey or football star, to be Robin Hood, or Thor with his thundering hammer. To be what was possible to be. And I didn't know what that was.

There's a penetration the brain possesses under particular conditions which I consider quite mystical. When the mind examines alternatives in writing, when it speeds up or gains added keenness, and a kind of abstract thinking takes place. Perhaps I have retained a certain cast of mind from that dreaming period which allows such qualities of the brain to flow into my fingers when writing a poem.

CHAPTER THREE

· · · · · · · · ·

THE IRON ROAD

PART 1

In 1936 I rode the freight trains west to Vancouver. It was year six of the Great Depression, called the "Hungry Thirties" in a later era. The poor were poorer, the rich sometimes hesitated before buying a third Cadillac; farmers traded eggs for groceries; the mood of nearly everyone was bleak and discouraged. Jobless Canadians by the thousands were also riding the freights from town to town, searching for work desperately.

I was seventeen in that dark year. An only son and much pampered by a doting mother, I had never been more than a hundred miles from home. What made me leave? Why didn't I stay in Trenton, where things were safe, comfortable and easy, going to church just often enough to silence neighbourhood criticism, pretending to look for work when I got tired of loafing? Why didn't I do that?

I don't know. I was bored. Besides, wasn't the west coast the evergreen Chamber of Commerce country, and Vancouver lotusland? Where drunks don't freeze in winter, they just lie on green lawns and gently mildew?

At first I hitch-hiked. West to Toronto, north to Sudbury, where I slept in a used car lot, raped by passionate mosquitoes. Then west again on the Trans-Canada Highway to a point just north of Sault Ste. Marie. And had to stop. There was no more highway. It hadn't been built yet.

· · · · ·

At Searchmont, a little CP Railway watering hole, I decided to ride the boxcars west, despite a nervous fear of railway cops.

The train arrived at midnight, a black thing with flashing lights, groaning painfully. It drank like an animal, great sloshing gulps from the dark water tower. Brakies walked the trackside cinders, swinging bullseye lanterns. Then a sudden shudder, the couplings' iron vertebrae jerking spasmodically in imitation of life; the far-distant engine sending multiple explosions backwards like firecrackers.

"It's gonna go, it's gonna go—," I whispered to a fellow wayfarer crouching beside me. "Naw, it ain't," he said in a normal tone. "Wait for the highball. That's what tells ya—" Moments later the engine's voice in the night went "Toot-toot" almost timidly. We ran for it.

I clambered into what seemed half a boxcar, the top half removed, a "gondola" that had once held coal. Wearing a waterproof canvas jacket, clutching a bag containing an extra pair of shoes, shaving cream and razor, and a large hunting knife. I was equipped for adventure, but for this kind of adventure?

Overhead the stars moved crazily. Dark trees rushed past in the bordering forest. All around me, coal particles danced invisibly on the gondola's wooden floor, my own bones shuddering in sympathy. And it started to rain, a slow drizzle whose velocity was increased by the train's speed into a barrage of stinging missiles against my face. Blazing cinders from the engine flew past, often crunching in my teeth with a bitter taste. North into nowhere we plunged, while I huddled miserably wet under the forward wall of the gondola.

Hours passed. I dozed and slept in acute discomfort, then awoke into an abnormal stillness. Dopey and half-conscious, I decided that the train must have stopped, leaving me feeling vulnerable, no longer a moving target. As if when trundling along at forty miles an hour, I had been unnoticeable, and hence, secure?

In half-light and half-rain I stirred, desperate to escape that dirty coal car and water that trickled down my neck in cold discomfort. Clambering down the steel ladder I searched for shelter, boxcars shouldering endlessly on either side. Ripping the strip of metal seal from a boxcar door with my hunting knife, I tried to haul it open. The thing wouldn't budge. With dull acceptance I went back to my own car, lost in bewilderment and wet misery.

A black-slickered railway cop materialized in the rain. He climbed into the gondola, regarding me with distaste. "You broke the seal on a boxcar." he accused. I admitted the charge meekly, knowing he wouldn't believe a denial anyway. He locked me inside a caboose with bars on the windows and a padlocked door.

Inside this railway prison I contemplated my fate, which didn't seem too terrible. After all, breaking a piddling strip of metal couldn't be very important, could it? But what would my mother think of all this, her only child locked in a backwoods prison and now beginning to get very hungry? Or the United Church minister who had awarded me a book-prize for attending services forty-four Sundays of the year?

At noon the CP Railway cop escorted me to his house nearby for lunch. Along the way people glanced curiously at the unconvicted but undoubtedly guilty criminal. And by this time I discovered that the little railway town I had landed in was called Hawk Junction, 165 miles north of Sault Ste. Marie.

I sat at table with the policeman, his wife and small daughter. He grinned at me, a little more human with his family present. Encouraged, I ventured to ask if breaking boxcar seals was a very serious offence. He grinned again. "You could get two years."

That was serious, in fact it was appalling. My face must have showed how I felt. They looked at me: the cop inexorably, his wife with sympathy, the child without understanding. "Tomorrow I'll take you back to the Soo for trial," the blue uniform said with finality. His wife gave me some Ladies Home Journals to read, and I was returned to the lock-up.

In my prison caboose I was jolted by the shock all over again: two years! What would my mother say? Or the neighbours think? And worse, to be shut away from sunlight for two years!

With a great deal of care I examined the car's interior again. It's windows were all broken, presumably by earlier prisoners trying to escape. The steel bars of these windows were firmly embedded in the frame, and moved not at all when I tried to shake them. The door was wood, opening inward, secured with a padlock and a metal hasp on the outside. It was discouraging. Other prisoners had apparently failed to escape, despite being older and stronger than me.

Still, they might have overlooked something. The window bars were obviously much too formidable. That left only the door. It was fairly heavy, with hinge keys outside so they couldn't be removed from the inside. I tried the doorknob, releasing the latch enough to allow the door to move inward a quarter inch or so, hearing the padlock rattle in its hasp outside. And ran my fingers along the narrow springy opening between upper door and sill, pulling tentatively inward. My heart was beating heavily, and I felt breathless. The door was flexible enough at the top to permit my fingers to work around its edge and close on the outside.

I swung myself off the floor, body supported by finger grip between upper sill and door, feet jammed against the sill near my hands. And pulled. Yanked inward as if I were about to fall off a cliff and my fingers were holding onto life itself. And scared, a scared boy, grown fully aware of the power and authority ranged against him, but finding the beginnings of strength in his own fear.

It seemed the door was too much for me. I hung high in the air for at least a couple of minutes, like a giant safety pin. And yet it was a kind of triumph to make this all-out effort, even if driven by terror. But stalemate. Then came a sound like ripping cloth. The door pulled inward abruptly, screws yanked from the outside hasp. The boy, who was not exactly me, plunged to the floor on his back, almost too scared to realize what had happened, lying there listening to a strange sound. My own labouring breath. Then peering outside, into an early Sunday afternoon. Into sunlight.

It was gloriously deserted, not a blue uniform or railway cop in sight. Everyone was digesting their midday meals peacefully, or snoozing on the sofa. Nothing visible but long parades of brick-coloured boxcars ahead and behind. I felt almost too nervous and hyped-up to take advantage of this freedom. And it would be much worse to be caught escaping; they'd lock me away for life! At least the caboose-prison supplied a kind of safety, demanded nothing of me but acceptance of events, passivity, destiny, and fate outside my hands.

I dropped quietly onto the cinders between cars. And started to walk south along the tracks. Mind in turmoil, nerves popping and pinging with the effort to control panic. No more freight trains for me. It occurred to me that the Trans-Canada Highway, ending north of Sault Ste. Marie, continued again farther west at Port Arthur and Fort William. I'd get there somehow. In the meantime, people were to be avoided; they'd report seeing a gangling youngster with nervous eyes, wearing a blue windbreaker, to the police. There'd be something in my face that would give me away. Something criminal? I couldn't believe I was really a criminal. Just rather stupid.

Furtively, and feeling very noticeable, I headed south toward Sault Ste. Marie. Slinking along close to the sheltering boxcars, peering back and forth cautiously. But the railway divisional point was quiet; only one sound, the crunch of cinders under my feet that sounded like small explosions. Then another patter of feet, small feet, like a child's, following me. The source of the sound was on the other side of those marching boxcars. But no use stopping now; that would indicate I'd heard them and was stopping for that reason.

Eyes fixed straight ahead, a careful lack of expression on my face, I hiked south. The footsteps continued, more or less keeping pace with my own. Surely whoever was over there, just out of sight, was aware of me, had some intentions toward me that meant danger. I tried to catch a glimpse of them in the openings between cars. Nothing. Just the sound of feet on cinders, without a clue to their owner.

The marching squadrons of boxcars ended. I emerged into open daylight, without protection of any kind against curious eyes. It was like being naked, exposed and vulnerable. But the mystery of those pattering feet was solved. A dog rushed out from behind the last car, frisking at my heels, wagging his tail, wanting to be patted. A brown dog. Knee-high and very friendly. He liked me, migawd, he liked me! I waved him off furiously: "Get away, get the hell outa here! I hate dogs!" At that moment I certainly did hate dogs. A man or boy walking quietly and blending into the landscape is one thing; a dog racing around him like a mad dervish is another. At least he wasn't yapping, at least.

The brown pooch dashed at me playfully, crouched on front paws, ready to leap left or right if I showed any inclination for fun and games. His bright eyes said: "Let's have some action, let's be friends and enjoy life." I groaned inside. And picked up a stick from beside the tracks, throwing it backwards as far as I could toward the miserable little railway town. A mistake. The dog chased it, brought it back to me, crouched again, the stick clenched between his jaws, wanting another throw. I ignored him, or tried to ignore him. That wasn't possible. He barked, not loudly, but enough to attract attention if anyone happened to be watching.

Thus far I'd done all the wrong things in my reactions to that dog. Resolved to ignore him, I marched south without looking at him. The last houses ended at a railway bridge across a wide river. The dog gave up on the town-side of the bridge. With a last disappointed bark he trotted off toward the houses. I wasn't the sort of playmate he had in mind; nor was he to my liking. But his tail was wagging again on the return journey.

· · · · ·

165 miles of walking railway ties, south to Sault Ste. Marie, a distance duly noted by regularly spaced mile markers on the telegraph poles. Walking the ties is rather similar to having invisible chains around your ankles, permitting only a certain length of step. The ties are spaced at

such short distances apart, that stepping from one to the next is too short a step, but stepping two ahead is too long. A small thing, but if you have to walk 165 miles it becomes more important. And I was afraid to return south again by freight train: they'd be looking for me.

Thick spruce and maple forest crowded in on either side of the tracks. It was late afternoon, and I was hungry again. I stopped at an isolated cottage, knowing I couldn't walk all that distance on an empty stomach. For a dollar, the housewife made me up some generous sandwiches, providing also a hunk of cheese and some cold meat. My jumpy nerves were quieting down now as I considered the possibility of pursuit. Probably I'd be safe for the rest of the day, but tomorrow the hounds would be in full cry. The hounds? Migawd, they wouldn't have dogs, would they? I dismissed the thought as ridiculous, but it started my nerves jumping again.

Thinking it best to take no chances, I decided to walk along the edge of the bush, just out of sight of the tracks. Follow the railway from a distance of twenty-five or thirty feet inside the woods. Keeping an eye on any possible activities along the right of way. Work crews had Sunday off, but the little two-man push-and-pull railway scooters might be abroad. Whatever. I plunged into the forest.

It was soft and spongy going. Trees and bushes had been cleared some distance from the tracks, but new growth was again springing into life. Angry little creeks occasionally sluiced from the forest and under culverts. Despite the fairly chilly temperature I was sweating, and flies buzzed around my head. After half an hour of plunging down hillocks or staggering up them, I headed back to the railway tracks. But there were no tracks. I had somehow mislaid them.

My mind told me the railway was only a short distance to the left, since I had veered right and away from them into the forest. But I'd wandered into the trees farther than intended; now everything looked the same. No landmarks, just trees. And never in my life have I been able to distinguish north from south or east from west. Other people may say casually, that's north; but I can get lost in a telephone booth.

The day had grown dark and gloomy; and without the sun to give me some small indication of direction, I was tangled in a maze of nowhere. I kept trying to veer left through the forest. Unless I had lost my mind completely, the railway was in that direction. And my left hand held some mystic clue to location.

After two hours or so of aimless wandering I knew I was lost, admitted it to myself. By this time all movement of my insides had speeded up: I was pouring sweat; blood seemed to be coursing at high speed through my body; my heart thumped heavily; my face felt hot, like the heat of a high fever. The process of rational thinking had stopped; images of home and fear of prison flew into my brain and out. I was nearly mindless. Nothing in previous experience had prepared me for this, a different reality, like suddenly being born with only scattered flashes of awareness, looking around and realizing that your mother's face and the faces of the doctors and nurses were trees. The world itself, nothing but trees.

I started to run. Up hill and down, slamming into trees full length and bouncing off, face whipped by stinging branches, tears pouring from eyes, panting and sobbing with fear. Fear not of being hurt, slammed by hard fists and pain, or the mental fear of being inadequate, incapable of understanding ordinary things—but fear of death. Leaving my body to rot in this brilliant green forest, mossy bones discovered years later by some woodsman or hunter. Fear of not being.

Running. I scooped handfuls of water from a creek, dashed it into mouth and over my face. And kept on running. Aware of hunger, I chewed at the sandwiches crushed in my canvas bag and kept running while eating. Legs buckling, face scratched and bleeding from whiplash bushes, lungs heaving with exhaustion I reeled through the forest. And with the onset of darkness collapsed finally on a hillside, wrapping myself around a tree trunk in nearly foetal position, as if the tree were a vegetable mother.

And started to think about God. All through childhood and early adolescence I had been afraid of Him. He knew too much, included all my secret thoughts, dislikes and weaknesses in the enormous cosmos of His mind. When I had attended church for forty-four Sundays of the year, receiving a book for reward, the reason for doing so had been this angry all-knowing God, not the book. I resented His authority, His omniscience, but never allowed my resentment to surface in conscious mind for fear of His vengeance.

But some of the irreverent books I'd been reading in the last few years began to have an effect. I was no longer very sure that God actually exists, that he hadn't been invented by men who wanted to keep other men in continuous subjection and fear. This was next door to atheism. But now I needed Him, needed help badly. And threw myself on His mercy, begged and prayed, mentioning heavy transgressions against His laws and His Holy Bible. The Bible had special significance for me, since I had studied certain passages for implicit sexual suggestiveness, in superstitious terror that He in His blue sky conning tower knew everything I was thinking.

"Get me outa here," I prayed, "and I'll do anything at all. Go to church, return to school, obey my mother, anything." And was vaguely ashamed of myself, for the appeal seemed to come directly out of my own weakness rather than conviction of the deity's existence. Never mind, take no chances. Just in case. Cover all the angles. "Please God, Please God—" And fell asleep.

. . . . .

The tree was an uncomfortable mother. I woke up several times in the night, having lost orientation, not knowing whether I was locked in a barred caboose, comfortably tucked in my own bed at home, or chilled and cold in the midst of an unknown forest. I floated in some dark limbo of the mind, shrunken and foetal, withdrawn into the basic spore of myself.

When grey light filtered among the trees, and realization of being lost sank in even more deeply, there seemed no reward or possible improvement in the situation by getting up and moving around. Conversely, staying there on the cold ground was equally uncomfortable. I debated the issues with myself, weighing the disadvantages of action or non-action. They cancelled each other out. And obviously, God was not going to take a hand, not just yet anyway. I was on my own.

As light increased to a grey ambience in which there was no visible sun, needs of the body became pressing. I had to piss. I had to piss. But that could be managed without altering the situation: open my fly and piss sideways down the hill. But I was thirsty as well, and thirst could not be satisfied while lying sideways among great trees on a hillside. Lower country with a creek or pond must be found. Thinking of these things, the silence began to enter my mind. A silence in which there was no sound whatever, only the small continual ringing in my head to which the brain returned occasionally with a question. As if there was a place in my mind, apart from the reasoning brain, where activities were going on that could not be fathomed, a place barred to me.

I was seized with curiosity: what could be happening in my head which I did not know about? Whatever it was seemed neither friendly nor unfriendly, just ignored me. And yet was concerned with me, its vehicle and necessary carrying case. My thoughts roamed around in my head, searching for the location of these and other activities, a point I could come back to and ask questions. Question: Who are you? Question: What do you want? No answer. Only that soft ringing sound, denoting the other was still there. Perhaps everywhere, co-existing and omnipresent?

· · · · ·

The forest was not dark and gloomy, but pervaded with luminous grey light surrounding green branches, and pooled below shadowy tree trunks. The ground spongy with dead leaves and rotting branches, tall trees interspersed with moss-grown stumps where loggers had been cutting years ago. I chewed on the last of my sandwiches and drank at a clear stream. A heavy depressed feeling in stomach and chest, trudging in any direction where I could push a thought through an opening between trees and hope to find it again later.

Among the trees some distance away, a dark shape appeared, and it was not my thought. A man, about the size of a man, wavering vaguely between grey tree trunks. I shouted, "Hey, this way! I'm lost, I'm lost!" No answer came, and perhaps my own thought had produced the dark shape.

Then another formless shape, as if a hairy man was stalking me like an unfriendly dog, glimpsed occasionally, working his way closer, trying to catch me when my back was turned. A bear? I'd be helpless if I encountered a bear. The CPR cop had, of course, confiscated my hunting knife.

Despairing and futile, I wandered through the woods, not rushing around madly any longer, but wandering slowly through a leafy maze in which everything looked the same. Then another shape I couldn't identify from a distance, which turned out to be an old hunting camp, built of mossy logs with the roof fallen in. About ten feet square. And so ancient there was no hope the hunters or loggers would ever return.

Having found my continual leftward turning was futile, I tried to straighten out the curve in my progress by sighting on a tree ahead of me to the right and heading for that. Then repeating the process. Reaching a hilltop, I climbed another tree to search for some landmark, anything that would orient me to a single direction. But at a height of thirty feet or so I could see nothing but greyness, nothing but nothing.

Twice more I returned to that same hunting camp, the woods myth of anyone lost in a forest tending to circle back again to the same place thus being verified. It was no comfort, causing sickness to rumble in belly and possible soul. It occurred to me that perhaps the circular route I was taking would get smaller and smaller, and become finally the circumference of my own head, causing me to reel and stumble from tree to imaginary tree. One possible plan: to close my eyes and stand perfectly still, fall down and not rise again.

· · · · ·

In a greyness like sleep but not sleep, I heard an alien sound. Muffled by mist and distance. Engines snorting softly, boxcars shuffling backward and forward, steel couplings jolting together. It came from the railway yards at Hawk Junction only a few miles away, but it might as well have come from the moon. Entirely directionless, the sound sometimes behind me, sometimes in front, fingernails scraping at my bones. I had a feeling of intense dislike at that moment, even hatred, of trains. I'd never ride another freight train. And maybe I'd never get the chance anyway.

"Goddam the trains!" I whispered in the greyness. Then "Goddam God!" But that last was sobering, using His name to blaspheme Him. And went contrary to my unstated but basic philosophy: Take no chances. I shuddered at the possibilities being raised. Vengeance is mine, saith the Lord. The angry spectre of the thundering preacher at King Street United in Trenton upreared from his varnished pulpit, pointing a bony finger at me: Sin! Sin! Sin! he shouted.

I walked tired, rested on my feet tired, walked in a dream—listening for any possible sounds besides the shunting trains at Hawk Junction. And ate my last cheese and meat when hungry, drinking at clear streams in the forest. The junk in my dufflebag was abandoned the third time I hit that hunting camp. An extra pair of running shoes, a tube of shaving cream with razor (I shaved only once a week), and other unnecessary items. They were extra weight to carry, useless when you might be dead soon.

Discovering old logging roads with renewed hope, I followed them until they tailed off into nothing or joined other old tracks that were equally ambiguous. They started and ended nowhere. A dozen years at least must have gone by since this area was logged over.

The passage of time could only be estimated. I had no watch, and the sun was invisible. My second night in the woods arrived as only a slow thickening of the greyness, which seemed more and more a likely prelude to rain. But there was no shelter, not even a stone overhang. And for some reason I can't explain, bugs scarcely bothered me at all. No animals either, except the odd rabbit and a few squirrels. The hunched bear-like figures I saw occasionally were certainly concoctions of my own brain—which reasoning did not make them any less fearsome.

A darker knot of consciousness inside the darkness, I chose the side of a hill again for a sleeping site. Low-lying ground I thought a vulnerable area. Which wasn't conscious thinking at all; but perhaps that different part of my brain which I called the Other was responsible.

Perhaps also when I slept the Other was in command, as some kind of guardian and warder. If I awoke suddenly and came to full control of my thought processes quickly enough, would it be possible to find out more about this Other, whom I was now convinced existed and functioned inside myself?

Night passed as a succession of uneasy dozings, stirrings into incomplete consciousness, a condition in which it was impossible to distinguish between shadowy night figures and the blurred images of my own night thoughts. That barred caboose-prison with broken windows flashed into my head. The moment when the caboose door exploded inward recurred, and I was again too surprised at freedom to be elated. Standing there shocked at success, when I had expected failure. In fact, expecting to fail at anything important, an attitude in myself that probably enhanced the chances of failure.

Rain whispering on leaves awoke me, a light drizzle that increased as morning wore on. My waterproof jacket ensured being mostly dry above the waist, but did nothing for legs and feet. I was half-drowned in less than an hour, plunging through undergrowth and ferny clearings. I was hungry, and kept trying to catch a glimpse of the sun, which I hadn't seen for two days.

A passage in the Bible occurred to me. Something like the text that runs: Shall a man by taking thought add one cubit to his stature? Maybe it wasn't that, but only a sharp realization that I hadn't been thinking to any purpose since being locked in this wide outdoor prison. Something bright flashed and glimmered in my mind, beyond all the greyness: that bright green river. The one I had crossed on a bridge from Hawk Junction, followed by a frisking unfaithful mongrel when I first headed south.

The river. The bridge. They formed two sides of a geographic triangle in my mind. The third side was this dripping forest, in which I had become the prisoner of mathematics.

Half-drowned, miserable and hungry as I was, a blessed euphoric bloom of hope: the odds two against one, and favouring me, that I could stumble on either the river or railway tracks that continued south after crossing the bridge. And paid myself the first compliment possible in several days, ego and hope reviving together.

A single glimpse of the sun was all I needed, even a bright spot where the fiery ball was burning a hole in the thick clouds. Climbing a hill, then shinnying up a tree with low-growing branches. Sliding back down the horny trunk again, trying to keep sighted on one silver-grey spot amid its surrounding dark-grey sky. Sighting from one slightly more prominent tree to another, staying on high ground, heading north, glorious north, glorious sun. Running again. That was a mistake. Slow down. Panting. Dizzy. A gamut of emotions, fizzing and alcoholic in racing brain and heart.

Keep thinking. Don't forget to think, the way you did before. But the mind wanders; it won't stay fastened to one thing or one place for very long. The thudding rhythm of my feet communicates with my brain. "Clementine" occurs to me. Who's she? "In a cabin, in a canyon, excavation for a mine/ lived a miner, a forty-niner, and his daughter, Clementine."

Singing. Not even feeling foolish about it. Rushing through wet undergrowth, roaring the chorus of "Clementine": "Oh my darling, oh my darling—" What was the rest of it? "Took her ducklings to the river, every morning just at nine/ stubbed her toe upon a sliver, and went down in the foaming brine." Why was it brine, how could the river be salt?

Wild eyed, dripping sweat and rain, undoubtedly a little mad. Hope will do that sometimes; despair is merely depressive. Two sides of an isosceles triangle—Name the other kinds of triangle? But I was terrible at mathematics. Name them anyway. I can't. And the rain rained, but with a definite bright spot in the sky over what might be the south-east. And I was, hopefully, heading north.

Squelching breathless through thick wet undergrowth on marshy ground, I nearly fell into a strange river. And still felt crazy from two days lost. What's your name river? Tell me your name. Oh yes, bonkers from talking to myself and Clementine.

The river gave no answer: only that it was a fast-flowing green river, and it was there, it was actually and blessedly there. I followed its banks to the right, and the right had to be more or less east. Rain stopped, the sun beamed down. There was a bridge, the bridge. My bridge, not Hart Crane's or anybody else's.

Soberly now, I walked south again on the CPR main line, careless of possible observers. My nose snuffling a little, body chilled in damp clothes. But they dried quickly in the reappearing sun. East of the railway tracks, some fishermen, taking down their tent and breaking camp. I asked them if they knew when there were any trains going south. They said: a passenger train just a few minutes from now on which they were returning to the Soo. They said: you could ride behind the coal car if you wanted to take the chance. I did want to. They were Americans.

One of them gave me a US dollar without my asking for it. He took me for a bum. I was. And grateful for warmth of any kind.

When the highball toot-tooted, boxcars and passenger cars hitched on behind stirred their steel bones, moving a foot or two indecisively. Then with deliberate intention, they chuffed south. In nearby bushes, a dirty hobo tensed his muscles, and dashed for a ladder behind the coal car.

And the rain of cinders began, stinging my skin, watering eyes, blackening everything like the Biblical rain of locusts. Feet braced against shuddering couplings, I endured. But still euphoric at having rejoined the world, even if rather crummy, my only world. Stung with cinders, hungry as an adolescent wolf, snuffling with incipient pneumonia, and damn glad to be alive.

We stopped a couple of times on our roaring progress south. Not for cities or towns, there were none. At small clusters of houses, perhaps for hunters or fishermen who had made appointments to be picked up, as had my own personal Americans. When the blurred mileposts slowed and a few houses appeared beside the tracks, indicating the Soo was just ahead, my nerves started to prickle. What if—what if—? Had the CPR cop wired ahead that an escapee was on the loose? Did the report say that he was armed and dangerous? Would a large policeman be waiting for me with handcuffs and leg irons? How much time would be added to the two-year sentence because of my jailbreak? And would my mother be able to visit me in prison?

·   ·   ·   ·   ·

Jumping off the train before reaching the station would be the best plan. But its speed was such that I'd be sure to break my neck and need a new skeleton after hitting the hard cinders. Courage and bravery were silly dictionary words not applicable to me, and I knew, I knew with certainty, that I didn't have the nerve to jump. Anyway, we were travelling much too fast.

The train steamed and roared past brick-coloured sheds, slowing now, but it still moved fast enough to make people into only pictures of people. Each brief glimpse between the cars left them standing stock-still, store-window dummies unable to move.

A wooden platform, the dull red station, drifting past slowly and ever more slowly . . . When the train stopped absolutely in the midst of its hesitations, a roaring wind existing only as an echo in my ears, my body climbed heavily down. It stood on the platform, thought to look natural and belonging there like the legal passengers.

And deceived no one. The inevitable cop materialized beside me. He was sausage-shaped, blue-coated and silver-buttoned. Pointing a school-teacherish finger at me he said, "Stay right here! I'll be back to deal with you after I've looked over the train."

Frozen stiff as a codfish on that railway platform, I stayed there for several moments while the well-dressed paying passengers looked at me as if I were an unwelcome foreigner. Then the voice of that Other, so knowledgeable about mathematics and triangles, spoke to me. And I felt a deep and abiding affection for him. He said, "Tarry not upon the order of thy going. Depart forthwith. Fuck off!"

And I did.

CHAPTER FOUR

· · · · · · · · ·

THE IRON ROAD

PART 2

S ault Ste. Marie is a steel town, a logging and pulpwood town, and
in 1936 a fairly roistering and sometimes drunken town. It seemed
to me remote from anywhere when I fled that railway cop and scam-
pered into the downtown Soo. I was shivering uncontrollably from
those two days in the woods, probably in danger of pneumonia. Since
there was a large Finnish population, there were also many steam baths.
I spent most of the day in one of them, emerging drained and enervated,
but not shivering any longer. Still nervous about being a wanted
desperado, I rented the cheapest room possible and signed in under
another name.

I felt that I'd been living at high speed, nerves twitching, temperature
high, peering into everyone's face on the street as if they had just arrived
from another planet. And also lucky, fortunate to have escaped those
woods around Hawk Junction! It was very close to being given a second
chance at life, after you'd already lost your first life. I was shaken-up
in all ways, and I expect my eyes were staring, sunken into my head,
since my weight was down to perhaps 165 pounds from all the missed
meals. If any of the people I stared at so earnestly in the Soo had asked
me a question, I'd have been liable to simply run away from them,
terrified.

Terrified? I think when you're in that heightened condition of nerves
and have foregone a few meals, been through a physical ordeal and are

very young, you're liable to fly right through the roof if anything alarms you. My sleep that night was broken and intermittent, hearing a man and woman quarreling beyond thin partitions, and a drunken party in another room—all this between sleep and waking. In dreams that night I was pursued by railway cops, feeling stinging cinders on my cheeks from the hooting engine far ahead of my roofless gondola, riding through the never-ending Northern Ontario forest all night long, someone whispering in my ear again and again: "You could get two years for this!" I woke to discover myself in a dingy bed; with an iron-hard erection—the kind you remember.

Still wondering if the police were looking for me, I took no chances on the railway any longer. Some of my small hoard of cash was expended to buy a steamship ticket from the Soo to Port Arthur, seven or eight hundred miles farther west. The lapping water quieted my nerves, at least something did. Lake Superior was calm for my sleeping benefit all that spring night, and the sleep removed more of my terror of being chased by cops. I caught another freight, and rode it west from Fort William.

. . . . .

All towns were rated by hoboes according to the belligerence or peacefulness of their local cops, whether the housewives were generous with their handouts—or even provided an occasional sit-down meal. Every freight train, whether heading east or west, always had at least a score of non-paying passengers. When they knocked on doors to ask for something to eat, it was of some importance to know beforehand what the likelihood was of being turned away empty-stomached or handed an axe and being directed to the backyard woodpile. And to know the location of each town's "jungle"—these jungles being woodsy spots near the railways where hoboes could sleep and boil their mulligan stew over an open campfire. Of course the town cops always knew where the jungles were located. If any crime had recently been committed in the area, the local constabulary descended first on the hoboes, rousting and sometimes throwing them in jail.

When I caught the westbound freight from Fort William, it had already steamed a mile or two from the marshalling yards. Peering from shrubbery beside the tracks, one could see the very long procession of jostling brick-red boxcars, with not a sign of any illegal riders. But ominously, walking rapidly along the catwalk on top of them, leaping the gap between cars, two uniformed figures passed each other going in opposite directions. At a no doubt pre-ordained spot, these cops jumped off the train. After which the trackside brush divulged a flood of shabby wanderers, most with a pack slung over one shoulder, a few with larger backpacks.

It's a delicate and precise operation to catch a moving train, and quite dangerous if it's travelling fast. I had thought of hitch-hiking west, but the trains were a much more certain and regular mode of transport. A few whispered colloquies with my fellow bums at trackside or in jungles provided me with train schedules, hints on the best ways of doing things, catching boxcars with least danger, where the cops were liable to be lurking. They were always generous to me with this very necessary information.

For instance, ordinary boxcars have steel ladders installed at the front end on one side of the car, at the rear end on the other side. And logically, you try to grab the rungs of the front ladder, not the rear one. If you should try to catch the train by grabbing the rear ladder, running at say fifteen miles an hour to match the train's speed, there's a good chance of falling between the cars and under the steel wheels in a mess of blood and screams. And I didn't kid myself: that particular unpleasant fate has befallen the occasional careless neophyte hobo.

It's a nerve-racking business, riding the freights. And there are all sorts of different places you can choose for the journey. Empty cars if you're lucky enough to catch one before the highball, the departure signal. Braced above the couplings sometimes, when you board a moving train; and later, climbing to the catwalks atop each car like spinal vertebrae. On refrigerator cars there's a small trapdoor front and back, beneath which you can ride if not claustrophobic. (One thinks of being trapped inside that tin box like a small coffin.) There are also long steel rods underneath boxcars. The public conception has hoboes travelling there, clinging desperately with fingertips while the roadbed blurs with speed just a few inches underneath them. I've never done that myself, or ever seen anyone else doing it. Riding the rods is not exactly a myth, but it is a very rare happening.

· · · · ·

Deep in the Great Depression, faces of people you encountered mirrored their economic circumstances. Blank unwritten-upon faces of the young, to the seamy visages of the very old. Most of the freight riders were looking for work, at least I thought so. Their clothes were often relatively clean, even if shabby, a mark of the amateur hobo, since riding trains is very hard on clothing. A few were out-and-out bums, moving from one place to another continually, who wandered for the sake of wandering. Occasionally I'd see one old man with a white beard who looked at least seventy, and I'm sure that riding freights has been the way he's spent most of his life. There's something distinctive about such people, and you don't see much of their inner selves looking out from their eyes.

This was the day of soup kitchens in towns and cities, work camps set up by the Bennett government, with unemployment statistics soaring. An aura and ambience of gloom and misery had settled over the entire country, the foremost thought in most people's minds being just survive, survive. The year before there'd been a big unemployment trek to Ottawa, with thousands of men riding the freight trains eastward to protest government starvation policies toward our own people.

Evidence of the desperate mood that inspired this trek was still visible everywhere. It was a mood in which the police were enemies, or at the very least, not to be trusted. In fact, the legends of police brutality were rampant among hoboes. One of these was a CPR cop dubbed "Capreol Red," so-named for the Northern Ontario town in which his activities centred. Capreol Red was said to club illegal freight riders from trains with a lead-weighted truncheon, inflicting broken bones and even death when his victims sometimes fell between cars and under the rumbling wheels. It was thought that the three branches of the police, Mounties, Provincial Police and railway cops took special delight in beating up more or less defenseless hoboes. Certainly the gap between police and ordinary citizens has never been wider.

I saw one example of police power—in fact I was involved in it—at a small NorOnt divisional point in the bush where trains changed locomotives before continuing west. The uniformed police with guns on their hips, either railway cops or Provincials, had lined up some thirty or forty hoboes beside the tracks, and one cop sat at a table like a businessman taking money from them. A couple of other cops had vacuumed the train of illegal passengers, then shepherded them to a spot where their money could be extracted with a minimum of trouble. There was no alternative, you either gave them your money and were allowed to proceed west, or refused and had your money taken anyway—but with the added danger of ending up in jail. My own tribute was fifty cents if I remember correctly, and that was a lot of money in those days.

·   ·   ·   ·   ·

By the time we reached Winnipeg I felt like a veteran bo. Of course, I had scarcely any money left after my extravagant splurge by passenger ship from the Soo to Port Arthur, with only a five dollar bill folded under the rubber patch on the ankle of my running shoe remaining. And felt nothing more than a small twitch of shame asking for a handout from some housewife, who was probably not very prosperous herself.

But that was the way things were done, the road to survival in a world where it seemed nobody cared very much and most people placed their own needs ahead of everyone else. Certain it was that the Ottawa government paid little attention to the shame and tragedy pervading the whole country. And you felt this—this climate and aura of acute melancholy in your bones. You didn't need statistics and suchlike evidences of poverty on paper; it was right there before your eyes. The mood affected everyone, a blight and plague like disease.

But I was young. The deathly terror at being an unregarded speck of dirt on the floor of the world was not always present in my make-up. Even the continual nervousness of riding freights and being chased by cops could sometimes be disregarded. I slept anywhere, in boxcars on sidings, empty section workers' sheds, riding flat cars, curled up into a foetus on the ground, literally anywhere—always with one eye flickering open at any possible threat to my personal living space. But still, among themselves, with a few rough exceptions, the freight-riders were a pretty law-abiding bunch. They had enough trouble scraping together the wherewithal to stay alive, and that was foremost.

· · · · ·

Poems ran through my head, scraps of them, things I had learned in school, other verses I had picked up from library books. I scribbled away on brown wrapping paper, working at a poem called "Reilly," about a not-entirely-imaginary freight train wanderer. The poem's protagonist was a picturesque hero of the steel roads, the doggerel soporific and cloying. Reilly was of course self-regarding, as we all were, writing "Kilroy was here" on boxcars and lonely water tanks in the bush. Gossip and rumours of crime and heroism filtered back and forth among the bums. When east-riding wanderers encountered western riders, stories of the road were exchanged in the trackside jungles, bad cops warned about, changes in the railway schedule, good and bad places to hit-up for handouts, and stories of women hoboes disguised as men.

Riding west out of Winnipeg, sitting in a boxcar doorway enjoying the sunlit morning, feet swinging loose and dangling, dreaming of nothing at all as houses grew scanty and green fields flooded into my eyes—a thundering pain overwhelmed my feet! And worse for me not knowing what had happened for a moment. The train was crossing a small river bridge, with low steel railings on either side, railings just high enough to collide violently with my carelessly swinging feet. If our speed had been five m.p.h. faster, I'd have been swept out that doorway; or failing that, my feet would have been broken. I'd been stupid. The penalty for stupidity in this case was being scarcely able to walk for a few days because of damage to pedal extremities. Well—I learned.

Sometimes there was exhilaration; it wasn't all grime and depression. Riding across western plains so flat that Winnipeg, Regina and Edmonton ought to have been visible to each other at the same time, the terrain seemingly without a wrinkle, every blade of grass a signpost on the horizon. At night, squatting in the shuddering boxcar, the lights of a prairie town approaching you from far away, like a great ship under all its canvas sailing toward you through the night.

I had heard about Broadview, Saskatchewan, long before arrival there. Only a small town, it was the point where time changed, all clocks were set an hour earlier at Broadview. But more important to the hoboes, it was a place where cops were said to be especially ungentle with a train's non-paying passengers. Our freight carried a load of farm machinery on flat cars, combines I think they were. I'd been dozing in the sun when the train began to slow, nodding awake to notice my fellow riders jumping off on all sides like fleas abandoning a stricken dog. I couldn't think of any reason for this, then remembered the formidable constabulary based just ahead.

Atop the lashed-down and floor-braced farm machines, I'd previously noticed trap doors. With hardly any delay I climbed inside one, entering a space of tinny darkness, metal gloom; hearing countless creaks and moans of metal rubbing against itself in ecstasy. There were blades and wheels and things inside that machine. I burrowed into the darkness under all of them, becoming invisible from the trap door through which I had entered.

The train crept and crawled, wheels' murmur transmitting itself to your bones, then so slow that movement became imperceptible, a coin or garden pea on the tracks might have stopped us. Only silence, broken by the engine's soft panting, which is like the susurration of crickets. And clangour of boots, banging against machinery. I remembered that old cry, "Cheese it, the cops!" from mythological childhood. And crouched in my metal nest, nerves taut, unable to cheese it, too frightened even to stir.

The trapdoor opened, someone peered down. Then the footsteps faded. After an hour or so of my entrapment, I heard bustling sounds of yard engines fussing around us, brakie's voices tinctured by my metal skin; then the jar and wham of a new engine coupled onto the train. And felt thankful these flatcar combines were not dropped off at Broadview.

In which case I would have remained behind inside one of them, a farmer's surprised face perhaps peering down at me eventually. And we moved, suddenly we moved, thanks be to some god of train schedules.

Calgary was memorable for a couple of things. I met a guy named Jim there, and we quickly became friends. He was twenty, medium-sized, dark haired and with a ready smile. One has empathy with a few people, but to say why is impossible. Jim and I were both sick of the dirt and lack of sleep endemic to riding freights. We both had a small amount of money, and therefore rented a cheap room above a Chinese restaurant. It had a couple of flimsy bunks. We collapsed on those bunks quite boneless, falling asleep almost as soon as our heads hit the pillows. And woke to a burning-burning sensation on every part of our bodies—not long after hitting the sack.

We sat on our bunks cursing and swearing, trying to figure out what could be wrong. It was, of course, bedbugs. They were attacking us in droves and congeries and regiments. Bitter complaints to the restaurant people were entirely fruitless. After a few minutes we abandoned the room, and spent all afternoon in a nearby park picking off bedbugs. And the little beggars were elusive, their fiery attentions being felt over most of the body, thankfully not in the crotch. I think I managed to get them all, but every time I itched thereafter, those bedbugs came to mind.

West from Calgary toward the high mountains. You could see them from atop the train as we trundled and chuffed toward British Columbia in bright afternoon sunlight. One chapter in my high school Canadian history had been entitled "The Shining Mountains"—about La Verendrye, a Quebecois explorer and fur trader, whose farthest western wanderings had brought him within sight of these same mountains. And when you think of it, there is something in history and human experience that is repetitive; your own mind is coloured by other men's reactions to the same thing, other men and women traversing the same country and experiences as yourself, again and again. And that is exhilarating to me.

I fell asleep somewhere west and south of Calgary, wearing a sweater and using my old windbreaker for a pillow (clothes that had seen pretty hard wear by this time, especially from those two days lost in the Algoma bush). A blank fragment of time was spent on a siding somewhere, with both Jim and I trying to shorten the journey with sleep. Shuntings in the night and lights flashing . . .

I awoke as if from a winter's hibernation, lost in the places I had been before. And where was I now? Surrounded and enclosed by complete silence. Stretched out on the splintery wooden floor of that boxcar, I could see a streak of sunlight that chopped a narrow hole in the dirt. And a wall of dark stone outside, extending from bottom to top of the half-open door.

It was the Crow's Nest Pass, many miles south of the Kicking Horse Pass. We had neglected to specify to the President of CP Railway which pass we preferred. All this country west of the Crow's Nest is a coal mining area. There was a depressed look about things, shabby buildings, people with scrunched-up faces and no joy in them; when it rained, coal dust blackened the streets and ran through the gutters . . . At Frank—still in Alberta—a whole mountain had tumbled down over the town. Like some vengeful god in the Christian Bible avenging himself on a sinful people.

When Jim and I knocked on people's doors for handouts, even the food was noticeably poorer in quality, or so it seemed. Of course, you hardly ever got anything but sandwiches, sometimes only bread and butter. We were grateful for that, and both broke. However, the five dollar bill inside the rubber patch on my running shoe remained intact, a kind of emergency life preserver.

At Fernie, a small mining town, Jim and I slept just beyond the outskirts, near what looked like an abandoned grain elevator. When our campfire died down after midnight, we heard savage snarling, very loud and very close. It jolted me into consciousness before all the parts of my body were ready, as if arms and legs were responding to the sound by waving wildly in the air, while the rest of me remained prone. My brain was elsewhere, still trying to process the frightful screaming which had replaced that crescendo of snarling. Then a dark furry body rushed past the nearly dead campfire, as large as the darkness itself. And so close you could feel the wind of its passage before it disappeared into the forest.

We sat there, I think paralyzed for a few moments, then one of us stirred the fire into life. "Mountain lion!" Jim whispered awesomely. "Mountain lion?" I repeated mindlessly. There was no more sleep that night.

·   ·   ·   ·

Riding the tops of boxcars by daylight all the way west, dipping down into valleys where the light turned pale green from lush shrubbery and surrounding trees. There was an illusion of being underwater, enhanced by the contrast between light and shade: you slowly climbed mile-long switchbacks on the sides of mountains, finally achieving air so clear you were suspended inside an immense crystal chandelier. I felt an exuberance from it, this geography of the spirit—like Achilles in Homer's *Iliad*, dipped repeatedly into invulnerability. And at that moment when you forgot where you were, the cops were most likely to appear.

It was probably riding those freights across the endless forests of Northern Ontario, the prairies rising in giant steps to the mountains, and then the Rockies themselves—such a wonder in the newly-arriving mind of a youngster—that some conception of what the country is was formulated for me. The actual physical presence at the eyes and ears replaces mere factual book knowledge; so many miles or hectares of a nation, then the land itself plunges into your mind. British Columbia was a revelation to me, more vertical territory than horizontal. If this whole kingdom of mountains, all those various angles and polyhedrons and rhomboids, akimbo tangents and tetrahedrons could be uncrumpled and flattened by your hands like a big sheet of wrapping paper, then spread out across the map of Canada, the resulting horizontal area would amount to an empire.

The towns strung out along the railway were a bit unreal to me, despite the grim social conditions of the "Hungry Thirties" and grinding music of steel on steel. All the parade of faces, faces that worried about things beyond themselves, faces that wore masks to prevent you seeing the owner. I really had been a child until I rode the freights, protected, sheltered, cocooned in all possible ways. By my mother as well as the conditions in which I grew up. Not rich, not poor. I suppose you'd call the condition lower middle class, in the English way of assessing social strata. Therefore it was magical to experience all this in such a brief time, the idea of a country taking shape in reality; although I'm sure this particular reality was a transient illusion. Certainly, those sunlit shapes of towns in the thirties in which I was a passing ghost—they were transitory. At the time, though . . .

· · · · ·

"Deadheads" are wornout railway locomotives. Passing through the Kootenay Mountains, Jim and I crawled inside the fireboxes of two of these defunct engines. They were being taken to Vancouver for scrap iron, probably destined for Japan. The reason for secreting ourselves in those dirty, cramped mantraps was the Doukhobors. Members of this strange religious sect were bombing trains, tearing up railway tracks, derailing peace and progress. The brakies had warned us about Doukhobor activities, other hoboes had warned us, leaving our own minds uncertain and unsettled. Houses were burning all over the Kootenays; Mounties lurked behind fence posts and town cops behind the Mounties.

Inside the guts of that deadhead, despite the grating rumble of steel on steel underneath, I heard nothing but smothering silence. When your nerves are keyed up, scared the train might explode, there isn't much else you can think of. That firebox was nearly soundproof and all you felt was continuous vibration, and fear a brakie might twist the outside latch and lock me inside forever. All in all, one of the more uncomfortable evenings I've enjoyed.

Many miles farther on when we stopped for water, listening to the chuff-chuff of engine and loud-sounding crickets, Jim and I looked at each other and laughed. Both of us were blackened by soot from feet to the top of our heads. We hurried to the water tank and washed as best we could without soap, while the incurious train crew watched. (And that was generally the case: it was quite rare if a brakie made any objections at all to the presence of non-paying passengers.)

Leaving the freights at Vernon—at one end of the Okanagan Valley—we started to hike south on the east side of Lake Okanagan. The big towns like Kelowna and Penticton were fifty or sixty miles away. When we reached those places eventually, we hoped jobs might be available. Jim had set his mind on getting a stake together, saving his money to that end. He'd decided to accept almost any employment anywhere at any time. I felt a little more choosy, but I liked Jim, now regarded him as a friend, and it was easier to go along with his decisions than to make my own.

Ten miles or so from Vernon there was roadwork. The highway was being re-surfaced with boiling tar, then gravel thrown atop the tar (or maybe the tar was actually asphalt). We got jobs there for a couple of days, at wages of twenty or twenty-five cents an hour. (Hamburger was ten cents a pound at that time, and a restaurant meal twenty-five or thirty cents). That job was a lucky break. We shovelled gravel from beehive-shaped piles beside the road, spreading it onto sizzling tar that would remove your skin if it happened to splash. A single drop of it stung like a red-hot needle. And the afternoon heat: it must've been well over a hundred degrees Fahrenheit. We tied dirty rags around our heads to ward off the blistering sun and soak up sweat; water was consumed by the gallon.

We worked on one side of a two-lane road, the flagman stopping traffic when necessary. After a couple of hours I heard Jim yell, "Look out!"—or I yelled, the yell seeming to come from both of us. An onrushing car headed directly towards us, just a few feet away. We dived for the roadside grass, tumbling head-over-heels. Somehow or other the car had gone past the flagman, then swerved in our direction, narrowly missing us even as we leaped for safety.

It seems odd to me now, that incident. I try to mentally place Jim's and my locations on the road to make it possible for that hurtling car to be so dangerous. I can't. Of course all this is over fifty years ago, so I can forgive myself for not remembering.

I do recall the road foreman blistering that careless driver's ears, listening with admiration to a flow of language I would have liked to emulate.

When the road work ended, we just kept on going south, now with some money in our pockets. Sleeping in cedar shavings at a sawmill one night was the most pleasant bed we found—the scent causing me to dream of cool forest aisles in summer. After the sawmill we crossed the lake on a ferry, along with some farm workers.

Orchards lined the lake's west side highway, apples glowing among the leaves, supplying us with fruit when we thought there were no observers. Sloping down beyond the greenery, blue water glittered in the sun. Lake Okanagan, eighty miles long and only three or four wide, said to harbour a monster called Ogopogo, which abducted unwary tourists, especially attractive female tourists.

At Penticton Jim and I stopped to look for work; there was none. But at Kelowna—we thought amazingly—a farmer stopped us on the street and asked if we were interested in working for a dollar a day and board. Or was it a dollar a week? In any event, I thought the wages were low, even for 1936. The farmer's name sounded like Skimmerhorn (a man who skims?). He gave us a ride on the back of his stake truck to the mountain farm, fed us and put us to work.

We did everything. Forking hay into a truck; felling trees with double-bladed axes and six-foot saws, then splitting them with steel wedges; shovelling manure and hoeing potatoes . . . it was hot. I weighed 165–170 pounds; the way sweat poured off me I was afraid I'd shrink down to 150. I looked somewhat like a fence rail. At night Jim and I were the sole occupants of a bunkhouse with two cots, a washstand and windup phonograph. The only two records, both 78 rpm, were John McCormack singing "The Far Away Bells are Ringing," and Wilf Carter doing violence to "The Strawberry Roan." We wore them out the rest of the way.

After a few days Jim and I discussed future plans. We liked each other, and wanted to stay together; but this hard work for a small amount of money didn't suit me. I wanted to head for the coast; Jim intended to stick it out at the job. With some difficulty I managed to extract one dollar from Farmer Skimmerhorn, then took to the road. The worst part was saying good-bye to my friend. I've never seen him since.

. . . . .

At Vancouver I went to a Dorothy Lamour movie, and hiked to Stanley Park where a parrot cussed me out on the waterfront. My intention, going there, had been to try and get a job on a gill-netter or long-liner. But a wave of restlessness overtook me, or it may have been homesickness. I don't know how to explain it. That same evening I slipped under the barrier at a level crossing near the waterfront, and hopped a freight heading east. I'm amazed at myself even now. Leaving like that made the whole westward journey seem pointless, an exercise in futility. I didn't even visit an unemployment office in Vancouver.

. . . . .

Homesick and restless has to be the explanation. A veteran hobo by that time, practised in begging handouts from housewives and soliciting stale buns at bakeries. Sometimes I was even daring enough to ride behind the engines of passenger trains, a much more rapid mode of travel than freights. You had to be especially agile at this, jumping off the train late since it approached stations at fairly high speed. And there were generally cops waiting on the station platforms.

I rode a passenger train east into Kamloops, disembarking when it had slowed down enough. I was too late. Two Mounties were waiting for me on the platform. I suspect some telegraph operator had noticed me behind the coal car farther west, and tapped out a telegraph message to the police. I was locked up for the night, and had a good sleep. Next morning before a magistrate, I was given a suspended sentence and ordered to get out of town. The Mounties made sure I did just that, their close surveillance making it impossible for me to board any variety of eastbound transport.

I walked the tracks, hiking along the railway ties to the first water tank east of Kamloops. It was twenty-five miles. Evening arrived before I did, and it was later still before a freight trundled up for a drink of water. I rode that train all night long, braced against couplings between cars. It was much too cold in the high mountains to ride the catwalks atop cars. Shivering at first light, I scrambled down to the cinders, confronted immediately by a railway cop. He said, "You wait here," then turned to examine the rest of the train for more illegal passengers.

These guys must've been reading each other's mail: that was exactly the same thing the cop at Sault Ste. Marie had said to me. I didn't pay any attention then, and didn't now either. But I don't think they really wanted me very badly, giving such a dangerous criminal a chance to escape and commit more horrible crimes. It'd be closer to the truth to say they didn't want to clutter up their jails with useless bums, who generally didn't care much if they spent a night or two in jail anyway. Jail was restful.

I started to walk again, heel and toe east over the railway ties. A highway running beside the tracks went up one side of the mountains and down the other; at least the rails were more or less level. Trouble was, when I spanned the distance between two ties at one step, that was a little too short a stride to be comfortable; but three ties were too much even for my long legs. And the distance from Golden (that was where the cop had divested my train of its fleas) to the next town was endless. The next town was Field, and Field was not many miles west of the continental divide, on either side of which the rivers ran in different directions away from the continent's high point. I was in pretty good shape, despite needing sleep, having walked twenty-five miles the day before. But the wearisome distance from Golden to Field?—I had no idea how far it was. But I thought there ought to be at least a water tank along the way.

Walking those ties, the sun blazed down, even in this highest part of the cold mountains. I had no hat, but improvised one from a newspaper someone had probably thrown out of a passenger train's observation car. I had nothing to eat all day, my stomach gnawed with hunger. Around noon I picked up half a slice of buttered bread from the tracks. Undoubtedly it came from the same source as the newspaper. Mountain streams under culverts provided drinking water. Sweat kept pouring down my forehead, despite the paper hat; my legs became wooden sticks around mid-afternoon. I had no socks; they had disappeared somewhere along the iron trail. I'd washed them in icy mountain water several times.

The tracks were normally at least forty or fifty feet higher than the forest on either side, with snow-peaked ranges soaring above everything. Far down below, I saw a large animal some time during that day of sun. It moved slowly on the edge of the bush, seeming in no hurry to either run or perhaps attack. My eyes were so glazed by the long day's brightness I couldn't identify it, nor decide whether to be scared or pay no attention to the beast. On fast reflection I decided it was wiser to be scared, and increased my pace eastward. If it was a bear, this was no place for me.

I trudged into the small railway town of Field just as it was getting dark. And managed to beg part of a loaf of bread from the CPR restaurant, then investigated outlying sheds used by section hands until I found one unlocked. A pile of greasy rags inside provided a bed. That night was probably the soundest sleep of my life. And thinking back, over those two days I walked a total of fifty-eight miles. I've hated exercise ever since.

In the morning, after chewing up the remainder of the dry bread and a perfunctory wash at a railway pump, I tramped east along the tracks to a point outside Field. I thought the gradient there was steep enough to slow down the trains and allow me to catch a freight. But they raced past me at around thirty miles an hour, with three engines supplying motive power. At the marshalling yards I'd just left, they'd hitched on an extra two locomotives: the height of land—i.e. the continental divide—was not very many miles ahead.

The speed of those several freights that went by was very discouraging to me; it would have been suicide to even make the attempt to catch one. But I did make an attempt, seeing the steel ladders at the front of boxcars flash by at dizzying speed. I didn't grab at the rungs. Doing so, a miss would have bounced me violently off the boxcar, into a collision with whatever was behind my back. So I sat down at the edge of the cinders, disheartened, while three more trains flashed by. I had no hope of making connections with any of them.

After that, I thought of returning to Field and trying to board a train right under the noses of the cops. "Kilroy" or my friend Jim might have done that. Not me. I was too chicken. Instead I sat on top of a dried-up culvert, thinking black thoughts and swinging legs idly over space. Then two black bears walked out from the culvert right under my legs, without seeing me above them. A tremendous wave of fear washed over me; if it wasn't fear it was about sixty-eight other emotions all colliding at once in my brain-pan. I was damn near paralyzed. I just sat there, trying to sort out all the info I'd ever picked up about bears before they sat down to a human meal.

They paid no attention to me, probably not even knowing I was there. The two furry backs disappeared in the greenery down the mountain-side, as my breathing began to reach normal again. Far below, the Kicking Horse River split into several different shallow channels; there'd been no rain for some time. Along the shoreline, after four or five minutes, I could see two small black figures, I'm sure entirely unaware of the emotions they'd evoked.

I must have slept, because the amber light told me it was late afternoon. My snooze had been uninterrupted by the sound of roaring trains a few feet away. It seeped gradually into my mind that there'd been no trains whatever going by, either freight or passenger. Then a couple of those gasoline "kickers" section hands use sputtered past, both loaded with passengers. Nothing else. And I thought that was peculiar. It was so quiet too, so very quiet. Something odd must be happening! Where? Maybe Field, but more likely farther east down the tracks. Else why would those men be going there on the section hands' kickers?

Something had happened, that was now obvious. Whatever it was had stopped all heavy traffic, freight and passenger. Walking a couple of miles eastward down the tracks gave me the answer: Landslide. Melting snow had loosened many tons of earth high up the mountainside, causing it to rumble down across the tracks with the sound of thunder in my sleep. I hadn't heard the earth and ice cascading down the mountain: but the sight of it reaching for more than a hundred yards across the right of way was awesome. The tracks were, of course, buried. Luckily no train had been passing when it happened; but now all east-west traffic was at a standstill on the CPR main line.

A small group of men were scratching away at the slide-site with pick and shovel, another man standing by obviously in charge. I asked the foreman for a job, then was teamed with another workman and became part of the emergency operation. My partner swung a pick, while I grubbed away with a shovel. He was very white-faced, a Ukrainian, and liked to talk. His nose wasn't a very good fit for his face, pushed around to one side. He was twenty, he said. Overhead they'd strung a few electric lines from which some light bulbs scattered the shadows. After we'd worked a while I was feeling very hungry; someone came around with sandwiches and someone else with drinking water.

In the darkness, on either side of my Ukrainian and I, were now scattered several dozen other workmen, all busily scratching marks on the mountain. We grubbed away with pick and shovel, steel clinking against stone, swishing rubble down the mountainside. Over the past several hours work trains kept arriving from Calgary eighty miles east, with additional crews. The one foreman in evidence was not in evidence very often, the job being largely without supervision.

I was both tired and not-tired, which means that the last two days of heel and toe tramping over the railway ties and lack of food had taken something out of me. But part of it had been replaced by last night's heavy sleep in the section shed, and a little more from snoozing beside the tracks waiting for an eastbound train. And besides, I was young. But around midnight, with floodlights providing scanty illumination for our monotonous shovelling and pick-swinging, the Ukrainian and I were both weary.

During the preceding evening we had noticed shadowy figures departing the work site, some of them returning a couple hours later. The grapevine whispered to us that a mining company power plant was situated close to the area, its furnace room warm and spacious. The foreman may have been sleeping too, since no one cried "Stop" when my friend and I left the job without permission. (I call my Ukrainian "friend" because that's the way it happens sometimes; you get along well with someone and do not question such good feelings.)

We must have spent three hours in that warm concrete womb of a place, engines throbbing nearby with the regular beating of a mechanical heart. Then sneaking back to the job as if our absence had been only to relieve ourselves, that was easy. (And if one says cheating one's employer is wrong, that is true: but making men work for seventy-two hours without relief is also humanly unmerciful . . .)

On our return to the landslide site, the moon was floating high among the clouds above the Kicking Horse River. A clear and windless night. Far below us the five or six arms of the river glittered—no, I guess they didn't glitter much, since there was no wind. They reflected the moon back at itself like giant mirrors, a silvery reduplication, a flame of silver moons. Quite magical for me. I worked with my eyes always on the river, always watching the moon, tired muscles taking sustenance from the sky. When increasing light made everything grey look even more grey, mist gathered on the mountainside across the river valley, and crept down behind the Ukrainian and I. By this time we were waving our arms like tired rag dolls, and swung our tools slowly, scarcely aware of what we were doing, renewed weariness gathering in our bones.

By mid-morning the water-carrier had been around, and a guy with more sandwiches (bologna, ordinarily unwelcome to my mother-spoiled appetite), the day bright and unending. I was questioning myself whether it was more wearisome to swing a pick and lift a shovel, or just stand leaning on the handle, a scarecrow without hope of being human. Blisters springing up on hands, legs wooden sticks, brain only alive when pain made you aware that some outlying province of the body was talking rebellion. But this dull continuous torture was not pain as such, since the torture itself blunted its own effects.

I began to forget everything, where I was, and why I was there; sometimes my Ukrainian stared at me and I at him with surprise that either one of us was still moving and distinguishable from trees. He was certainly as weary as me. His wandering nose in a face growing pink in the sun, swaying body in its lift to the sky and swing back to earth, they aroused my deep concern. I can't say for sure, but I think we laid our hands on each other's shoulders when the noon sun was near its highest—and said to each other: "For chrissake, keep going! I need you to be there in order for me to be here!"

Did I say that? I guess it's not likely, but I felt it. And the earth swung its earthen body another several degrees into afternoon, then early evening. With my shirt removed, the strong sun tattooed my back and shoulders until protection became quickly necessary. Blisters broke, and I complained bitterly to anyone within hearing. But again, I don't know if I actually did that. If God had existed, I would have called his name. I would have said, "Get me outa here, God! If you do, please sir, I'll break my own personal record of attending King Street United Church forty-four Sundays out of fifty-two. And I'll double that every Leap Year!"

Another half-awake snooze leaning on shovel that evening. But it permitted me to endure. Water came, food, foreman, some big shots who just stared at us. My Ukrainian was nearby, face haggard and drawn. Another night. And throb-throb of the mechanical heart, from somewhere down the mountain. The river spread its octopus arms under the moon; my own arms dipped and lifted and pretended they were working. And summer wore into fall while the river shone and the sun turned red and slipped down behind a mountain. Then it came up again, and I lost all track of time . . .

There was no relief, not another shift coming to work; and there was no one to push you, no slave-driving foreman with whip tongue. The foreman was there, in the near vicinity, but we seldom saw him. Evening of the third day, and neither one of us had given up the ghost. Through bleared eyes we saw that the track was clear. Fresh workmen from Field and Golden worried the last few rocks and shovelsful of earth from the right of way and down the littered mountainside.

Emergency work crews and hired-on labour like myself all lined up at a little table to receive their pay cheques. There were no pay cheques. You received a small pink card which had to be exchanged for either money or a cheque at the CPR offices in Calgary. A work train, with the interior of its cars lined with bunks, waited for us at a siding a couple of miles east down the tracks. My Ukrainian and I swallowed a last sandwich and fell into those bunks, asleep so quickly its effect was like a blow on the head.

I never heard the engine when its couplings banged onto our work train. I slept and slept. In the morning, coming to bleary consciousness, bearings of time and place mislaid, it took several moments to assign everything to its proper slot. This was Calgary; everyone else in the train was gone, including my Ukrainian friend; I was very hungry again, and still.

Wandering out of the railway marshalling yards into a crummy district of shabby store fronts, and greasy spoon restaurants beside the tracks, I spent all the money I had left for a fifteen-cent breakfast. And started out looking for the CPR offices in order to get paid. But today was Saturday; everything was closed. Discouraged, I started back to the railway yards, and met an apparition. I could see it coming from far away, clothes flapping as it moved, an immensely fat man, so ragged and dirty and smelling so bad that any self-respecting skunk on a Calgary street would phone the cops.

The apparition said, "That cocksucker, Aberhart—" That's all I remember. I fled, escaping the unpleasant smell.

A train was being made up in the yards when I arrived back; a kind brakie told me it was bound for Regina and points east. Rather than spend a weekend without money in this cowboy town (everyone I met in Calgary, then and later, wore high-heeled boots and a Stetson hat), I boarded the train.

All the incidents and minutae of the trip back to Ontario, cold journeys at night with cinders stinging the face, handouts from housewives at backyard doors, good and bad brakies, cops, everything has faded into some mental limbo. I can't remember. Back in Trenton, I cashed my pink card at the CPR offices there, and felt briefly rich.

Now, long after this youthful hullabaloo of nerves and travel and journeys through the shouting wind at night, I am nostalgic. I know well that everything I've been through, all my fear and trepidation, all my exaltations and euphoria, have changed me much, have left their indelible imprint. As they say, as most people seem to say, I wouldn't have had anything different.

Not to be smug about it, not many people get to ride those boxcars, run away from cops and try to outfox them, beg for handouts during the Great Depression, reach the blue Pacific and then turn their back on it with youthful scorn, heading back the same day towards the grey east. At least not many people alive today did those things. Hugh Garner rode the freights, but I know of no other writer who did. They fascinated

me, those trains; the undoubted danger, the rail music that has pounded
and throbbed into a long silence . . .

I rode the freights west again during the summers of 1937 and 1938.
During the fall and winter of those years I worked at whatever odd jobs
were available. And every year I awaited spring with bored eagerness.
And the iron road waited for me.

> Riding the boxcars out of Winnipeg in a
> morning after rain so close to
> the violent sway of fields it's
> like running and running
> naked with summer in your mouth and
> the guy behind you grunts and says
> "Got a smoke?"
>
> Being a boy scarcely a moment and you
> hear the rumbling iron roadbed singing
> under the wheels at night and a door jerking open
> mile after dusty mile riding into Regina with
> the dust storm crowding behind you and
> a guy you hardly even spoke to
> nudges your shoulder chummily and says
> "Got a smoke?"
>
> Riding into the Crow's Nest mountains with
> your first beard itching and a
> hundred hungry guys fanning out thru
> the shabby whistlestops for handouts and
> not even a sandwich for two hundred miles
> only the high mountains and knowing
> what it's like to be not quite a child any
> more and listening to the tough men
> talk of women and talk of the way things are
> in 1937
>
> Riding down in the spit-grey sea-level morning
> thru dockyard streets and dingy dowager houses
> with ocean a jump away and the sky beneath you
> in puddles on Water Street and an old Indian woman
> pushing her yawning scratching daughter
> onto a balcony to yell at the boy-man passing

"Want some fun?—come on up"—and the girl just
come from riding the shrieking bedspring bronco
all the up and down night to a hitchpost morning
full of mother and dirt and lice and
hardly the place for a princess
of the Coast Salish
(My dove my little one
tonight there will be wine and drunken suitors
from the logging camps to pin you down
in the outlying lands of sleep
where all roads lead back to the home-village
and water may be walked on)

Stand in the swaying boxcar doorway
moving east away from the sunset and
after a while the eyes digest a country and
the belly perceives a mapmaker's vision
in dust and dirt on the face and hands here
its smell drawn deep thru the nostrils down
to the lungs and spurts thru blood stream
campaigns in the lower intestine
and chants love songs to the kidneys
After a while there is no arrival and
no departure possible any more
you are where you were always going
and the shape of home is under your fingernails
the borders of yourself grown into certainty
the identity of forests that were always nameless
the selfhood of rivers that are changing always
the nationality of riding freight trains through the depression
over long green plains and high mountain country
with the best and worst of a love that's not to be spoken
and a guy right behind you says then
"Got a smoke?"
You give him one and stand in the boxcar doorway
or looking out the window of a Montreal apartment
or running the machines in a Vancouver factory
you stand there growing older

—*Transient* (1965)

CHAPTER FIVE

. . . .

PER ARDUA (ET CETERA)

In mid-summer of 1939 I was twenty. When war was declared, everyone joined some branch of the military, army, navy or air force. At least it seemed they did. People I knew disappeared from my knowing; familiar faces on the street were replaced by strangers; men marched and counter-marched at district armories. There was quiet hustle and bustle everywhere, but not much actual excitement since the war's beginning was more or less stalemate.

I went to the RCAF base just east of Trenton and took the physical; the blue air force uniform looked more attractive to me than brown khaki. My reasons for joining up were not patriotism, at least I don't think so in retrospect. It was the climate and mood of the times to join some branch of the military. One just did, because that was the way things were. In newspapers and on radio there was no special emphasis on death and destruction, the terrible futility of war. In fact there was often a lightheartedness about the way people regarded this oncoming Armageddon, which was still only play-acting at war. Wearing a uniform was thought of in much the same light as an ordinary job, with the added benefits of free clothes and medical care.

. . . . .

I was not called up for actual service until January 10, 1940. I was given a badly fitting blue uniform and a number, R52768. My trade category was "General Duty"—which meant that my time could be spent doing anything at all, literally anything. But after initial uncertainties I was assigned to the Airmen's Mess, which was the responsibility of Sergeant Knowles. The sergeant was a small lean Scotsman, whom nearly everyone liked, including me.

The Mess was in two separate sections: a huge dining area with Knowles in charge, and the sizable kitchen with a sergeant-cook directing things. Of course, those two sergeants had completely separate responsibilities: the reason I mention this was that I became involved with their divided jurisdictions, entangled in them.

Most of the General Duty guys working in the Mess—all Aircraftsman Second Class like myself—were of local origin; I knew quite a few of them, at least by sight. Our duties were many and varied: sweep and mop the dining and cooking areas; become beasts of burden at the orders of both cooks and Sergeant Knowles, convey food to counters or wherever it was needed; clean tables, fill salt cellars and pepper containers; keep the large white enamel jugs filled with milk. In fact, we did just about anything.

It had been pounded into our heads, of course, that we must obey superior officers, those airmen of higher rank than ourselves in both kitchen and mess. And it was inevitable that some of the non-commissioned officers began to fall in love with their own power and authority: they liked giving orders and seeing them obeyed. One of this breed among the cooks was Corporal Chase, who took particular delight, I thought, in making me do things that were not my direct responsibility.

Chase wore the white cook's clothing and distinctive hat; he was medium size, about twenty-five, with a florid face and very full red lips. His attitude toward me was, let us say, unfriendly. There were big stainless-steel, electrically heated cooking pots in the kitchen, about five feet in height, a long row of them for boiling whatever it was. Beneath them was a lengthy gutter and drains to take care of anything that boiled over. This was the scene of my downfall.

The easiest place to empty coffee grounds was in the drains under those steel cooking pots. Sergeant Knowles had told me that was okay when I asked him about it. But Corporal Chase said nix, don't do it. This was a dilemma for me, divided authority. Who should I obey, superior rank or the guy who gave the last order? Corporal Chase gave the last order. Far as I was concerned, fuck Corporal Chase. Besides, sergeants eat corporals. (Of course I wasn't quite so carefree when all this happened.)

Anyway, I emptied coffee grounds under the cooking pots after Chase had expressly instructed me not to do it. He happened to have a water hose in his hand at this time, and turned it on me with considerable wetness ensuing. I happened to have a large white enamel pitcher in my hand, which I'd just emptied. I propelled this heavy pot toward my superior officer's noggin with considerable velocity. It made thudding contact. After that, things got a bit confused.

I was immediately placed "on charge" for striking a superior officer, despite Sergeant Knowles' earlier permission to empty, etc., etc. But Knowles had a higher rank than Chase. And in this particular case there was some provocation: Corporal Chase and I were decidedly antithetical, which means I didn't like the prick. While all this was going on, the charges being figured out and so on, I was behind bars. And suddenly forced into being an adult, given no time to adjust, and feeling very sorry for myself.

Two days later I was quick-marched into the presence of a commissioned officer, with Sergeant Knowles and Corporal Chase for and against AC2 Purdy. It would've been a scene right out of Kafka if I'd read Kafka at the time. They took my wedge forage cap away from me, as if headgear was the trademark of being a free man, and it was not possible to flee the premises hatless. The barking voice of the NCO in charge of that detail still rings in my ears if I shake my head a little too vigorously.

"Prai-soner and aescort, quii-ck mahh-rch!" and "Haww-lt!" (It's an odd fact which I have researched extensively that the NCO in charge of such details sounds different every time.) "Layy-ft tawn!"

The officer, a bored flight looey, who had sold used cars on civvy street, looks at the documents on his desk and says, "Do you accept my punishment?" (This in lieu of a full-dress court martial.) Well, do you? Sure, man, whatcha think—I wanta go through this crap the rest of my life?

Two weeks confined to barracks: I was lucky, I guess. And for the remainder of my time in the Airmen's Mess, Corporal Chase and I walked on eggs when we approached each other, wary of enamel jugs and water hoses. Then I was posted—which means transferred—to Uplands Air Base at Ottawa for a disciplinarian course of instruction. Doing well at Uplands meant I would come away from there with twin stripes designating corporal. This was an outcome devoutly desired on my part, in order that I would not be quite so vulnerable to guys like Corporal Chase.

.   .   .   .   .

All along, of course, I had been writing poems. Writing them was—and I guess still is—a condition of living for me. Not like breathing or my heart beating, which sounds literarily pretentious anyway. I take writing for granted. The words: "I must write a poem" never come into my head, I just do it.

At Uplands in Ottawa I ran into LAC Bob Terence, who also wrote poems. He was a couple of years older than me, had been writing most of his life. And perhaps, looking back at him, Terence had a plodding quality about him. He was much concerned with change and improvement, getting better and better with his prosody. And was also interested in my stuff, read it, commented on it, without appearing to be greatly overwhelmed. I don't blame him a bit: my poems were simply awful. But the important thing was: Bob Terence encouraged me at a time when I needed encouragement. I can't remember his own stuff at all, but there's a warm memory of the man himself.

Just before the war, and for a while after, I was sending poems to US magazines, like *Driftwind* (which used wallpaper for its covers), *The Lyric West*, and *Florida Poetry Review*—names like that. A few were published, giving me the exalted feeling that I was one of the literati; it kept my ego at a level which allowed me to tolerate myself.

.　.　.　.　.

On return to Trenton, wearing the proud badge of corporal, saluting officers wasn't quite so demeaning. (And I did keep my eye open for Corporal Chase.) Then, accompanied by another corporal, I went to Toronto and bought a 1927 Whippet automobile, a car of ancient vintage even in 1940. I drove it back to Trenton without ever having driven a car before. And obviously, a driver's license was an immediate requirement. This didn't present any problems.

Visiting my old school friend Harold Wannamaker in Trenton town, we went swimming together at Oak Lake. And met a girl there named Shirley, already known to my friend. She rode the old Whippet's running board back from the lake to the parking lot, clinging to the door frame and exuding an aura of sex and femininity.

All those curves, the swell of breast and girl-scent and enticing cheek just inches away while I drove the car—and nearly plowed it directly into a large tree. I was badly smitten, but had scarcely ever dared speak to one of these strange female creatures before. To do so would be to take the chance of finding yourself less than nothing, if she refused to acknowledge your existence. To do so would be—well, anyway, I did so.

Shirley and I drove to the sand banks near Picton a couple of days later, with the ostensible purpose of swimming. I ran the car out of gas along the way, and had to walk to a service station for more, at considerable loss of dignity. At the beach we undressed far distant from each other; not for propriety's sake, but from a kind of reversed prurience in my head. Just as it was getting dark we waded out into the shallow water extending a quarter mile into Lake Ontario. I didn't even dare hold Shirley's hand while we waded into the semi-darkness.

I seemed to exist in a separate cocoon from the girl, moving with jerkiness, stiffness, half-frozen and half-thawed; knowing all the time I was acting like a stupid ass and could do nothing about it. Shirley tried to break into my robotic stiffness, probably because I made her nearly as uncomfortable as myself; talking about her girl friend and her girl friend's romantic life.

And yet, however far from communication you are, this is the time when you are most intensely conscious of that other human being. For the first time in my slightly retarded life I was on the verge of contact with another mind and body, the invasion of self when you feel those delicate tendrils from another universe touching inside your defences. And I blew it.

Shirley tried to make things easier, but we drove home to Trenton in near silence. When I tried to speak with her again, she wouldn't come to the phone. A day or two later I went out with another girl, and this time my inhibitions had vanished: I crawled all over her. The second girl knew the first girl, and told Shirley what I'd been like. Shirley didn't believe it. And I don't blame her a bit.

On the streets of Trenton I ran the old Whippet into a garbage wagon when its brakes failed. It sat for weeks and months at Clegg's Garage awaiting repairs that never came. To replace it I bought a 1939 Ford coupe with a rumble seat. When I was posted to Picton in Prince Edward County, in charge of the security guard there, I was twenty-one years old and, if still not entirely comfortable with other people, had learned to get along with them. Living in barracks ought to do that for anyone.

Before my Picton posting came "Colonel Bogey," who was almost entirely mythical. His voice shattered glass and woke sleepers miles away; when he said jump, you damn well jumped; when he said "About Turn!" you better had . . . Every morning on the parade ground I heard Bogey's music while airmen marched and counter-marched; the flag was raised and the national anthem blared. Faintly and then more strongly, emerging from sleep, I heard him coming: "Dah-Dah!—dah-dah-dah!" and it was like marching armies paraded inside my guts, small men with drums and horns whose music stirred my turbid innards—"Dah-Dah!—dah-dah-dah!" And there was Shirley, laughing at me.

· · · · ·

Warrant Officer Second Class John Silver was the Trenton Base sergeant-major. He was the parody of a sergeant-major, not a bit like Long John Silver in Stevenson's *Treasure Island*. In his late fifties, face like a potato, body like the sack it came in, he was loved (apparently) and respected. I never knew why. WO2 Silver was succeeded by WO1 whatever-his-name-was. WO1-Whatever was the opposite to Silver: between thirty and forty, body like a tapering wedge and trim as a huge weasel, height about 6'2", brown-faced and moustached, it was said he had once been the light-heavyweight boxing champion of the Canadian Armed Forces.

WO1-Whatever was a fearsome creature. I never knew if the myths about him had any basis in fact. I did know that his commands on the parade square in front of the administration building trembled the bones of my inner ear. Sleeping late, I'd sometimes hear the marching columns, a picture of them forming in my brain, transmitted by Colonel Bogey dancing in my vertebrae. Then a savage screeching "HAW-LT"—like the sound of a faraway train wreck.

In the big white stucco barrack blocks, with their long corridors, it was said that WO1-Whatever ordered that garbage cans with open mouths be situated at one end, then he rolled beer bottles into them from the other end (I didn't believe that, but I wondered). And that in a Toronto night club, encountering some new air force recruits, he had ordered them to drop their pants and given them a "short arm" inspection. ("Short arm" is a military term meaning to strip the penis in order to ascertain if the man has gonorrhoea). Any of this may or may not have been true.

· · · · ·

And the war in Europe continued. Yellow Harvard training planes took off and landed on the air field across #2 Highway. Before the Picton posting I was a corporal of the guard, escorting airmen with Ross rifles to tall skeezix guard towers for their four-hour shift; waking them and verbally chastising them if they fell asleep.

A soporific existence, but one in which something nagged at me always. I was unhappy, and could only identify a few of the reasons. Sex, of course. I was a virgin, unless you say that masturbating fairly constantly alters that virginal condition. Going out with girls steadily now, none of them made much impression, despite my continuous unsuccessful attempts at defloration. But Shirley, my love—ah, Shirley. My other reasons for unhappiness sank and died in the smelly marsh of bad poems I was writing. But Shirley, ah *Shirley* . . .

Then Picton. The army barracks there had previously been headquarters for the Hastings and Prince Edward Regiment (which is Angus Mowat's and Farley's "Hasty P's"). Promoted to the temporary rank of sergeant, I was the NCO in charge of a hundred or so candidates for air crew, who were awaiting their turn to get into the training schools for pilots and navigators. And some of them navigated to the nearest pub with minimum delay.

My character at that time was changing rapidly. I don't really know now what sort of person I was then. The Hitler war both real and unreal to me. When I hear people I knew long ago say something about me, I am generally amazed at their opinions. The fumbling and rather idiotic self that fluctuates between that identity and aging writer cannot be replaced by these opinions; but I become very uneasy about myself. The fraction of one per cent anyone really sees of another human being is often embarrassing to me now. Still, I am *Me*, soon to be extinguished by time, only important to myself, and then not for very long.

At Picton, I promoted a number of air crew trainees to the rank of acting NCOs (corporals) for security guard duty. And guards were posted at various, seemingly vulnerable, spots on the military base's periphery. Most of the trainees were American, and I got along well with them. But I played favourites, left, right and centre. Whatever a sergeant was not supposed to do—I did. Including cruising the sleepy farming county seat of Picton looking for girls. Driving my little Ford coupe on gas ration coupons, dashing and I'm afraid predatory. And probably behaving aggressively—still a virgin, but not really more than a small town hayseed with literary and sexual delusions.

There was a girl, of course. She worked in a Picton variety store. Small, dark, delicate features—taking the time machine back to 1941–42, I think WOW! She and I went to Oak Lake near Stirling. After swimming, we perched among thick evergreens at the lake's edge, still in our bathing suits, chatting about very little. I had hoped to relieve this intolerable burden of pseudo-virginity from myself. The luscious dark creature responded to my queries regarding her comfort and well-being with low-voiced monosyllables that were too transparent for me to translate.

On the wooded shores of Oak Lake in bright moonlight, I did my best to remove the lady's bathing suit for immoral purposes. In the midst of these earnest efforts, I was still inhibited by a United Church upbringing—I couldn't. The girl didn't exactly co-operate, but didn't resist very hard either. We went swimming later at the sand banks near Picton (scene of my earlier embarrassment with Shirley). I continued my seduction attempts very seriously. Same result, no dice.

In bright moonlight, parked on the romantic sandy shore of Lake Ontario. Acting Sergeant A. Purdy: "Dear (whatever-the-hell-her-name-was), Let's drive farther down the beach where it's quiet (read, darker). Okay?"

"Okay."

The Ford wouldn't move. Migawd, what's happening? Wheels are spinning around in the wet sand. I give it the gun, they spin some more. We were mired in the sand, permanently, or at least an hour of permanence. I had parked the car where the small and harmless waves made sleepy soothing noises which I thought might be romantically helpful.

Someone in another moonlit vehicle knew the girl, so I ditched her with them. Then called a farmer with tractor for hire nearby to haul me out of the sand. When I paid for the service, my girl was long gone. I think of her occasionally in that early time for both of us. She was very lovely. If she happens to be still alive, I say to her: "Lady, lady from long ago, forgive me."

. . . . .

At Picton I began to burden myself with the opinion that I was a very important person. The air crew trainees flattered me immensely, some of them; two or three even hung on my words in a manner that suggested I possessed great wisdom. And I was, in effect, the commanding officer of Picton Air Base. It went to my head. The war, which had always been unreal to me, receded even farther. And there was no one around to say me nay, or so I thought. But fate unbeknownst to me, was even then preparing my downfall. Not far distant from the base lived an ex-Indian Army colonel, whom I now suspect focused a very expensive set of binoculars on me a couple of times a day to monitor my activities, or lack of them. But more of that later.

For a carefree interim period, I was on the town, Picton or any other town nearby. Between desultory inspections of the guard, I slept, polished the necessary buttons and boots, wrote poems (sometimes), ate hugely (I was up around 195 pounds at this time), and investigated the girl-possibilities within a twenty mile radius. The prospects looked pretty good; and three stripes was a big help.

However, despite having learned how to get along with the male gender, females still induced a choking sensation in my throat at times. They were so *other*, thought differently and lived differently. Besides, in talking and associating with them, I generally had ulterior motives. Oh, not always, but sometimes. There was no hope in my mind of ever understanding them, but I might get lucky and tumble one or two into bed, though not simultaneously. To understand women, at least to some limited extent, seems to me extremely important, although sexual motivation is no longer a dominant factor. If you are male and fifty per cent of the human race remains a cipher to you, what hope do you have for your own humanity?

Anyway, as the Picton NCO in charge of things, I used to go to Belleville sometimes, flanked by two or three of the American guard boys. We drank some beer, and a few of them continued to defer to me. On one occasion we "picked up" three girls on the street, wandering down to the waterfront park with them. At the grandstand we did the requisite nuzzling and flopping around on the floor with them. (As I recall, there was some dogshit in the corners of that grandstand, of a particularly redolent nastiness retained by our clothing.) The girls were extremely young, and when confessing their ages added on a couple of years. The name of my girl was Eurithe Mary Jane Parkhurst. I dated her again a few times.

One morning after a hard night on the town, I was sleeping in. And became aware of harsh voices slamming into my consciousness, voices that were decidedly unfriendly. On the edge of sleep I felt indignant. Who were these underlings, these less than nothings, to disturb their superior officer at his well-earned rest? Scraping eyes open with one trembling hand, glimpsing a patch of sunlight on well-polished shoes, I pursued blue trousered legs up to torso and unsmiling face with three bars decorating its uniform. Wow!—chain lightning flicked in my brain—three bars designated a flight lieutenant (same rank as army captain).

With a sinking feeling I jumped to my feet, not so much confronting the officer as cowering before him. I stuttered and stammered, and everything I said meant the same things: I was guilty—of whatever it was. Besides, just coming out of sleep and wearing only underwear shorts, you can't be very rational and reasonable. I was caught, snared, trapped and cornered: dereliction of duty, asleep, comatose and flummoxed. And posted back to Trenton Air Base forthwith.

This time I was brought up before a squadron leader, in view of the seriousness of the charges. It seems that this ex-Indian army colonel had been spying on my activities or lack of them for some weeks, and finally phoned Air Force headquarters in Toronto to inform the high command that the Hitler war was about to go down the drain because of Acting Sergeant A. Purdy. Because of him and because of myself, I stood at attention and hatless, flanked by an armed guard. Awaiting my condign punishment.

The gold braid slowly raised its head and became a stern voice: "Reduced in rank to acting corporal."

Lo and behold, it was so.

As one among several guard corporals at Trenton, my duties were to supervise men with rifles at guard towers on the air field's periphery. These towers were perhaps forty feet high; you climbed to the little cabin-shelter on top via a precarious ladder, rifle slung over your shoulder. The guards were relieved every four hours, fresh ones driven to their posts in a panel truck. During the night everyone slept in the darkened guard room, except the corporal (yeah, I'd learned my lesson). And again, these men were often US air crew trainees.

Two exceptions were a couple of Toronto football players, Jake Gaudaur and another guy whose name I've forgotten. I used to horse around with them, waking them for duty late at night. Both were huge men, and our good-natured pseudo-wrestling bouts always ended in my crying uncle. Or "Enough, time to get out there and save Canada from Hitler." Years later I met Gaudaur when he was commissioner of the Canadian Football League. It had been proposed that I write an article about him for *Weekend* magazine. However, he didn't remember me at all.

Returning from Ottawa after that disciplinarian training course in the spring of 1941, other NCOs had also been appointed. And when I came back from Picton in disgrace, they were running the guard system at Trenton. Corporal Parkes, a short, brown-faced first world war veteran in his early forties, was soon promoted to sergeant. And like other first war veterans I encountered, Parkes had a tendency to throw his weight around, handing out unnecessary orders, making others aware of him unpleasantly. Corporal Elkins was fresh-faced and helter-skelter in manner, but I don't remember him well. Corporal Bill Botham was short, fat-faced, pimply and oily-skinned, talked rather effeminately, and was promoted to sergeant in charge of the security guard orderly room. Roland ("Rollie") someone, whose last name I can't remember, was sergeant, then flight sergeant in charge of day-to-day guard operations at Trenton. He was a large handsome man, French Canadian, quite young for his rank, with many likeable qualities despite a tendency to swagger.

1941–42 was a boring and highly dramatic time at Trenton Air Base. Boring for me and others like me who had a newly developed dislike for military service; but high excitement for officers and sergeant pilots. The commonwealth Air Training Plan was coming into full effect then. Camouflaged Lancaster bombers lounged on the tarmac; British Mosquitoes, Fairey Battle fighter-bombers lunged and swooped, practised firing at targets over the Bay of Quinte. Yellow Harvard trainers climbed like vivid moths in the sun. The white stucco barrack blocks and hangars swam in waves of summer heat; blue uniforms marched and counter-marched, everyone looked purposeful as if the outcome of important events depended on them.

If you could imagine yourself hovering above that air base, high above it and looking down, officers and men would have lost clear definition and movement, become stick figures, motionless. It's an alien thought, in which the mind enables you to briefly escape time and space.

And saluting, saluting (longest way up for the arm, and shortest way down—yes, I *remember*)—so much, so often. There was a story I heard about Corporal Tombs' Victoria Cross. Anyone awarded that prestigious decoration must have the minimum rank of corporal and be saluted *first*, by everyone, including officers. It was said that Corporal Tombs proceeded to the administration building every morning in order to receive his quota of salutes from officers and make himself feel important. I have some sympathy for him. It would have tickled me, in like circumstances, to do the same thing.

But it was an uneasy life. An airman walking around the base with a button undone or his brass buttons unpolished or looking sloppy in any way—that man was bound to be stopped by an NCO or officer, lectured scathingly, and perhaps placed on charge if he answered back or even looked sideways. The amount of power residing in military rank has much the same influence as money in civilian life. That sort of thing frays the nerves, made you feel furtive and vaguely guilty of something or other.

· · · · ·

One afternoon when I escorted a guard detachment to #9 Construction and Maintenance Unit a couple of miles distant from the base proper,

I encountered fame. In the person of one John Gillespie McGee, an American air crew prospect awaiting room at his training school. I'd never been shy about writing poems; everyone who knew me knew about that. I guess McGee did too. He'd written a poem called "High Flight," which achieved a modicum of attention. I made a point of hunting him up at 9 CMU.

McGee and I showed each other our poems, our manner toward each other circumspect and wary. We paid the expected polite compliments which cost nothing; he about to become an officer, as designated by the white flash in his wedge hat, I remaining a lowly corporal or less. He was slender and young with a small moustache. At the time, I thought "High Flight" was pretty damn good, and felt envious; it has been reprinted since in quite a number of anthologies. But since then, I thought those first lines:

> O I have slipped the surly bonds of earth,
> And danced the sky on laughter-silvered wings

— and ending with, "Reached out my hand and touched the face of God" were pretentious crap. McGee himself died in the skies over Europe. It was not a bad death, if any death can be so designated; but I wonder what he'd be writing like now?

A magazine of RCAF interest was published at Trenton Air Base. Its masthead had the air force motto, *Per Ardua Ad Astra*—"Through Difficulties to the Stars." The magazine published a sort of doggerel poem called "The Flying Instructor's Lament," which, years later, I couldn't be sure I hadn't written then, I wanted to have written it so much. The first two verses go like this:

> What did you do in the war, daddy,
> How did you help us to win?
> Circuits and bumps and turns, laddy,
> And how to get out of a spin.

> Woe and alack and misery me,
> I trundle around in the sky,
> And instead of machine-gunning Nazis,
> I'm teaching young hopefuls to fly!

Well, I didn't write it, at least I don't think so: my memory isn't that bad. In fact, there was not a single thing I wrote in those wartime days at which I can look back on with pride. McGee, in his carefully disguised opinion of my poems, was absolutely right.

But songs from the airmen's wet canteen used to echo in my sleep along with Colonel Bogey, a man who requires no quotes. The songs were simply hilarious in that presbyterian-puritanical repressed era (which has since swung around to nearly the opposite condition). Drinking beer was generally part of those songs, as in "I've got Sixpence": "Oh happy is the day when the airman gets his pay / And we go rolling, rolling home / Rolling home, dead drunk—" And another with a list of numbers, of which this is one:

> And this is number three,
> how ashamed I was,
> I touched her on the knee,
> she said you're mighty free,
> oh god amighty how ashamed I was—

Bawdy and obscene, but not completely divorced from reality. They stick like glue in the mind.

That summer of '41 it was decided that I might make a pilot, navigator or gunner, given sufficient incentive and training. I took the air crew medical, twice. Both times my blood pressure shot up nearly as high as an eagle can spit. I'd been excited at the idea of hobnobbing with Billy Bishop and the ghost of the Red Knight of Germany. Sadly the realization came to me: shit, now I'll never be able to slip the surly bonds of earth.

Harold Wannamaker had joined the RCAF not long after me. He got into his training school quickly, became a sergeant-pilot, and was posted to Trenton prior to my last demotion. At this time Sergeant-Pilot Wannamaker was flying training missions, and wanted to give me a "flip" (air force jargon for brief flight), since I'd never even been up a four-storey building at the time.

My maiden flight was in a two-motored plane (this was before jet engines were invented), not a monster bomber like the Lancaster or Flying Fort. And while Harold was strapping a parachute on my back before takeoff, I noticed a mischievous look in his eyes. That look boded something, even if not ill. Then in the skies over Trenton Air Base, I discovered I was upside-down, quite suddenly, trying to keep my lunch in its proper place. And yep, I felt a bit scared. When he did it again, I started to curse Sergeant-Pilot Wannamaker. But it's difficult to properly express your feelings when you're upside-down.

Everything was changing around the security guard orderly room at Trenton. Sergeant Botham at his paper work or duck-waddling in barracks—his pimply face was smug, smugger and smuggest. He spoke in a mincing meeching voice that made my teeth grate together. Sergeant Parkes, the first war vet, left on two weeks leave and never came back (I think he'd had a heart attack). Corporal Elkins was posted elsewhere. Flight Sergeant Roland, the French-Canadian NCO in charge of the guard, did something the higher-ups thought reprehensible and got demoted to just plain sergeant. It affected him terribly—he lost weight, his ruddy complexion paled a little, and one never saw him smile. I think he was not able to see ahead, past the present trauma and into a happier time. Previous to the demotion, Roland took such joy in being himself, in confident day-to-day existence. His subsequent depression inexplicably had an effect on me as well. And I think, "how strange!"

I had been going out with Eurithe all that summer, but fairly occasionally. A couple of other girls were also among those present. I pursued them all earnestly, and without success except for smooching in parked cars. Then Eurithe left town, having gotten a job as waitress in Niagara Falls. That seemed to do it for me. I suddenly got romantic, cupid hovered over my Ford coupe; a blinding light from the sky, and I was in love. I drove to Niagara Falls, talked, smooched some more.

When Eurithe returned for the weekend to her home in Belleville, I was on duty as corporal of the guard; I couldn't get away to see her nohow. That preyed on me. Just a word from the lady would ease this inner hunger. I drove the guard panel truck to Belleville, wearing the full regalia of webbing and side arms. Though nobody stopped me at the gate or said: "Nay, Corporal Purdy, thou mayest not desert thine assigned post—even now at this fateful moment, sixteen German saboteurs are crawling through the grass at Trenton Air Base's outer periphery." Nobody said that.

Ann Street in Belleville, about one a.m. A terrace, one of whose houses had Eurithe's upstairs window facing directly on the street. I whispered to wake her, shouted softly, and threw some small stones. She came down wearing a night gown, and got into the guard truck. I pressed side arms, webbing and brass buttons hard into her soft flesh. Some more whispering, then I drove back to Trenton.

But my escapade with the guard truck had repercussions. Charged with dereliction of duty—I can't remember all the charges, but there were several—I was again ushered into the presence of the Officer Commanding. He was a flight lieutenant with a little moustache; he'd been a school teacher in Toronto before the war. His face was entirely expressionless, and from what I'd heard of him, if he were to undergo suspended animation, there'd be no change.

The NCO commanding the guard detail gave his orders in a curiously muffled voice: "Prisoner and escoort, HAW! Raight tau-nn!" I think he had a cold. And all of this felt like a dream at that time, until someone said: "Do you accept my punishment?"

This time I was knocked down to LAC, which is the rank called Leading Aircraftsman. I didn't lead long. Successive demotions brought me down to AC1, then AC2, and it's hard to imagine what depths I could have achieved if the war hadn't ended first. Weeks after my crime and punishment, when I was finally allowed off the base, I encountered a very drunken civilian. He regarded me somewhat sneeringly, probably despising all uniforms—when his eyes were able to focus. I saluted him.

· · · · ·

Despite my most recent demotion, the romance with Eurithe made progress. I met her family (very numerous progeny) including the *pater familias* who was six feet three and large. Eurithe and I got married that fall in 1941. I requested a week's leave for a honeymoon. Sergeant Botham refused. I requested a weekend pass, which was grudgingly granted by my erstwhile guard buddy.

We rented a house on Dufferin Avenue, Trenton town, a house my mother owned. I was, of course, living off the military base with permission. We owned a 1940 Chev by this time, and my teaching Eurithe to drive resulted in a trauma still affecting both of us many years later. Next year I was posted to the Manning Pool in Toronto for re-assignment to some other RCAF base.

In a dull and depressed mood I was domiciled at the Toronto Exhibition grounds "Horse Palace" for the next week, along with a few hundred other airmen, I made some casual friends there, with whom I roamed Sunnyside amusement park on the Lake Ontario beach, and drank beer with a few times. But my spirits were too black and dismal to enjoy anything much. Having been married for several months, I was used to that condition and resented being deprived of it.

Eurithe and I talked on the long-distance phone a few times. She said she'd try to get to Toronto, although I didn't really expect that to happen. But it did. And I went AWL (absent without leave) when she got a room in a beachfront lodging house, where we spent a couple of blissful nights.

Of course it had to end, with me placed on charge for the nth time it seemed, getting paraded before yet another bored officer and listening to the prescribed ritual. Of course, I hadn't gotten over being scared, despite the repetitions. This pseudo-legal situation is calculated to set your nerves on edge, make you think you've been unutterably wicked and a decided detriment to the war effort. It's impossible to think of myself as having been fully adult at that time, despite my chronological age. And for just about anything I can think of, I've been a late-developer, delayed for years at the starting gate. Which means that all my reactions are liable to be slightly different than other people's.

Posted to Vancouver at a less-than-civilian rank, I was assigned to guard duty at #2 Equipment Depot, which shared the base with #9 CMU, a construction unit, under the shadow of Burrard Bridge. Then at Hastings Park, I took the night shift at a Pacific Exhibition grounds warehouse stuffed with military equipment. The place was enormous. For the first few nights I roamed the echoing aisles on the lookout for saboteurs. Then I slept, albeit slightly uneasy from memory of other occasions when my sense of military duty was less than perfect.

In the morning at Hastings Park waiting for my relief to arrive on the streetcar, frowzy and dishevelled, I'd stumble outside the warehouse to piss, staring across Burrard Inlet and the Second Narrows to glimpse mountains capped with shimmering snow. First light touching the brilliant peaks—not to lift the spirits exactly, but to make you aware there were other things besides dirty concrete floors and your hand scraping over unshaven jaws.

Then on duty back at the base, I paraded to and fro after midnight on the dock near False Creek mouth, Sten gun slung over my shoulder. It was shift work, and I seemed to invariably receive the graveyard assignment, any possible sleep secured by day with drawn blinds. Nearby was a streetcar repair depot; overhead on my right, the blacked-out Burrard Bridge with an occasional rumble of late traffic.

The trouble with this semi-public job was—you couldn't get a wink of sleep on duty. An NCO or Duty Officer was always prowling around in late evening. If you heard or saw anything even slightly suspicious, you were supposed to yell at it: "Halt! Advance and identify yourself!"

Or something like that. No, you couldn't sleep, but I would dream awake. My questing spirit lifted above Burrard Bridge in geographic omniscience, roaming thru past and future, ignoring this present condition of being a bug guarding a bug-city against other insects.

The moon drifting down in a silver track on False Creek around three a.m., ducks swimming from light to shadow, making sensible ducknoises, unalarmed in this peaceful place. Then the sudden noise of a Sten gun chattering at them, black water speckled as if a handful of peas had been flung into it. The ducks stared uncomprehendingly, unable to believe anyone would wish them harm. And departed unhurriedly, flying under the bridge where it was less noisy. I reloaded the Sten gun, trying to think of an excuse besides boredom for firing it; and a separate excuse to the guard sergeant to account for the missing cartridges. And an apology to the ducks.

Eurithe came to Vancouver, after an exchange of letters and long distance calls. My womanless condition was ameliorated; I was joyful, even slightly contented. We found an apartment, adjusted to each other all over again, although I'm not sure how well we ever knew each other. Then I got sick, some form of arthritis whereby you have either too many white blood cells or too few. I could hardly walk, in fact couldn't without the balls of my feet feeling like they were on fire. And zoom, into the hospital at #2 ED I went.

I was placed in a ward with quite a number of other airmen. For the first few days fever raged in my blood. There was a nurse in that hospital, Sylvia Weaver, from my hometown of Trenton, now holding a commissioned rank in the RCAF. I thought we might be able to talk to each other, but apparently she felt her officer status very strongly. When my fever was worst in the early morning hours after midnight, I rang the bedside bell and tried to attract Sylvia's attention. She acted toward me like someone in high society and refused to believe I needed anything. I've always remembered her behaviour—when I thought I was going to die and she wouldn't bring me a drink of water.

When I was recovering, Eurithe came during visiting hours. And there was a non-commissioned nurse or orderly on duty in the daytime. Her name was Sammy. In the morning she used to give the patients of my ward—of whom there were at least a dozen—alcohol rubs under the blankets. She'd reach under there with handful of cold fire and massage the stuff into my stomach. And I would achieve the most fearful erections, tumescent penis reaching toward her hand and aching to shoot the moon.

I'm damn sure she knew. Chattering about almost anything, her small body doll-like in the white uniform, face animated and innocent and somehow indomitable, seemingly quite unaware of the turmoil and shattered calm her presence induced. Sammy, Sammy, you with the chubby figure and incipient double chin at age twenty, after fifty years I still love you.

From the base hospital in Kitsilano I was sent to Colwood on Vancouver Island for convalescence. Before the war Colwood had been a country club with a big golf course, just outside Victoria, about as nice a place as you could imagine. But I never did take up golf. Doctors there tried to identify the bug that had nearly killed me. I think they were quite baffled.

After my recovery and return to Vancouver, I was posted to Woodcock in BC's northern interior. There had been no warning or previous intimation this might happen. Perhaps the high command was concerned about my health. But it was a shock. Not long after retrieving my new wife from far away Ontario, I was about to lose her again. This time she'd be only nine hundred miles distant in our tiny Vancouver apartment, and me lost in the middle of the mountains, about 150 miles inland from the sea on the CNR's northern route. I damn near wept.

. . . . .

#9 Construction and Maintenance Unit, to which I was attached, was building an air field in this remote area. A Japanese attack was thought to be a constant menace. Perhaps one house or two constituted the village of Woodcock itself, not even a whistlestop on the railway line. Looming overhead on either side of our small valley were mountains like the legends of mountains, a presence always in your mind and waking eyes: almost the same as being aware of invisible persons in the room with you, but much more awesome. One of these was called "Rocher de Boule." A name that sounded like a spell.

Beside the nearly completed airfield, a swift cold river poured past on its way to the sea. This was the Skeena, from whose snow-fed water giant Chinook salmon were hauled by the Tsimsyan Indians in their dugout canoes. I saw the salmon being caught, and their slab-like size seemed incredible to me. Later I visited Indian villages, Kispiox and others, marvelling at the totem poles so crowded with manifold activities, both human and animal, that it was easy to think of the legends they depicted as still happening.

The fly in this paradise ointment for me was the NCO in charge of the base. That was Sergeant Jackson, who'd been a typewriter mechanic in civilian life. We disliked each other on sight, and a sergeant was well able to make life miserable for all lesser ranks. Jackson was black-haired, medium-sized, in his late twenties, with an unpleasantly penetrating voice. He gave me all the dirty jobs he could think of—pick and shovel stuff, sweeping floors and cleaning toilets. Duty Watch is a kind of military penalty for doing something you shouldn't, but which really isn't very serious. I got that punishment every time I looked at Jackson sideways. We both felt antagonistic to each other. And I don't know why. Jackson also had some of my own bad habits when I was in charge of the guard at Picton: he played favourites. He was a prick, in my considered opinion.

> In the long grass lying
> there in 1944
> hating that sergeant for thinking
> three stripes made him so superior
> he could get away with anything
> peering thru tall grass at him
> hoping his face might alter
> flush or grow pale
> and he'd double over with agony
> from the force in my eyes
> VOODOO thoughts
> of an RCAF airman
> —trying to make the self-important
> bastard throw up his dinner
> contract any ailment untrivial
> like a permanent dose of clap
> or imaginary fleas
> approx. the size of rats . . .

—from *Sergeant Jackson* (1968)

My closest friend at Woodcock was Leo LeBlanc, easygoing and dark faced, a guy who got along with nearly everyone. On weekends, when Jackson couldn't avoid handing out forty-eight-hour passes, Leo and I would ride the freights that chugged past on their way to Smithers (eighty miles) or Hazelton (thirty-five miles). We'd catch the trains on the fly, when they slowed but didn't stop on the way past Woodcock. Drinking beer with Leo and others of Jackson's non-favourites at pubs in those towns could sometimes be fairly exciting.

Leo and I once escorted a couple of nurses back to their hospital about two miles outside Hazelton late at night. Their local boy friends had imbibed too much booze earlier, and weren't around when the nurses needed them for the dark and rather lonely hike. The nurses sat Leo and I down for coffee and biscuits in the hospital kitchen, cautioning us to make as little noise as possible. I've forgotten how it happened, but I managed to knock a large glass jar off the table. It detonated on the floor with a terrible bang. The four of us, two girls and Leo and I, we just sat there and looked at each other with blank faces.

Then the nurses magically disappeared, first motioning Leo and I to depart the premises with all speed. We took to our heels, running through the midnight darkness blindly, heading toward the road without knowing exactly where it was. I was a little ahead of Leo, then BLAM!—I stopped as if I'd run into a concrete wall. I'd smacked straight into a wire fence, quite invisible, and hit it in such a way that all parts of my body stopped at once. There was scarcely any slack in that fence to take the shock—and the shock was considerable. Leo had been warned by the *oof!* sound I made, and stopped behind me.

We stood there a moment, looking back at the hospital. Lights were coming on all over the building. "Migawd," Leo gasped, "I hope those girls didn't get caught."

"How about a little prayer for us as well," I said.

It was still a couple of miles from that hospital to the place where freight trains stopped to take on water. We walked, stretching it out into a slow gallop, sobering a little in the cold night air. When lights of a car showed up behind, we dived into brush at the edge of the road. The Mounties insignia and outline of a hat visor was visible as the patrol car passed slowly, its spotlight passing over our heads.

"They think we're criminals," Leo said.

"Well, aren't we?" I wanted to know (there's something about acting guilty that makes you *feel* guilty).

Back at Woodcock, watching Indians hoick those barndoor-size salmon into their canoes made me envious enough to become a fisherman myself. I scrounged some tackle and fished from the shores of the cold Skeena, managing to catch a few Dolly Varden and cutthroat trout. They went to the cookhouse.

Amusements and pastimes in that remote place were not abundant. The nightly poker games in barracks never attracted me; but watching the mountains change in the changing evening light, that was magic. And when the brick-coloured freights trundled by on their slow trip west to Rupert, or reversed themselves moving east to Smithers and south to Vancouver, I was lonesome for Eurithe.

Leo LeBlanc and I got together with several others to concoct homebrew. We begged canned peaches and dried fruit from the cookhouse, used a big concrete pipe with wooden plugs at either end for a container, poured boiling water over the mess, adding yeast later, then buried the pipe among rocks beside the Skeena. All this at night. Some giggling went on during the brewing process. Someone had a bottle, and we thought we were being very clever, making home brew. Much later, I heard that no one could remember where the stuff was stashed: all participants in the project had lost their memory for that night.

From Woodcock I fired off letters to Eurithe urging her to secure an RCAF travel warrant (which paid the cost of the ticket), and take the train north to assuage my woman-hunger. (I didn't use that last term, of course.) At the same time, I was writing to a flight sergeant I knew in the #9 CMU orderly room, asking that I be posted back to Vancouver on compassionate grounds. Those letters must have been killers. Anyway, they got results.

Shortly thereafter I was transferred back to the Kitsilano air base, and started south by train. But what I didn't know at the time, Eurithe had also secured her travel warrant, and started north to Woodcock nearly simultaneously with my own southern departure. We passed each other going in opposite directions somewhere along the CNR northern route to Prince Rupert.

． ． ． ． ．

And something I still feel badly about. Years later, I saw my friend, the orderly room flight sergeant, again. He was a uniformed guard at the Winnipeg railway station. Our glances passed across each other, but he didn't seem to recognize me. I didn't want to embarrass him by saying hello, and have wondered ever since if I should have spoken. I hope he got a better job afterwards.

Back at the military base I was attached to the service police (because of being over six feet, I suppose), dividing my time between night building patrols and daytime main gate duty. Revolver strapped around my waist, boots and buttons shining, saluting officers and examining airmen's passes, it was not unpleasant. But the small apartment I'd rented was very empty: Eurithe had discovered she liked Woodcock, got a job waitressing at the airmen's mess and wouldn't come back to me. I coaxed and cajoled by letter, tried to phone a few times, wandered Vancouver long-faced and doleful. Sleeping alone didn't agree with me. But the lady was obdurate, while I imagined all sorts of immoral goings-on with the women-hungry airmen at Woodcock. It must have been a full two months before she stepped off the train at the Main Street CN station, looking marvellous.

All this time I had been writing poems. Looking back from the vantage of now, I ought to be embarrassed by them: they were atrocious poems. Blessedly, I didn't know that. But they had a kind of serene purity and unawareness of their badness; my poor cowering little ego clung to them and made them beloved:

> I saw the milkweed float away
> To curtsy, climb and hover
> And seek among the crowded hills
> Another warmer lover.
>
> Across the autumn flushing streams
> Adown the misty valleys
> Atop the skyline's sharp redoubts
> Aswarm with coloured alleys—
>
> I caught an echo in my hands
> With pollen mixed for leaven
> I gave it half my song to hold
> And sent it back to heaven.
>
> Now oft, anon, as in a dream
> O'er sculptured heights ascending
> I hear a song—my song, but now
> It has another ending

> —*The Enchanted Echo* (1944)

I was sending them out and getting published in places like *Drift-wind*, *The Lyric West*, and around the end of the war to the *Canadian Forum*. I treasured them when they appeared in magazines, the only thing I'd ever done that awoke some personal pride.

During the war the *Vancouver Sun* ran a complete page of poems in its Saturday edition, paying a dollar for each one published. The *News Herald* also had a continuous competition in its weekend edition, one that involved completing limericks after being provided with the first couple of lines, but adding the names of the particular advertiser, dry cleaners, clothing stores and suchlike. Of course the lines you wrote were always complimentary to the advertisers. The prizes for this contest were two tickets to the Vogue Theatre on Granville Street, which meant that Eurithe and I got to see a lot of mediocre movies. As well, over a period of about two and a half years, I appeared in the *Sun* poetry page over forty times.

I cut out all my own poems religiously, gluing them into a scrapbook. Northrop Frye was then some kind of editor on the *Canadian Forum*. I asked him for criticism on my stuff, and he sent me a full-page letter analysing it. I included his letter in the scrapbook as well; but the whole collection got lost on one of our moves from one lodging place to another.

All these dollar poems in the *Vancouver Sun* caused me to be in touch with Joan Buckley, who edited the *Sun* poetry page. I met her in late 1943. Joan was perhaps thirty-five years old then, her legs crippled by polio years before; she was therefore confined to a wheel chair. Her face was dark brown from many hours of sitting in the sun, and sometimes it wavered from side to side. Her parents operated a lily farm near Langley Prairie; they drove her to Vancouver to attend meetings of the Vancouver Poetry Society every couple of weeks.

Occasionally I'd take the bus to Langley to visit Joan and the Buckleys. I'd sit with her in the sun or beside her bed, talking about everything and learning much. Joan had self-published a couple of small chapbooks of poems, and another on how to write poetry. They sold well locally.

Through Joan Buckley I joined the Vancouver Poetry Society, meeting Ernest Fewster, the president, among others; and Tom McInnes, a very old man whom I remember staring out the window at nothingness. And the Duncan family, mother and daughter, the latter working at a Robson Street radio station, writing and editing. The daughter soothed my quivering nerves when I read poems over the air, feeling very big-time.

In 1944 I paid $200 to publishers Clarke & Stuart on Seymour Street to print a 500-copy edition of my own poems, called *The Enchanted Echo*. It was sixty-four pages, soft-covered, and perhaps seventy-five to a hundred copies were sold or given away. Having already stated certain opinions of my own work, there's no need for repetition here.

. . . . .

Our son Jimmy was born July, 1945; I was discharged from the RCAF that same month. I emerged from the air force with an abiding dislike of uniforms and uniformity, but certainly better able to get along socially with other people. However, my personal insecurities remained, perhaps a legacy from childhood.

But there were good things to remember, and good people. Among them, Sergeant Knowles, who is unlikely to remember me at all. Sammy of the alcohol rubs at #2 ED hospital, with her little smile on the edge of a sob. And Shirley, who might remember me to my own extreme embarrassment. Leo LeBlanc, never seen again, but cherished for friendship and midnight escapades in Woodcock, Smithers and Hazelton. That flight sergeant at #9 CMU who was responsible for my being posted from Woodcock back to Vancouver. Seeing him at the train entrance of the Winnipeg railway station made me feel such warmth for him all over again. I hope his life has been a good one. LAC Bob Terence at Ottawa—a man who didn't write very well himself, but encouraged me to do so. And Joan Buckley. She was one of the kindest and most gentle people I've known in my life.

It very nearly amounts to a summing-up, when all that was unpleasant in other people, and the times when you were at your own personal worst—these are completely unimportant. You do remember them, since the great rolling surge of the past can never be escaped, nor would we wish it to be. But perspectives alter, morning changes to evening, while the morning music lingers—How could I forget Colonel Bogey when his *Dah-Dah!* was a substitute for Beethoven at age twenty—until Beethoven himself picked up the beat when I was thirty. *Dah-Dah!* and the Harvard trainers take off from Trenton Air Base, flying into my blood stream like yellow seagulls. *Dah-Dah!* and I remember everything, as if it were happening yet.

> Remember the early days of the phony war
> when men were zombies and women were CWACs
> and they used wooden rifles on the firing range?
> Well I was the sort of soldier you couldn't trust
> with a wooden rifle
> and when they gave me a wooden bayonet
> life was fraught with peril for my brave comrades
> including the sergeant-instructor
> I wasn't exactly a soldier tho
> only a humble airman
> who kept getting demoted
>   and demoted
>   and demoted
> to the point where I finally saluted civilians
> And when they trustingly gave me a Sten gun
> Vancouver should have trembled in its sleep

for after I fired a whole clip of bullets
at some wild ducks under Burrard Bridge
(on guard duty at midnight)
they didn't fly away for five minutes
trying to decide if there was any danger
Not that the war was funny
I took it and myself quite seriously
the way a squirrel in a treadmill does
too close to tears for tragedy
too far from the banana peel for laughter
and I didn't blame anyone for being there
that wars happened wasn't anybody's fault then

Now I think it is

—*About Being a Member of Our Armed Forces*
(1965)

CHAPTER SIX

·　·　·　·　·　·　·　·

THE TAXI BUSINESS

Looking back on it, I remember the ending better than the beginning. There's a Japanese historical movie called *Gate of Hell*, in colour. Its opening scenes had all the confusion of the ending of my first (and last) business venture. Fires were blazing, people rushing in all directions, confusion, chaos—I'm talking about the Kinugasa movie. But in 1948 the Diamond Taxi was real. And I was losing it.

The reasons for losing it were simple (or they seem so now). Bad management, on the part of both myself and my father-in-law, Jim Parkhurst. Bad drivers who kept crashing cars. Debts for both gas and repairs were beginning to overwhelm us. And our reputation was bad, since there was bootlegging on the part of both drivers and management.

And my marriage was falling apart. There was tension under and sometimes on the surface whenever Eurithe and I spoke to each other. I don't know why exactly. It was very painful for me. I see myself standing facing her in the little one-room apartment, which was also the taxi office. Her eyes said that she detested me. And how can a man understand that a woman whom he has loved and cherished despises him—like a slug, like spittle underfoot? Like nothing.

So we busted up. That was maybe 1947. I don't know for sure. But living was at a high pitch then; there was no doubt about being alive; things hurt too much not to know. Writing about it now, the urgency and uncertainty and tension all seem to return to a degree . . . But details are vague in some areas; bright and clear in others.

The bailiffs were seizing everything on behalf of the garages, service stations and finance companies to whom we owed money. They had already taken nearly everything. I was driving the last unseized taxi, a tan-coloured 1946 Dodge, quite an unremarkable car in every way: but its tail lights winked when it caught sight of me, its seat comfortable to my behind. It knew me, and would've wagged its tail if it had had one.

Belleville, Ontario, just after midnight in the fall of 1948. There's been rain earlier in the evening, still a trace of it remains on the pavement. I am driving the old Dodge down Bridge Street, going nowhere in particular, feeling very depressed about myself, about Eurithe, about the taxi business, and it was maybe just about to rain again . . .

Then I spotted that car behind me. Couldn't see who was driving, half a block behind and going faster than my Dodge. Not a cop, not the look of a private citizen either, and not another taxi since there was no roof light. It made me uneasy to be followed, especially since I had nearly two full cases of beer in the car, with a few more stashed under the front seat where I could get at them easily.

I turned right on Pinnacle Street and headed east. The other car was still behind me and closing fast. It kept turning its bright lights up and down, as if I was meant to be terrified from being followed and pull over. Well, fuck him—or her, as the case might be. I zipped down Pinnacle at about seventy, turned left with a shriek of tires at a narrow lane that exited on the main drag. The guy—it was a man—was less than a hundred yards behind when I wheeled her right at Front Street, clipped an ornamental shrub on the curb, then whipped over the Moira Bridge to North Front and floored her on the way north.

The last bailiff, the last car, and me, the last human being on a dying planet. And sure, I felt melodramatic and histrionic, kind of excited too. This is the way to end things, a marriage, a business, maybe even a lifetime. Bullshit didn't occur to me. That damn car behind had gained and then lost ground, its driver a hunched shape, visible only if my rear vision mirror and street light coincided.

There were headlights behind me, but I think it was just someone who couldn't remember where he lived after a few beers. I saw the bailiff again on the way north, at least I think it was him. He'd stopped dimming his lights, hoping I'd stop. By that time my blood was racing too hard to pay attention to anything except what the voice in my brain was whispering, "Don't stop! Don't stop! Don't stop! . . ."

"Highway 62 in red October." I drove north on the new highway to Bancroft, went whispering through the little villages of Bannockburn and El Dorado with all windows dark at two a.m. This is my grandfather's country, or so I like to think of it. Swigging at the beer. (What kind? . . . I can't remember.) And where was the guy who intended to take my car away from me? Somewhere behind, far behind, I hope. Ex-wife back there too. And Jim Parkhurst as well—Wheeler-Dealer Jim couldn't deal his way out of this one. Dodge purring along at a steady eighty, no sweat, no worry, and have another beer.

Only a mile ahead Highway 62 branches off left: I make the turn onto the old Hastings Road just in time. It used to be the main highway to Bancroft and Maynooth, but now the roadbed is potholed and crumbling. It twists and turns, zigzags up and down hills, reverts to gravel then back to paved surface again, dense bush crowding in on either side. A road that seems to have a mind of its own, and decides every turn by itself. Once there were subsistence farms here, weathered log barns and cabins, a few more pretentious structures. All are crumbling back into earth. Animals and people, where are they?

I catch a glimpse of headlights a mile or so behind; then they dip under the crest of a hill. But I made the turn, off Highway 62 before those lights could reappear. It couldn't be the bailiff—miles and miles north of Madoc and a hundred thousand miles south of the moon.

Slow down to about twenty, then have to stop the car and move a dead tree fallen onto the road. Have a piss, off to one side of the road for modesty's sake, the moon a pale neutral onlooker. Another beer, and sling the empty bottle into the bush to await future archaeologists. Then migawd a beaver dam in front of me, its water crossing the road ahead. How far ahead? I maneouvre the Dodge until its headlights appear to illuminate a hill, which is maybe fifty yards farther on. A hill? That means the water in front can't be very deep? Well, does it mean that?

Very slowly I aim the old Dodge into shallow water, and slowly, slowly my sweating mind and body accompany the car. With a beer held tight in my crotch, peering intensely ahead where the road appears to go—or once went and now doesn't go at all. And maybe Grey Owl's favourite beaver family is eating willow and poplar soufflé on disposable plates ahead, and me about to interrupt their dinner?

Yep, it's a hill. And the car feels like it's working hard at the top. And there's a lake on my left. I pull off into a cleared place, once perhaps a scenic lookout, and look down on a white eye of water that stares up at the moon. Twenty feet below the lake appears deep; but I can't really tell for sure.

The Dodge is now sobbing in neutral for what is to come, emergency brake on. I find a fifteen-pound rock, adjusting it above the accelerator pedal until the motor is growling hard. Standing by the door, I smack the metal roof goodbye, release the emergency brake and stand back to watch. (Of course I haven't neglected to liberate what remains of the beer.)

The old Dodge hits the water and sinks, but slowly, as if it feels reluctant to go. Bubbles of air come popping up to the surface. I feel emotional about it, as if I've betrayed the poor beast. Well, better some nameless lake than nagging creditors. The car sits down there in maybe thirty feet of water, headlights still shining upward. I think they won't last long, and will die with the car.

I gather up the beer into an old windbreaker, sling it over my shoulder and start back toward Highway 62. At the beaver pond, I have to roll up my pantlegs and my shoes squish like wet cardboard wading through the moonlight.

Something ending. I mourn for that mechanical thing as if it were human flesh. And have another beer. Black Label. Walking toward my grandiose destiny, which is not Diamond Taxi, not Eurithe—and just what the hell is it then? South to Highway 401 in early dawn; drinking the last beer a bit north of Madoc, then catching six winks of sleep beside the road.

Hitchhike to Toronto? Sure. Well, how about writing a novel? Yep. And start a new life, leave the old one behind. And this is the way the world begins, not with a whimper but the bang of broken glass from my last Black Label empty. The novel? I shall dedicate it to my dead grandfather, Ridley Neville Purdy (miserable old bastard)? Why not? (He saw through all my pretences so well—) To Ol Rid, then.

. . . . .

When the Diamond Taxi came up for sale after the war (four cars and four licenses), Jim Parkhurst proposed that both of us should drive cab and manage the business together. And I supplied all the money to buy the outfit. Our arrangement was that Jim take no salary, not until we estimated that the amount of work he'd contributed amounted to the same value as my own cash investment. That seemed quite reasonable to me at the time, and I had no other plans for making a living. And my wife seemed to go along with the deal. I did have a few forebodings about it myself, since I had no management experience and quite a few doubts about myself. Anyway, the taxi business in that late summer of 1945, with Jim Parkhurst and I (supposedly) in charge, became my life for the next three years.

A sandy-haired man named Lorne Munro had owned the Diamond Taxi previously. Its cars were old and decrepit, none having been replaced or adequately repaired over six years of war. Of these cars only an old green Hudson, a now defunct species, had any attraction for me. The shock absorbers of all the cars gave passengers a bumpy ride; even the tires were unreliable; and wartime gas was still rationed. However, Jim Parkhurst seemed to have the answers, reassured my nervous queries, gave one and all the strong impression that things were going well and he had the business under complete control.

Jim was a study in character contrasts. Born on a farm in the Bancroft area eighty miles north of Belleville, he joined the army at age fifteen during the first World War. A lanky six feet three inches in height with a mature manner and appearance: recruiting officers passed him with little more than a quizzical frown regarding his proof of age.

World War I and the Canadian Army were the big adventures of Jim's life. He loved the army, romanticized European places, was promoted to Sergeant, suffered serious shrapnel wounds, and was discharged with a pension in 1918. Disliking farm life, he became a door-to-door salesman for *Maclean's* magazine. He sold encyclopedias and whatever came to hand. Shortly after the war he married Ethel Ryan of Montreal. A production line of procreation was set up, and produced eleven children. They were still arriving when I met Eurithe in Belleville in 1941. She was the second oldest.

Somewhere along the line Jim Parkhurst had acquired small expertise in nearly everything imaginable. Hating to work for anyone but himself, he hauled cordwood from the north with an old truck when the sales jobs petered out. The wartime shrapnel wounds had never properly healed, remained suppurating and had to be treated and bandaged daily.

Our taxi office was an upstairs room with sink and small toilet, which doubled as Eurithe's and my apartment. It was at the south end of Belleville's main drag, right beside the London Lunch. There was also a phone in the downstairs hallway, where drivers took calls and reported in. Two doors away was another taxi office, Grotto's; this one much different in character from our flighty and sometimes irresponsible operation. Grotto's had been in existence for some forty years. It was owned by two brothers, both elderly, one with greyness showing under his skin even when closely shaved; the other you never saw at all.

I mention Grotto's because Diamond was such an opposite number, its drivers seemingly recruited from race tracks; bootlegging by all of them including the co-managers (booze was very scarce and continued to be rationed immediately after the war, a twenty-five-ounce bottle selling for ten bootleg bucks, a mickey for five). Still, I personally must have felt a great sense of freedom, of beginning to think for myself again after six years of close military supervision. In the midst of it, Eurithe and I were perceptibly drawing apart, a situation not of my choosing. And I suppose my mind was chaotic. I was drinking some beer at times—which translates to mean that I drank too much every couple of weeks. Above all, I had no plan or design for my life, as some people appear to possess. I had no confidant, or really close friends. I lived from day to day. One may call this pragmatic or existentialist, which is perhaps a way of dignifying chaos.

It was an era of clichés—I was a disorganized and lost soul. On the other hand, it's difficult to say that I wasn't actually "blossoming" in full possession of this unaccustomed freedom. Freedom despite drinking bouts and driving twelve-hour shifts seven days a week. I was writing some pretty awful poems. None survive now, scribbled frenziedly when the ideas came, sitting in rented rooms or idling taxis outside the taxi office, often just before sleep, at rare times in pubs on napkins and beer-splashed tables. I remember none of them, just the fact that they once existed and vanished quickly.

. . . . .

Lorne Munro didn't vanish, remaining in the offing after he sold his business. I'd run into him sometimes that late summer with girl friend in tow; and occasionally picked him up at the Queen's Hotel, the Docter's Hotel, carting them to Munro's apartment on Belleville's west hill. He was obviously rootless and lost himself. About forty, a casual man with offhand conversation, waving his hand languidly to emphasize a point that nobody cared about anyway. His girl friend, Edna, dark haired, spasmodic in speech, close to an alcoholic, as Lorne was himself.

One day he hired me for an afternoon trip into Prince Edward County, taking me into his confidence about the project he had in mind. "She's an alcoholic," Lorne whispered in my ear confidentially, "and I gotta break her of the booze habit. I've got it all planned out, and this afternoon you and me, we're gonna make it happen."

I was fascinated and bemused by all this, also extremely curious. The husky alcoholic voice whispered in my ear from six feet away; the rehabilitation scenario unfolding, cause and effect, beneficial result a mere matter of time.

I took Lorne Munro and his Edna into Prince Edward for several miles. We stopped at a sunny farmer's field complete with grazing cows; we unloaded a trunk full of groceries, bottled water, Coleman lamp and sundries; we set up a tent in the middle of the field while cows watched in cow-wonder . . . And left her there. Edna said on our departure, "I have nothing to read," in a whiny voice.

"Ya can't read anyway," Lorne said.

Walking away from the tent in memory, I look back. Her forlorn little face stared after us, her expression saying better than words that she didn't know what was happening to her. And maybe she didn't.

In the car Lorne Munro said, "We'll pick her up again two days from now." He glanced at me sharply. "You'll see. She'll be a new woman."

But I never saw Edna again, whether she was new or old. He must've got someone else to pick her up from where she was marooned in that farmer's field. Or perhaps he changed his mind and went back again the same day. There are some cold nights in Prince Edward County, even in the summer.

. . . . .

At war's end with men pouring out of the armed forces, eager for freedom and the fleshpots of "Civvy Street," the streets of Belleville were blue, brown and white with airmen, sailors and soldiers. All thirsty for booze and women, aching to spend money, wanting excitement and novelty, wanting, wanting, wanting . . .

Bootlegging flourished—I think all the taxis except Grotto's sold booze. Trains kept arriving from Toronto and Montreal jammed with discharged military heroes, some spreading out to northern towns, Madoc, Tweed, small villages and farms along the highway to Bancroft.

Undoubtedly there were scams and confidence operations; certainly a few of these people were cheated of something or other. Nearly everyone you met was good-humoured, eager to see again a face they loved, a place they remembered. I had felt much the same myself on returning to Trenton to find my mother old (she would have been sixty-seven then, five years younger than I am now), and alone, turning more and more to religion for solace. (I have a twinge of guilt when I think of her.) Anyway, at Trenton I tried to find again all the old places mentally joined to my own youth—Weddell's tugs, B.W. Powers coal sheds on Front Street, ruins of the munitions factory east of the river . . . Not that I loved them as such, but they were part of my past, lost fragments of myself.

Jim Parkhurst's older sons, Gordon (the eldest) from the army, and Alvin from the navy, were also eventually discharged. When Mike's Taxi and LaMorre's Taxi (four cars and licenses each) came up for sale,

Jim used his sons' military credits to add them to our growing fleet. Neither son possessed enough money to take over Mike's and LaMorre's on their own, but pyramided onto Diamond Taxi the wobbly financial structure was almost viable. The two ex-military sons joined us as drivers, Jim and I remaining as managers. There were perhaps two dozen, or slightly more, taxi licenses in Belleville in 1945. Jim Parkhurst and I controlled nearly half of them.

One would think such percentages ought to ensure success; but it was a recipe for disaster. Jim and I got into more and more disagreements, struggles for control, under-the-surface wrestlings, out-and-out fights for simple domination. After Eurithe and I separated, around 1947, say, I don't think she was completely aware of the duel her father and I were waging. It wasn't very often obvious, only once or twice were there any shouting matches between us, just this continual slipping away of any power or influence in my own possession.

Of course it disturbed me. I was twenty-six, and had spent nearly six years having nearly every move I made dictated by superior officers. Then very suddenly I had to act on my own, make my own decisions with no help from any quarter. Neither previous experience nor my own psychological make-up was a preparation for this situation. I felt lost. And yet, on the outside I was brash, confident and sometimes overbearing—I think I was, I *believe* I was like that. Probably my outside character was fairly unattractive. (Think back on your own past selves: do any of us really know what we were like then, that misty and unresolved person long ago, from whom we have somehow evolved to what we are now?)

I was ex-military, and shared all the weaknesses of other ex-military personnel who thronged the streets in 1945. I had developed a taste for beer; I liked women, and found it difficult to meet any after the breakup with Eurithe. I was directionless, suddenly released from the confines of marriage. (That word "confines"?—yes, I think there are bonds and shackles attached to all relationships.) I am introspective now, not so much so then. At the time, I think I was—somehow—"panic-stricken" at being alive. Can that be understood? What does it entail to live in the world, alive in the solitary conning tower of the brain, pondering all the why and wherefore questions we must ponder? Of course, no answers at all present themselves.

. . . . .

The Diamond Taxi office was directly adjacent to a restaurant, the London Lunch. This was a favourite parking spot for cabs, a place where potential customers came to mix food with the beer they had often previously imbibed from nearby pubs. My own drivers and I used to duel with Smith's Taxi drivers for any available parking spaces. Smith, a very large and formidable looking man, had a partner whose name I've forgotten. Call him Smith Two.

The protocol for securing a parking spot was that you backed in, and Smith Two on this occasion was doing just that, backing into the one spot open at the London Lunch. Then I arrived, thought of all the times he'd beaten me to a spot in the past few weeks, and just dived headfirst into that forty feet or so of pavement. Smith Two stopped in the nick of time to avoid crashing into my lovable old Dodge. Both of us jumped to the sidewalk and confronted each other.

We glared, ominously silent. There was the feeling that if one or the other spoke first, it would be like blinking your eyes in the face of danger and you had lost. We continued not speaking. I was, of course, completely in the wrong; I had no business preempting that parking spot. (On such events world catastrophes hinge.) We glared.

Smith Two was obviously going to hit me first or I was going to hit him first. But we delayed, sort of dancing around each other in a slow waltz. Smith Two was short, heavy and built close to the ground—er, pavement. I was tall, heavy and closer to the sky. I was also long-armed, sort of, and much younger. I picked him apart with a left jab, jab, jab, jab, and saw his face grow bloody and felt sick. I left the London Lunch to take a call and felt uncomfortable while driving. On investigation, I found I'd shit my pants.

. . . . .

I think some people look at you and see only a stereotype. But there are others to whom you were not completely invisible, although they see the version they want to see. In Belleville there was this woman who lived with her husband at a restaurant they owned and operated on Dundas Street East. Actually she wasn't more than a girl, and very pregnant. When I drove her to wherever it was, she would look at me meaningfully. She wanted to leave her husband, and had selected me as a replacement. Her glance was languishing and seductive.

But I didn't get all this info from her, the part about wanting me to run away with her. She'd confided in another driver, and he gave me the story. The other driver also mentioned that the girl's husband was jealous and wanted to have a word with me. All this was flattering in a way, but quite amazing. I'd scarcely spoken to the lady, but she apparently regarded me as potential suitor and possible husband. Nothing happened, no follow-up to this, but there must have been a story I never did hear.

* * * * *

Despite our acquisitions, the Diamond Taxi office remained at the south end of Front Street; Mike's and LaMorre's at the other end. Marshall, a cripple from polio, manned the phone for Mike's and LaMorre's, with a parking lot behind and a cobbled alley beside the office. Drivers would park at either office, depending on their locality at the end of a call.

Gordon Parkhurst, who'd spent the war in the army and was the eldest of Jim's sons, quite suddenly took a dislike to me. I never did find out the exact reason for this. I'm not sure if he knew the reason himself. Perhaps because Eurithe and I had broken up. In any event, he kept making uncomplimentary remarks about me at the Mike's / LaMorre's office when other drivers were present. And yes, it was uncomfortable, that situation, and became more so as time passed.

I decided this situation couldn't continue, and invited Gordon to come outside with me to the parking lot. The implication was that we would fight. However, I had also made up my mind that fighting would solve nothing, might even make the situation worse. My plan was simply to talk and to talk and to talk, on the assumption that if we were talking we couldn't be fighting at the same time. Besides, if we did fight, I would very probably lose, since Gordon would make a very formidable opponent, with muscles on top of his muscles.

I have probably never talked faster and to more effect. Gordon just stood there in a menacing attitude, watching and listening. I had stirred him into anger with my original invitation to come outside, as if he had somehow lost status himself. His jaw was thrust out, forearms raised and tense with expectation of violence. The outcome of what I said was always in doubt, as I talked desperately on and on. Gordon and I must have stood in that parking lot for at least half an hour, nose to nose, he glaring at me while I talked placatingly.

I can't remember a thing I said. But it worked. We made our peace, and there has scarcely been the mildest argument between us since that time. Of course I defer to Gordon in all situations where there might be one. Besides, I've grown rather fond of him. Words have seldom worked so well for me.

* * * * *

The drivers of our triple-headed business had the bad habit of crashing cars, which didn't help with our insurance rates. Bob Gannon, a likable

Irisher with red hair, smacked into another car head-on coming down the long Oak Lake hill one night in a rain storm. His wiper had stopped working. Gannon died in the crash. His girl friend, who was riding with him, was severely injured. Another driver, Jim Brown, bashed up a car but walked away from the crash unscathed. Later he took care of this omission by committing suicide. Our creditors were beginning to be insistent.

I think there's something demoralizing to human character about certain occupations (the Grotto brothers notwithstanding). Lorne Munro, original owner of Diamond Taxi, drifted away as people do and was lost to my knowledge. The same with Barney LaMorre, who moved to Trenton twelve miles away. I have the strong impression that both were men without purpose or intention in life; they drifted, and drifted nowhere.

Mike Lucas, previous owner of Mike's Taxi, was briefly my friend. Mike had somehow gotten to know Senator Fraser of Trenton. Fraser, according to Mike, had a lot of influence and was instrumental in Mike's purchase of a motel operation three miles east of Belleville on #2 Highway. This, of course, after selling Mike's Taxi to Diamond.

Mike was chunkily built, active and yet relaxed as a cat, blue-eyed, and he bragged about himself almost continually. We talked in the manner of intimates a few times. His wife was a good match for him—busty and not shy, they slanged each other often when I was with them, giving me the impression that this was a warm give-and-take sexual relationship. Not long ago a passage of lyrical stuff came into my mind, and it might even be mine: "We came like water and like wind we go." I use that about the people I knew in the taxi business. They're gone, all of them, except Jim Parkhurst's sons. I'll never escape Jim Parkhurst's sons.

· · · · ·

There were always hangers-on, people who attached themselves to the drivers and taxi office; perhaps because they thought it was glamorous. Most of them were female. One Burl (sic?) Hill rode around with Gordon. The Hill girl was a vision, someone I'd be proud to introduce as "my girl" in any society. She floated rather than walked, talked little, was outside her own milieu, the Indian reserve near Deseronto eighteen miles east. I fell in love with her just watching her shadowy face behind the glass windshield of Gordon's car, the epitome of all the princesses I'd ever dreamed about, when the word "princess" meant to me a beautiful and desirable woman. But the Mohawk princess disappeared after a few months, and so have all the others.

It's the ugly and unpleasant aspects of driving cab that I remember best. The nasty things in which I was personally involved. Our business consisted largely of house calls: somebody would phone the office and ask for a cab at such and such an address right away or else at some specified time. On one of these calls I remember pulling over to the left side of this residential street (the wrong side) to make it convenient for both customer and me, without going to the bother of finding a driveway and turning around so that I was facing the correct side of the street.

After I'd knocked at the customer's door and was on my way back to the car to wait a moment, another car pulled up in front of me, just about headlight to headlight. The man driving this other car, a stocky and heavily built person, got out and confronted me. "You're parked on the wrong side of the road," he said challengingly. Yes, that was true. I had to admit it. And a jawing match ensued, during which this guy was fairly screaming at me, with the rotten stench of booze on his breath. Then he uttered the key words, the key words, mark you, after which any red-blooded Canadian, American or, as the case may be, Lower Slobovian—decides that physical combat is unavoidable. ("You're yellow!")

I hit the guy. He hit me; or being slightly drunk, perhaps he missed. We brawled disgracefully. (Although now I see some humorous aspects to all this —) The passenger I had called for emerged from her home, disturbed by these antics.

Anyway, what happened was nothing much. The other guy's wife also made her presence felt, and bawled out her husband. She then seized her erring spouse by the metaphorical ear and dragged him away, perhaps to church. I ferried my own passenger off as well. Around midnight, when business was dying down, I went back to the taxi office, to find—whadaya think? Yep. It was him. He'd remembered the name on my taxi, looked it up in the phone book and tracked me to home turf. Still spoiling for a fight, if he wasn't spoiled already.

We fought. In the alley beside the office. Right and justice prevailed. I ended up on top of the guy, and about to bang the bastard's head on the cobbles to inculcate better manners. But Jim, my esteemed father-in-law, pulled me off before I could accomplish this fell design. I guess I didn't mind him doing that. It was ugly, and made me feel wrong about doing the only thing possible. Afterwards, I heard the usual rumours: the guy was busting up with his wife; he was an ex-boxer who needed exercise; he was an escapee from Kingston Pen. Take your pick.

. . . . .

There were a few peaceful moments—driving north in winter, turning off the main highways onto narrow tree-lined country roads, with snow creating its mindless lovely sculpture on evergreen branches. The Canadian Shield loops south about twenty miles north of Belleville, almost capriciously. Its dark Precambrian rock as much a stone mood as a geologic period. For me, the knowledge that life had not yet appeared here or mere traces of it, three billion years ago, casts a solemn note over the present time. Driving through a rock-cut on the highway, I still have the strange feeling of being submerged briefly in prehistoric seas. We humans are such transient creatures . . .

For a couple of years after the war ended, certain varieties of consumer goods remained in short supply. And men and women in uniform were still trickling from trains and buses. You could feel a kind a sadness about them sometimes, as if an era of their lives had ended. And it had. The Hitler war had supplied purpose and meaning to the lives of a great many people, and this was now removed. Military discipline too had occupied a large place in the psyche of some, which enabled them to feel that time itself was filled—with schedule and measurement of the hours.

My own life, despite often moving swiftly over Belleville streets in early morning, then the succeeding torpid calm—my life often made me feel nearly invisible. As if I touched no one, not in any way that made them know I was me. At three and four a.m., whispering down the city centre of Front Street in a light rain; joining the rush of Dafoe's, Grotto's and other taxis to the railway station for an early train. Or just cruising, slowing for a lone figure walking home on the deserted planet at one a.m., waiting for them to flag you down. I tried to fill this peculiar emptiness with activity, as if activity in any direction, however meaningless, would serve as a substitute for something I couldn't remember . . .

The poems I wrote then were a habit as much as anything:

> An ominous length uncoiling and thin.
> A sliver of Satan annoyed by the din
> Of six berry-pickers, bare-legged and intent
> On stripping red treasure like rubies from Ghent.
> He moved without motion, he hissed without noise—
> A sombre dark ribbon that laughter destroys;
> He eyed them unblinking from planets unknown,
> As alien as Saturn, immobile as stone.

—from *Rattlesnake* (1949)

I had not yet achieved anything close to "my own voice," the way of writing which is like a signature, unmistakably yourself. That sounds like a bit of artsy nonsense when you say it, but there is a tone of voice that rings true, behind which your own face and mind hover and cling always to the written words. But that didn't happen for me. And therefore this three-year chunk of my life produced poems that I think worthless. It's the I—me in poems, whether first person poems or not, that is most valuable and valid. It's the lack of a single personal human face behind E.J. Pratt's epics that leaves me indifferent to him and them. This despite "The grey shape with the palaeolithic face." You have to reach the Neolithic Age to attain complete Cro-Magnon Humanity.

My friend Harold Wannamaker appeared in the Diamond Taxi office one day in 1947. Now in civvies, his beautiful wavy hair was nearly all gone, but his grin remained. He'd stayed in the RCAF after the war—or maybe it was with the Royal Air Force?—flying Lancaster bombers in Egypt. Although I don't suppose he'd been bombing anybody lately.

We went out on the town to celebrate Harold being a civilian again. But before this celebration, there was an incident which had a direct bearing on our festivities. I'd had a couple of passengers in my taxi, and shortly after we started off the man began to hammer the woman with his fists. I told him to stop, in fact insisted that he stop, instructing him with some vigorous gestures. The guy paid no attention, just continued beating on the woman. Whereupon I drove them to the police station in the Belleville market square; and the cops made sure there was no more such nonsense. Later on I was informed the beater-up-of-women was looking for me, intended to serve me likewise.

Back to Harold Wannamaker. With jollity and rejoicing on account of Harold's release by the Egyptian Pharaoh and air force high command, the two of us wandered down the main drag and into a pool room. This place was no doubt the haunt of low types with brutish foreheads; I've haunted such places a great deal myself. As things turned out on this occasion, my other friend, the erstwhile violent passenger, was also an *habitué* along with a friend of his. They cordially invited us outside to a nearby alley to sample the night air. It was implied very strongly that my health was in some danger.

As it chanced, the beater-up-of-women was occupied by Harold. I took on his friend. Shortly after hostilities commenced the friend fled; whereupon I motioned to the beater-up-of-women that I was free for the next few moments. Perhaps half a dozen punches were exchanged when this man fled as well, disappearing in darkness at the opposite end of the alley. Then a cop made his presence known, having detected suspicious noises emanating from the darkness. This cop insisted strongly that something untoward had been going on. Harold and I reassured him that we were friends, and seized with a sudden desire to urinate, had entered the alley to do so. Deciding that this version of events was not unreasonable, the cop gave us his blessing and departed.

After a brief conference, Harold and I decided to continue our celebration at a locality where cops were not so plentiful. I drove the cab a couple of miles outside town, parked on the edge of a farmer's field, where Harold and I settled down to finish off the two mickeys of rye I had secured for us. We'd been at this field only half an hour when a car approached us with all the ominous earmarks and flashing rooflight of the dreaded constabulary.

I managed to hurl an empty mickey bottle some distance away, hoping I was unobserved. The full bottle was hurriedly stashed under the car. But I hadn't deceived anyone with these feeble manoeuvres. The cops escorted us back to town, throwing Harold and I in the hoosegow. We were, of course, frankly and unabashedly stoned, while doing our best to speak without slurring the words. Things whirl around a bit when you're in that condition. I settled down on a greasy looking bunk in an attempt to allow the whirling motion time to stop. And fell asleep.

I awoke to hear this loud pounding noise, very hard on the ears; but for a few moments I was unable to summon speech. It was Harold, of course, beating his fists continually on the cell door. This door was steel, and emitted a *vroom-vroom* sound like tribal drums beating in the jungle less than a foot from my ears. I was moved to protest. Perhaps I was in imminent danger of being eaten by savage Indians in the Brazilian jungle—our native Indians in Canada having been weaned from this unpleasant habit.

Harold pounded frenziedly at the cell door. His back was soaked with sweat, his shirt nearly black with it. The dim wire-protected light on the ceiling reflected on his bald spot (again I thought of that beautiful wavy hair with dark red lights when the sun shone at the right angle). I had an overwhelming feeling of wonder that this should be us: the high school football hero and veteran of the war in Europe: and me with this marvellous entire world in my head whose secrets I hadn't figured out how to reveal. But sadly, the two prisoners were indubitably us.

The jungle drums in our cell continued, eventually attracting a uniformed guard. Harold clutched the bars with both hands and addressed him passionately. "Let me outa here! Let me out! I know the magistrate's son in this town! Let me out!"

Then, perhaps feeling that those sources of influence were insufficient, Harold yelled, "I know the mayor! The mayor is a good friend of mine."

The guard just stood there.

Earlier in the morning, Harold and I had been permitted a phone call, as per the malefactor's code or something. Around five or six a.m. our wives appeared, both Harold's and mine (this had to be before the break between Eurithe and I was *fait accompli*; but as a result of the incident, my repute and status with her suffered greatly). Anyway, they bailed us out of jail.

Harold and I were subdued, perhaps even humble in demeanour. The heroic daredevil pilot and great writer *manqué* had received their comeuppance, or comedownance as the case might be. The cops eyed us inscrutably as we departed their dark domain, shackles knocked off. Some of those cops were probably married men. They may even have known how we felt.

Years later I wrote a poem about this experience, a poem differing in some respects from the incidents just described. It was called "The Drunk Tank." Later still, when I was writer-in-rez at the University of Western Ontario in London, Ontario, some students wanted to make an amateur movie dramatizing my poem. They got permission from the local cops to use an empty cell in the city hoosegow for staging their movie. The students had me down in their thespian endeavour in the part of the guy hammering on his cell door who knew the magistrate's son and thought he should be especially favoured because of that.

Cameras were set up, all the actors *in situ*; the student director said whatever directors say. Then I got panicky. I was overwhelmed with fear; all I could think and say was, "Let me outa here!" And this despite having been in jails a few times in my life, the play-acting had gotten to me. A great wave of terror. And I have no explanation for this, despite my explanation. The fear was like sexual lust or screaming rage: everything else fled from my mind. A feeling that is indescribable unless you're actually feeling it at the moment; and if you are, you're too drunk with it to even think. From that part of your mind called the "limbic brain," the pre-human areas of being alive? I wonder.

I changed places with the uniformed guard, listening with a drained feeling to the frenzied prisoner screaming, "Let me outa here!" And yes, I had been stripped down to some essential kernel of myself, the self always behind whatever I think I am.

So few of us have or will have any living remembrance of the dead. Or so it seems to me. And why should we, what good does it do; what point? I try to answer that question—with a response that is mostly for myself despite this context—and say that we humans try to balance our memories and feelings against oblivion. I say to myself—and in these words now—that my feelings and memories are important. They're all I have that is me—a woman's face in a particular light, the triumph of some things making sense when you thought they didn't, the repeated failure of knowing they don't. The woman in your mind who will always be there, inhabiting empty skull and printed on bone as a continual absence, then a crumbling place in the earth. Chemicals dissolved in rain.

Harold Wannamaker became a flying instructor in civilian life, probably late in 1947. He crashed and died in his light plane at Oshawa. I heard about it long after.

· · · · ·

The people you met in the taxi business, the majority of those you drove hither and yon and everywhere—these were generally poorer people. In England, I suppose, they would be called the lower class. They included the drunks, of course (despite the previous episode, I didn't drink myself silly very often), those people who seemed always to be clinging to existence with their fingernails, the shabbily dressed and badly housed people, who always found money for a cab. Others who needed help with groceries or awkward burdens; and the motel clientele, the young with money and urgent sexual needs. People who were ferried to and from their places of work in morning and evening. The Sunday churchgoers, street pickups, passengers from railway station and bus terminal. You got a pretty complete cross-section of humanity in this business.

After the breakup between Eurithe and I, she found someone else and no doubt needed that someone else. I "went out" with three or four girls, the relationship with some enduring for a while, one lasting longer. The disagreements and outright quarrels between Jim Parkhurst and I continued. Drivers crashed their cars; gossip and rumour permeated existence; the routines of living, morning and evening and sleep.

Call this next incident a penalty for my sense of humour (Eurithe would have another name for it). The town cops were continually watching our taxi office doorway beside the London Lunch for evidence of bootlegging. Aware of this surveillance, I was unable to resist playing a joke on them, thinking the cops would take it with good humour. I filled a mickey bottle with water, handing it to a Diamond Driver stealthily but at an angle the watching cop could observe.

Halfway down the block my cab was stopped and the driver hauled off to the slammer. They had to let him go free shortly after, when they discovered the supposed booze was tap water. But after that, Belleville's finest watched me closely for any least transgression of city or federal laws.

It was very silly on my part. I can only plead boredom at the time and avoid the word stupidity. Those long hours of hanging around a nearly deserted taxi office; lounging outside the London Lunch waiting for customers; on long drives fighting sleep by allowing cold air from an open window to blow onto your face and deliberately open mouth; the sloppy drunks and con men on the make you encountered periodically; living in a rented room, eating bad meals in bad restaurants . . . A mollusc hanging onto a tide-washed ocean ledge precariously.

The cab drivers were an interesting bunch. Some were older semi-permanent veterans; these ranged in age anywhere from twenty-five to fifty. Others were fill-ins, generally quite young, taken on for a day or two, who might achieve steady employment if proven reliable. Bill Donohue was probably late in his fifties, wore glasses and liked his booze. But that conveys nothing of his dry humour, the unexpected twists he gave to nearly everything he said. A little guy, everybody liked and protected him from being pushed around.

Roy Hoard was fat and phlegmatic; he drove the Dodge when I wasn't driving it. Roy wore a tweed cap, the kind with a visor; I believe he thought it was stylish. There was something very cold and considering in the way he looked at you. Eric somebody, a man strong enough to lift one end of a car; we looked on him with awe. Clarence somebody, a man with vertical lines running down his thin face; a loner who always stood apart from the rest. But they are like sand in the mind; their memory runs away and escapes you.

In late summer of 1948 it was fairly plain that the Diamond Taxi, and the other eight licenses as well, were in danger of bankruptcy. Attempting to delay our downfall, I borrowed a thousand dollars from my mother in Trenton. But nothing worked. The drivers hired by Jim

Parkhurst either bashed fenders or got into other kinds of trouble. My own disagreements with Jim had become bitterly frequent. His early "understanding" with me that he would take no money from the business until his own investment in time and work equalled my cash investment—that agreement between us was never kept. One understood that he needed money to live in addition to his army pension, but there was no financial accounting, no coherent plan of operation, and very little communication between us.

To like someone is different thing than having them as a business partner. Of course Jim Parkhurst was attractive and generous—on the surface of things. But his organizing abilities were more apparent than real. He spent much of his time at poker games. If he lost money disastrously, this was played down; when he won, no figure was given, but the implication was that his winnings were considerable .

Jim wanted to be the central figure in any situation, and generally was; the way other people thought about him was always extremely important to him. An imposing figure, his reticence often made him seem even more impressive. However, the fatal flaw was that he never stuck with anything to its finish, whatever the project might be. I think he often depended on his veteran's pension to take care of emergencies. If he went broke in a poker game, the pension was still there. Of course, it was the reason his proposal to take no money from the business sounded as if the arrangement might be possible.

But I blame myself equally for the failure of the taxi enterprise. A pyramid operation, it depended on trust, co-operation and hard work. There were few of those qualities between Jim Parkhurst and I. Much later, and in a different situation, I received valuable help from him while building our house at Roblin Lake. Relations again became coolly cordial. However, my overwhelming impression of Jim is that he never achieved any degree of genuine self-awareness. He saw himself always the way he thought other people viewed him. Reality in the assessment of himself was beyond him.

As for myself, I was completely out of my depth in the taxi business. And despite its occasional rewarding moments, I disliked nearly every part of it. Whatever I have since become—and of course even that is debatable—is a matter of late development.

Bankruptcy is a sort of *dénouement*, a dramatic ending whereby all is changed afterwards. We did everything we could think of to stave off this ruin, which had stigma and disgrace attached to it. Creditors were given excuses and promises, none of them reliable. Drivers' salaries were delayed for a week and often more than that. But finally it was like fate, like death, like the medieval sailors' concept of a flat earth and sea over the edge of which you finally plunge without hope. I think of Malcolm Lowry's pessimism, although I am not a pessimist. I think of myself driving and drinking beer in the old Dodge, pursued by a vengeful bailiff, racing north on Highway 62 in red October. Turning onto the old Hastings Road, its upkeep abandoned by time and the parsimonious township reeves, the forest primeval swarms in from either side of the road, beaver dams are taking over . . .

And there I am, aiming the worn-out old car over an embankment, driving it into a deep moonlit lake, its headlights shining into black nowhere. Then walking south to Highway 401, drinking beer and throwing the empties onto the road allowance. Off to Toronto to start a new life; and write a novel dedicated to my grandfather, Ridley Neville Purdy, Ol Rid who was dead and wouldn't deign to even look at the fancy words if he were alive . . .

. . . . .

Very dramatic, a fitting *dénouement*! And something I completely imagined to make things bearable for me.

What did happen—everything veered sideways, details of factual things became uncertain, their status cloudy and vague; the financial situation indefinite, but about to be catastrophic. Weather clear, but clouds in the offing. For a long time, doubt about things happening just beyond my knowing, decisions made that I wasn't immediately aware of. And probably I have never felt more inadequate.

But things weren't entirely disastrous. The differences between Eurithe and I were repaired, at least covered over during the next few years. Roy Hoard died, I think from a heart attack. As mentioned earlier, a driver, Jim Brown, committed suicide by hanging himself. Gordon Parkhurst went to work for the CP Railway. Alvin started a delivery business. Jim continued his poker playing, went back to odd jobs and temporary projects, his pension assuming more importance.

. . . . .

And slow down to about thirty, swig half another beer and hold the bottle clenched between my thighs. Like a story, which I intended it to be. A fox dashing out from underbrush, running full-out thirty feet ahead of the car, caught like a moth in the headlights; but unlike a moth, unable to turn right or left away from the road. A prisoner of light, its tail riding straight out behind in the self-created wind. Does the fox think it's being pursued by a man or a metal monster, as auto and animal race into the darkness? Is the fox's mate waiting somewhere far behind, alone in the forest, one of the junctures of their lives missed, their coming-together delayed, perhaps for a very long time?

Of course I know all this is a fantasy, but does the fox on the old Hastings Road know it too?

CHAPTER SEVEN

· · · · · · ·

ON BEING A WAGE SLAVE

What happens in your brain when the personality changes? What causes the change to happen? Can you pinpoint the moment in time when all this took place? I mean go back in time and examine yourself in the mirror—memory?—the time and place and you, all swaying like seaweed in dim green underwater light . . .

Of course I'm talking about myself, but some changes take place in all of us. However, they are far more ghostly in humans than invisible growth rings at the hearts of trees, or the sockeye salmon turning crimson on returning to its birthday waters. One says, how, why, when, where? But I'll never find out for sure, since no god will tell me, and my own investigatory apparatus is like a compass full of iron filings: I can't look at myself from outside, observe a duplicate self with clear eye and neutral judgment.

I have a basic assumption that I must make before going farther: that my writings changed and became more complicated; I hesitate to say "better," but I must say it. And my motives for conducting this self-examination are all purely selfish. Most of us are more interested in ourselves and our own thought processes than in any other person, with the possible exception of times when we are besotted with love. And besides, I believe I "think" more efficiently when I'm writing on paper than when I'm talking (say), musing pretentiously *on the awesome shores of eternity.*

· · · · ·

My wife Eurithe, our small son Jimmy and I arrived in Vancouver in early fall of 1950, the year of the Big Freeze. Reasons for coming were several, one being that life in Belleville and Trenton seemed a financial dead end at that time. Another, we were nostalgic and homesick for the west, having spent three years there during my wartime RCAF service.

> City at the continent's edge
> where everyone was born three
> hours younger than the grey east
> and sometimes light is so luminescent
> the air glows glows internally
> and nobody breathes for a moment—

—from *Vancouver* (1984)

The first experiences we had on our return to Vancouver were enough to remove all sentimentality from my character. We had little money and rented an unfurnished apartment on 2nd Avenue near Cambie Street. I bought a standard-sized second-hand bed at a store on Granville Street. The store owner assured us faithfully that he would refund the purchase price if we went broke. That possibility was not unthinkable. We'd been living on potatoes, blackberries that grew around False Creek, and crabapples from a vacant lot across the road.

A week after the bed purchase we still had no jobs and no money. I had to return the bed whence it came: carrying the wretched thing on my back from close to Cambie Street for what must have been at least a dozen city blocks to Granville. What's the Biblical tag line—"Take up thy bed and walk"?

Anyway, the used furniture guy would only refund me half-price for the bed after I lugged it back to his establishment. Five measly bucks. My pitiful tale of being broke and hungry failed to move him at all. I took the five bucks. We bought some groceries. I drank a beer, but didn't write any poems. It was a bad time. I feel lachrymose and savage just thinking about it now.

Eurithe and I took turns going out to look for work, since one of us always had to stay behind with our five-year-old son. One of the many places the UIC people sent me to was Sigurdson's Lumber Co., a couple of blocks from Granville near False Creek. They took me on for the minimum wage, and I worked nights.

At Sigurdson's I was sometimes the "helper" for a leathery old journeyman carpenter, whom everyone respected for his expertise with wood and most feared for his bad temper. I think he rarely even glanced at me during all the time I was with him, and hardly spoke at all. He still seems to me the prototype for Milton Acorn's "mumbly old carpenter, shoulder-straps crossed wrong"; but I hung on the two or three words that old man muttered in the course of an evening, generally about my own mistakes.

When I got laid off from Sigurdson's, it was a blow to my ego—not that I'd expected to make the place more than a whistle-stop on the way to something better. But I had to find another job quickly. And the absolute low point of life for me is looking for work and not finding it. Tramping the streets in Vancouver rain, filling out forms with your own vital statistics that were vital to no one else, realization slowly dawning that nobody wants you, you're unqualified for anything even an idiot could think of in his worst moment. Talking to personnel managers at factories, talking to their assistants, the underlings of underlings. At day's end wanting to confess to your wife that you were useless, nobody wanted you, and why the hell should she be any different? But keeping your mouth shut.

Eurithe got a job first. Office staff at St. Paul's Hospital. (She even looks efficient, especially if I'm not with her). I've compiled a long list of her virtues, but such a list eventually begins to sound the opposite to what's intended. Therefore, I'll just mention her one drawback—she keeps interrupting what I haven't said yet.

. . . . .

I found a job at Vancouver Bedding, a mattress factory on Clark Drive. My first job there was menial, as a wrapper of mattresses and box springs, very low-paying (less than a dollar an hour). Therefore, I studied the machines during lunch hour trying to get a better job, asked questions of their operators, even tried to run them myself for a few minutes when the foreman wasn't watching. And I shouldn't have been surprised when the machine operators thought I was trying to steal their jobs: they wouldn't supply any helpful household hints to their machines. But I was surprised! And perhaps, in a sense, I was trying to steal their jobs.

They were metal puzzles, those machines. The roll-edge consisted of a wooden table on which you placed the mattress. And included a grey-painted hunchback machine of ominous aspect, running around the table's edge on rails. It had steel jaws that opened and closed in two-inch bites, and stitched a sausage-shaped rolled-edge onto the helpless mattress. The machine operator lifted the mattress edge into those jaws with a sharpened ice pick, racketing steel almost catching your soft fingers as you walked backward all day long, in a kind of monotonous trance. The process was rather like feeding a hungry Bengal tiger several thousand meals a day, snatching your fingers back from the meat every time. And yet I sometimes fell asleep walking backwards like a zombie, then yipe-yiped as steel nipped my fingers.

> A hunchback shape
> mounted on rails
> with clacking jaws
> into which you shoved
> the mattress edge
> with sharp ice pick
> lifting it hard
> while the needle stitched
> a quarter inch distant
> from my soft fingers
> All day all day
> walking backwards
> continually pursued
> but never quite caught
> by a grey hunchback
> that seemed to spit at you
> because it was steel
> and you were flesh

—from *Machines* (1984)

The tufting machine wasn't nearly so dangerous, despite a similar monotony. A giant needle affixed metal buttons above and below the mattress in a pre-determined pattern. You moved a sliding table to the left and then to the right, shoving the mattress to a spot where you wanted to place the button. The wooden table made a noise like "oompah" every time you moved it and the needle plunged down, and you moved it continually. The noise imitated an iambic or trochaic metrical foot, like in a line of poetry; a stressed syllable, then a non-stressed one, spoken under my breath.

Therefore, when the giant needle tufted a mattress, I kept time with a poem I had memorized:

Do not go gentle into that good night

(or reversing the metre and distorting it:

"oompah—oompah—oompah")

Old age should rave and burn at close of day—

(Dylan Thomas could never have anticipated this use of his poem, keeping a factory worker more or less sane.) Sometimes I would even verbalize a poem aloud (*"From the hag and hungry goblin that into rags would rend ye/And the spirit that stands by the naked man in the book of moons defend ye"*), and fellow workers would look at me with a peculiar expression. Thus every mattress I tufted became one very long line of blank verse when I wasn't thinking of a specific poem. But the machine's "oompah" sound could not furnish end rhymes. Therefore, I would stamp my foot on the wooden floor when a rhyme seemed called for. All I lacked was applause at the end of a mattress-poem.

The filling machine was much simpler, and used for cheaper varieties of mattresses. On a few occasions I helped run a mattress through the filler, sewed its end on the tape-edge, roll-edged it, and finally tufted it. There was some satisfaction in that, like following a plant from seed to flower to mature fruit. An incongruous comparison, since machine operators were nothing like gardeners.

I became fairly expert at running these machines, but never learned to do anything more than simple repairs. And that caused problems. When machines broke down the factory manager, Arthur Watt, became a repairman. He didn't like the job and blamed the machine operator— me, in most cases—for causing the breakdown. He'd work at the roll-edge and tufting machines, probing their innards, his face growing red with anger at the clumsy workman and imperfect machine.

Arthur Watt had married into the Hammond family, who operated Hammond Furniture Company, and for which Vancouver Bedding was a minor subsidiary occupying a small part of the same building. Of course, the extent of his financial interest in the mattress company was forever beyond the knowledge of a humble employee like myself. But it must have been considerable, for Watt often worked on the machines or wrapping table, or with the shipper when things became hectic.

He was a tall man, about six foot two, age around forty, and worked always in grey pants and white shirt. His manner was completely detached with employees, his reddish-coloured face remote and slightly austere. But when customers or personal friends visited the factory, Watt unbent and became obviously charming. My own relations with him were always formally correct, neither of us betraying any personal feelings toward the other—except when my machine broke down. Then he boiled inside, a pressure cooker under imperfect control.

During that period in my life, the time of sumptuous youth, I was physically ebullient, as if there was no limit to my energies. At the same time, I never learned how to use those energies most efficiently. I expended too much of myself on even the simplest job, and threw all my strength into difficult things. I was enthralled by work, and yet I hated it.

When Arthur Watt and I worked together, sliding mattresses and box springs down a second-floor chute to the shipper below, I worked my hardest to show him up. Which no doubt at all was exactly what he wanted. One tipped a mattress onto its edge, then gave it a little practised flip toward one's body, shifted hands to its central point and lifted it at arm's length over the head. Sometimes we worked in tandem, then raced together on tip-toe to the chute, like ballet dancers.

Only once was there ever a situation in which I could cause Arthur Watt any personal discomfiture. As has been obvious, my own feelings about him were ambivalent: I both admired and detested the man. On this occasion: I found myself with another worker facing Watt and two more from opposite sides of a table. The exact logistics of this situation are now vague to me, but each little group was pulling against the other, hauling on ropes in order that a very tight mattress cover would slide around a spring that was much too large for it. The delightful part of this tableau for me was that I faced directly opposite to Arthur Watt, and what pulling power I had would affect my boss directly.

By an act of will, I changed myself into a steam locomotive. Not a diesel: I have no use for these fancy engines that break down in moments of stress. For one instant the engine of me became a steel thunderbolt. I yanked so hard that Arthur Watt's chin forcibly contacted the table between us. No blood, of course. Then I physically withdrew from the situation, apparently unaware of anything out of the ordinary. And changed back to the holder of time card 168.

It was a moment of ineffable and unrepeatable sweetness. I felt Arthur Watt's eyes brush against me with just a hint of speculation. And lowered my own gaze from innate shyness. Work continued.

With cobwebs between elbows and knees,
I say that I hate violence:
there have been street fights;
two wills glaring eye to eye arm
wrestling—;
hours struggling for my soul or hers
with a woman in a taxi;
whacked and bloody and beaten in a poolroom,
playing pool with the winner and winning,
then walk home, and fall down like a broken chair,
that kind of pride.
All violence,
the inner silent implacable defiance
of money or god or damn near anything:
but it was useful once
to the middle-aged man with belly and ballpoint
getting drunk on words but sobering ah sobering.
Remember the factory manager Arthur Watt,
big, charming smile, attractive personality,
who worked alongside his crew,
to increase production,
wearing a white shirt and tailored trousers:
one day Watt and four others
pulled against three of us across a table,
hauling the cover onto a mattress
much too big for the cover, with ropes,
a workday job delightfully turned to a tug-o-war:
me, digging up more strength than I had,
aimed it at Watt especially,
yanked the bastard toward me,
dragged an extra ten pounds of myself
from the guts and yanked
the boss till his head banged wood with
both arms stretched towards me on the table praying
to Allah there is no god but Allah
                              W. Purdy . . .
The trick was to keep an absolutely straight face,
no expression whatever hold
the chortle to a goddam whimper
of pure joy that started in the balls
and raced 90-miles-per-hour to the angels' antennae

where it sang sweet songs to female cherubs
emerging in the factory dust as a deprecating tsk-tsk,
a normal cigarette cough,
successfully dishonestly solicitous.
As a matter of course he hated me,
which I accepted modestly as my just due:
I've drawn it after me down the years,
that sobbing violence,
ropes to the mattress past like cobwebs
that break with a sudden movement or gentle smile:
or, tough as steel hawsers,
the ropes drag me inch by inch
to the other side of the table,
where the factory manager awaits
his unruly workman with a gun,
to watch with amazed eyes
while I write this poem,
like blossoming thistle.

—*Notes on a Fictional Character* (1968)

I have a mental picture of myself at that time, riding the interurban from our small house on Vanness Avenue near Burnaby to the mattress factory on Clark Drive. I am reading the *Collected Poems of Dylan Thomas*. A gangly thirty-to-thirty-five-year-old, hair receding at the temples, and an expression of mixed interest and puzzlement flits across my face while reading. And glancing around self-consciously at other early morning travelers to see if anyone has noticed these intellectual proclivities, and again to see if there are any good-looking girls on the interurban. A poetry-writing factory worker with pretensions to culture.

Somewhat earlier, an ex-merchant seaman named Doug Kaye came to work at Vancouver Bedding. Doug was an expert tape-machine operator and commanded top wages. His voice was low and gravelly, not easy to understand above the clatter of machines. Something about him though: he too was afflicted with a monumental discontent from his lot in life. A small man, I sometimes got the impression Doug was a medium-sized volcano awaiting the right time to blow its top. He smoldered underneath.

We became friends. To which friendship add Curt Lang, a precocious teenager I had met at a science-fiction fan club gathering. Curt was one of those preternaturally brilliant youngsters who antagonize their elders by being too obviously intelligent. He was also a science-fiction buff. Curt admired my rather puerile poetry, which really doesn't speak well for that aforementioned intelligence.

I suppose the three of us were a bit enthralled with each other, and there was some novelty in an ex-seaman with musical ambitions (Doug took violin lessons), a pre-embryo writer, and a hedonist youngster of fifteen finding each other available and interested. We met once a week, generally at Doug's place, wives also in attendance. (Curt hadn't achieved one of those as yet.) Doug played operatic records and German lieder; we drank beer and talked a great deal.

Up to that time my own literary gods were Bliss Carman, G.K. Chesterton, W.J. Turner, etc. These were not exactly household names even at that time. But suddenly I found myself reading T.S. Eliot, Dylan Thomas, W.B. Yeats, Ezra Pound and others. I had realized that my own writings were, if not precisely mediocre, certainly not immortal literature either. I simply wasn't saying things that I should have been capable of saying.

. . . . .

And I met Steve McIntyre, a Davie Street bookseller who liked good literature and sex. He must have lived with a score or so women—not all at once—over the years I knew him. He seemed to have read and have an opinion about every book I'd ever heard of; if he hadn't read it, then he was about to. Steve talked in a jerky and halting manner, with pauses not where you'd place commas in writing, but right in the middle of a subordinate clause, leaving you looking at him expectantly and feeling foolish. His voice was a husky cigarette burr, like someone scraping a chair over a wooden floor.

All of Steve McIntyre's friends regarded him as a combination of Socrates and Plato, a very wise man. Among these friends were Wayne Thompson, a champion beer-drinker who once managed to procure a pair of Egyptian mummies from Woodwards Department Store, then tried to raffle them off at twenty-five cents a ticket. And Alec LaFortune, who had hitch-hiked west from Toronto, had an abiding grudge against the police, and who wrote poetry. And Raymond Hull, an ex-Englishman with literary ambitions, who later collaborated with a UBC professor to write *The Peter Principle*. And to this menagerie could be added Curt Lang and myself.

I spent many afternoons then and later, listening reverently while Steve McIntyre expounded on literature, his own opinions, other people's opinions, providing all his friends with the final word on philosophy and truth. At one point he informed me that my knowledge of great books was almost nil. And he meant "great" in the early twentieth century classical sense. Proust, Dostoyevsky, Woolf and the like. I have no doubt at all that he was right about me. Most of those unread writers would never use one word if ten would suffice. Proust, for instance, filled several pages to describe a man waking up in the morning. And one of the sentences in Swann's Way is at least a page long.

The McIntyre effect was to send me to the Vancouver library and book stores, grimly determined to discover what I was missing. I choked on Mann's *The Magic Mountain*, loved Woolf's *Jacob's Room*, and nearly died of old age reading Proust's *Remembrance of Things Past*. And those—along with quite a few others —were it, finis, the end. I never went back to them; and I've forgotten nearly all of them. I started to read completely coeval stuff instead, feeling like a traitor to Steve McIntyre. Nevertheless, I think he would have loved Garcia Marquez's *One Hundred Years of Solitude*.

·   ·   ·   ·   ·

One of Curt Lang's high school teachers was a guy named Downie Kirk. He in turn knew an obscure writer who lived with his wife somewhere in the wilderness across the Second Narrows Bridge. Kirk had translated the man's novel into French, and had a high opinion of his writing abilities. This hermit-writer in the rain forest was also said to be a notable consumer of alcohol, but was morose and hard to get along with at times.

Curt got an expedition together to visit the writer. It happened to be on a weekend, so my own time was free. And we took along two bottles of Bols Gin, when Downie Kirk mentioned that our reception was likely to be less than cordial without it. The high school teacher, a fussy rotund little man, found it necessary to say nearly everything twice, then look at you inquiringly as if you had to pass an examination. When I asked about the writer, Kirk said, "Yes, he's a genius! O my, yes, he's a genius!" And looked at me as if I'd doubted it. As a matter of fact, I did doubt it.

We turned right after crossing the Second Narrows Bridge, there was a lot of water on our right; we passed an Indian graveyard; there were a lot of trees too. Maybe fifteen miles of trees and water, then we parked my little English Prefect at a wide spot on the road. Downie Kirk located a path that led straight down into the middle of thick woods, and seemed to know the way. We walked about a mile, caught the gleam of water again, and a sort of driftwood house appeared out of the greenery. It was built atop log pilings on the beach, and looked almost like a houseboat.

The man who emerged from the driftwood shack looked short because he was so heavily built. Sporting several day's beard, pants held up with a piece of rope, bloodshot blue eyes, face nearly beet-red, he seemed a drunken bum. And I wondered: how can this guy be a great writer?

His name was Malcolm Lowry; his famous novel, *Under the Volcano*. Margerie, Lowry's wife, wrote detective stories. It was mentioned that she had once been a Hollywood starlet, but fell in love with Lowry and abandoned the movie capital. I thought she must have looked a little different in Hollywood: her face was now an interlaced network of tiny wrinkles, a cobwebby kind of face, as if the skin had been shattered like a teacup then glued back together again.

Lowry had been lonesome and was now convivial. We sat on his porch drinking, across the inlet from "the loveliest of oil refineries," a silver plume of smoke from one tall chimney touching the sky, a spurt of flame from another signaling the daylight moon. I was nearly hypnotized from listening to Lowry talk: about his wanderings in Mexico, being jailed in Oaxaca ("where they cure syphilis with Sloan's Liniment/and clap with another dose"). And about wandering the bone-dry hills, searching for the one, the ideal thirst-quenching alcohol; sighting the gates of Paradise at the bottom of his glass.

Sometime during the long afternoon of Bols Gin and talk Lowry recited his poem, "Sestina in a Cantina," his thick very-English voice bearing the full weight of archaic fear and horror, far beyond the complacent British Empire; how the world is a giant prison, ruled by tossing mooseheads and witch doctors in business suits. And he talked about the weird sorcerers of Central America, walking on red-hot coals while demons stared at you from non-human eyes.

Then becoming silent, he stared at nothing directly in front of him, as if he was alone on that porch. And thinking of tossing mooseheads that ruled the world? Of ships that sailed the seven seas, revisiting old ports over and over, their crews vanished and the ship's bell ringing the same time forever?

We ran out of booze. Lowry and I went back to Vancouver for more. At the all-night liquor store on Hastings near Main, Lowry bought six bottles of Bols Gin. Then he said, "There's a church with beautiful windows near here."

We searched and found it. But a man in black clothes—some kind of priest, I suppose—was standing guard at the door. He explained to us that a wedding was about to take place, and delicately pointed out that we were not invited. Of course our appearance was against us. Lowry wore scruffy old corduroys held up by a piece of rope; I was just marginally better dressed. The Man of God had no doubt decided we were bums; there were plenty of those around this Hastings Street area. I explained to the priest, speaking very carefully on account of my own precarious sobriety, that my friend thought the windows of his church were very beautiful and wanted to see them again.

Lowry stood by silently, while I talked and tried to convey my own version of working-class respectability. It was difficult. We were both pretty well sloshed. But I kept talking, thinking that if Lowry spoke just once, a bottle of Bols Gin was liable to pop out of his mouth and float high away over Vancouver's skid row. At which the Man of God would excommunicate us, and rightly so.

I talked some more. I was perhaps a little carried away in my compliments to the little waterfront church and its undoubtedly artistic custodian. Lowry and the priest listened. Then a car drew up at the curb during my unpersuasive discourse, disgorging some wedding guests. The Man of God hurried to greet them. While he did so, I was shocked to realize that Lowry had disappeared as my harangue continued, and simply walked into the church unhindered. I'd been the unflattering red herring for his entrance, as now the wedding guests were for mine.

Lowry was kneeling on the floor between pews in the rainbow-coloured light, praying to some god or other—with six bottles of Bols Gin in a brown paper grocery bag on the seat behind him. I thought of Coleridge's "Ancient Mariner." And Lowry was transported back to that time: dressed in strange medieval seamen's clothes instead of his frowzy sweater. Hung around his neck, instead of a dead bird—six bottles of Bols Gin. Then, while I watched in fascination, he began collaring wedding guests at the curb outside, whisking them away from the officious priest. "Listen," he would say to the wedding guest, "—once in a Mexican town called Quauhnahuac, there was a consul—"

After Lowry's death years later, and after it was decided that he was a genius, I reviewed his *Selected Letters* for *The Canadian Forum*. One of them was to Ralph Gustafson and said to Gus: "—two wild poets from Vancouver came to see me one dark and stormy night. The one, Curt Lang, was very good and so was the older man whose name was Al-something-or-other." (It wasn't a "dark and stormy night"; the day was bright and the sun shining.) I signed my review Al Something-or-Other.

．　．　．　．　．

For a few months in 1952–53 we rented a house near the Sikh Temple on 2nd Avenue. Eurithe's sister came out from the east to live with us, for some forgotten reason. And Eurithe's sister was a sight to behold, especially if you were male. About 5'10", but otherwise quite indescribable; so beautiful and so unaware of it that all ordinary occasions and idle conversations became stilted, infused with a prickling sensation. The inevitable suitors gathered.

At this time we had a female cat which entered and left the house via a hole in the bathroom floor. One early morning we heard the most awful caterwauling; male cats from Kitsilano to Jericho Beach had foregathered to pay court to our cat in the kitchen. We chased them out. On another morning I found the earth under our apple tree covered—not with apples, but male cats gazing longingly upward at our feline Cleopatra ensconced in the upper branches. My wife's sister's name was Norma.

Curt Lang was an immediate casualty, if I may so term it. A future famous New York playwright was another; his name was Victor—uh, something-or-other. And I fell in love for the hundredth time with my wife's sister. She is now in her 50s and has gained weight.

．　．　．　．　．

Doug Kaye, Curt Lang and I decided to manufacture our own booze. Weekly consumption was straining our triangular resources unwontedly, not surprisingly. Doug had this plum tree in his backyard, its fruit the size of baseballs. He also possessed home brew expertise gained from his merchant seaman days, and thus took complete charge of the operation. Several weeks later in the Kaye basement, Curt Lang and I gazed in neophyte wonder at plastic garbage cans full of young wine working hard and musically for our future pleasure.

The adolescent wine was divided meticulously by Doug, between the three of us; although I had to remain custodian of Curt's share because he was under age and his mother felt strongly about her child's recreational pastimes. And we began to sample the stuff. A few of my bottles seemed a bit "off," perhaps a quarter inch from the vertical. In fact it tasted lousy. It so happened that two other Vancouver Bedding employees lived just down the road from me at this time; one of them, named Glen, having taken over my old job on the wrapping table.

Anyway, Glen came to visit me. Being of a hospitable nature, I fed him some of my wine, including the "off" stuff. He liked it, and drank a couple of bottles; I gave him a couple more when he left. Glen didn't show up for work the next day. His landlord gave me the story. It seems our boy had become a little excited after drinking more of my wine: to the degree that he tore out the bathroom fixtures, then went on a noisy rampage through the living room and communal kitchen.

There were consequent plumbing charges, plus other expenses of one kind or another. As he listed them with accusing forefinger, Glen's landlord fixed me with his most meaningful stare. It meant you're responsible: the guy expected me to pay for damages his tenant had caused through the agency of *my* "off" wine. Well, I couldn't accept that. One has to be responsible for one's own actions. But Glen's landlord didn't see it that way. He even threatened me, in an oblique manner of course.

. . . . .

I was writing a verse play during my last couple of years at Vancouver Bedding. It was a fantasy based on my own childhood, and partly derived from Dylan's *Under Milk Wood.* Lorne Pierce, the editor and manager at Ryerson Press, Toronto, asked me for poems for an anthology he was co-editing, along with the deceased Bliss Carman. (Presumably Carman's editorial work was limited in scope.) After the antho, he asked me if I had enough poems for a small chapbook. I gulped and my insides churned with delight. It came out in 1955 with the title, *Pressed on Sand*, and was slightly less lousy than my first self-published book.

In 1954 also, Doug Kaye began to whisper seductive union noises in my ear. He'd been responsible earlier for a union implant at Restmore Mattress, and been made to feel so uncomfortable afterwards that he came to work at Vancouver Bedding.

I was a confirmed right winger then, in both thought and politics. But I was very impressed by Doug. We used to punch out at noon hour, drive to a grassy place overlooking the harbour, watching freighters loading and unloading as he worked on my social conscience. I have no doubt that some of Doug Kaye's ideas, expressed in a gravelly voice that made you lean forward to listen—I have no doubt they became part of the accelerating changes in myself.

Anyway, Doug wanted a union in our factory. He couldn't work for it openly himself, since he had little seniority; therefore he selected me as his alter ego and chief executive arm. Long afterwards, I think the reasons for planting that union at Vancouver Bedding rested on fairly shaky grounds. Wages were on a par with similar establishments elsewhere; working conditions were no hell, but what did you expect, the worker's Paradise?

However, and a big however: Arthur Watt, the factory manager, coming out to work on the floor, a white collar among the blues. That was an irritant. And it was annoying to me personally that Watt had once entered the john, where I sat on the throne to have a quiet cigarette. He'd leaped high enough above the cubicle door to observe my nicotine orgy, then waited for me outside with a threat of dismissal.

Doug talked me into it or perhaps he *silenced* me into it. That unstoppable voice and its hoarse condemnation of capitalism (although he wasn't a communist) as a political system—they began to make me discontent with contentedness. But he was wise enough in his manipulations of me to allow periods of silence, wherein I could chew over what had been said and make allowances for this passionate nay-sayer, and admit the reasonable side of things he said. Besides, I wanted to please him. Which is a trait in myself that has always warred with a basic antisocial character. (Sometimes I think the human mind is split into so many fragments it's impossible to ever figure yourself out.)

Okay, the union.

I talked to the six or seven male employees about joining up, always before or after work or at lunch hour. And I'd notice Doug getting in a surreptitious word to girls in the cutting room, where mattress and furniture covers were cut and sewn together. He talked especially to Rita, who was a sort of boss girl (I don't know what else to call her), and had the sort of face and figure you rarely see when awake.

Workmen of the Hammond Furniture Co., at the other end of our own block-long floor, were already members of the Vancouver Upholsterers' Union. We had to be very careful about this proselytizing; but management found out about it somehow. I suspect the filler operator, Tony, had whispered in the ear of Arthur Watt when the latter was doing some of his casual helping-out on the machines. At any rate, Tony later became foreman. Built on the ponderous lines of a railway boxcar, wearing horn-rimmed glasses, Tony kept his thoughts to himself, but seemed to go along with the rest of us. There's a word for this sort of guy in union lingo, but I can't remember it.

Everything went well. The day came when the union was in, everyone signed up, and despite my objections I became shop steward. I didn't like it, since I'd never taken a leading role in anything before.

But obviously, Doug had no seniority; I was stuck with the job. When ushered into the boss's office later, accompanied by the union representative, Percy Lawson, I felt like a bridegroom newly bereft of genitals.

Lawson was spokesman in discussions with Arthur Watt. Sitting in the boss's office I felt stiff and frozen, much the same way I was when I read poems in front of an audience for the first time. Somehow, completely naked. But Lawson, a short, fat, bald man, with an assured and unshakeable calm, took over completely; I scarcely said anything. There's a certain slick protocol to such discussions, expected clichés and cold politeness. Lawson was expert with them. I admired him.

> Sitting with Lawson in 1954
> > sitting with Percy Lawson
> ill at ease in the boss's panelled office
> after work hours talking of nothing
> talking of practically almost nothing
> a lousy nickel raise that is
> > haggling over a lousy nickel
> . . .
> Thinking of Lawson
> up from the coal mines
> on the island and gotten fat
> since talking and haggling and
> being afraid of practically nothing
> but death and his wife and damn near
> > everything but not
> not bosses
> not Watt
> . . .
> In a tactical pause between the chop
> of words Lawson turns
> the little fat man probably dead now
> turns then and gives
> me a gold-toothed grin

> —from *Percy Lawson* (1965)

Anyway, we settled for a small raise and I scuttled out of the boss's office quickly.

Then I was maneouvred into becoming recording secretary for the big union. And found myself sitting in a union hall with other officials on a raised stage, in front of a workers audience, taking down minutes and motions and stuff like that. And thought, what's going on, why am I sticking my neck out like this? Is this what I really am, a union official? Not that I have anything against union officials, except I'm not one. I resigned after two meetings. And Doug —I'm sure he was laughing all the time at what he'd gotten me into.

· · · · ·

Earlier than this I'd been writing admiring letters to Irving Layton, the Montreal poet. I introduced his books onto the shelves of Vancouver book stores, becoming Irving's west coast rep. I was still working on my verse play *A Gathering of Days* (much influenced by Dylan Thomas). It had already been rejected by the CBC.; then John Reeves, a director-producer, wrote me and accepted it. But he also asked for certain changes in the manuscript.

During the spring of '55, one of Curt Lang's friends was the sound effects man for a production of *Mister Roberts* at a small theatre near the old Vancouver Library on Hastings Street. The play was directed by Dorothy Davies, with Bruno Gerussi and Hollywood's Craig Stevens among the actors. After hanging around rehearsals for a few days, Curt and I were conscripted into the play as actors. We played drunken sailors hoisted back onto the ship in a landing net after shore leave at the islands of Tedium and Ennui. We had to work hard to stifle laughter while supposedly unconscious.

My thespian career was brief. I'd been saving money to go to Europe for over a year, and the spring of '55 seemed the right time. Being so obviously unpopular with factory management, I decided to quit before they fired me. After the excitement of *Mister Roberts*, Eurithe and I sat up all night working on my own play, she typing and I scribbling madly, and crossing things out in a high fever of hurry. Next day I caught a Greyhound bus heading east.

· · · · ·

There was the feeling that things had gotten away on me somehow; I was no longer in control of my life. I'd quit that crummy job at which I made the top wages of $1.65 an hour, and was terrified to be leaving it! That job had been a large part of my world, at least had made the other more important parts financially possible. My feelings before leaving Vancouver Bedding must have been exactly the same as those of millions of other people stuck in boring poorly paid jobs and who keep working at them all their lives. Now I was making a discovery, the same one other quitters make: it's terrifying, but also exhilarating. Quitting is a word with disgrace attached, but it frequently makes good sense. I was terrified, but also rode a wave of exhilaration and freedom on the Greyhound bus heading east.

In Toronto I stopped a few days, meeting John Reeves at CBC and some of the actors in my own play, drank beer with a few of them; most notably, I met Alice Frick, a wheel in the CBC script department. Later on she was kind enough to coach me in the essentials of play-writing. I stayed a week in Trenton with my mother, then on to Montreal where I slept on the studio couch in Irving Layton's living room. And Irving's kids, Naomi and Maxie, kept begging for nickels and dimes, then graduating to quarters.

I loved Layton on first meeting. He was fascinating and maddening and silly and egotistic. He was the best and the worst. Roly-poly small or massive and ridiculous, Proteus or Chaplin. His friend Dudek was skeezix in Academia (McGill), a vertical rail fence right out of the comic strips. When Frank Scott was added to the mix over drinks at the Ritz Carlton, I became entirely hypnotized. Scott had purchased all the remaining copies of his first book from Ryerson Press at a good price, when the publisher intended to sell those books to a remainder outlet. He gave me one, and I felt good.

Then Dudek, who had been reading the stuff in my first book (except for a privately published one), *Pressed on Sand*—Dudek looked up and said about the poems, "Why Hardy said the same thing fifty years ago." My feeling that I too was one of the literati elect vanished damn quick. When I got the chance, I read a lot of Thomas Hardy.

I've left out the most important person, Betty Layton, Irving's wife. Quite tall, with a dazzling smile, and warm, that warmth perhaps the most memorable thing about her. If we couldn't have mixed someone like Betty (and there was no one like Betty) into that almost entirely masculine household and circle of friends, much would have been lost. I think Leonard Cohen's poem about her is entirely inaccurate, makes her a cartoon. She was not a cartoon.

·   ·   ·   ·   ·

I have a vague memory of being whisked through downtown Montreal in Layton's little baby carriage with a motor, arriving at the docks in early morning. Curt Lang and his friend Jim Polson, who were on their way to Europe as well, had already boarded our ship, the *Ascania*.

I stood at the ship's railing in Montreal harbour, trying to glimpse

Layton on the docks below. But he'd probably left right away, to teach the kids at his Hertzeliah high school. I had quit everything: job, marriage (temporarily), and there I was, perched on the awesome shores of eternity. Snickering a little. But also scared as hell, since that crummy job had anchored me to a kind of reality. And the planet I was standing on no longer felt entirely stationary. I didn't admit it then, not exactly: but yeah, I was scared.

And on our slow passage eastward down the St. Lawrence, while light faded at day's end, I watched the Quebec shoreline despairingly: homesick before I ever left home. I felt like a ghost in transit from life to death. It was the first time I'd ever left Canada, and whoever was wearing my clothes was almost a stranger to myself.

CHAPTER EIGHT

. . . .

EUROPE

So there I was, pretending to be a writer, on my way to Europe in
1955. I wasn't at all sure what a writer was, or if I might be one. I
had visions of the real and indubitable writers, of Proust and Joyce, and
of Yeats with his mission to recreate Irish mythology in Holy Ireland.
And I was scared stiff at the idea of abandoning the flowing udder of a
permanent job.

By the end of my five-year jail sentence at Vancouver Bedding, I
was drinking a quart of home-made beer every morning before going
to work, and sometimes two. My temper was so frayed and ragged from
such continual exhaustion that even my sweet-natured wife had betrayed an eagerness for me to get on my way.

But this decision to pack up and leave for Europe wasn't as simple
as it might sound. I was nervous as hell about leaving my badly-paid
job and trundling off with two equally hare-brained friends. I agonized
over going and not going for weeks, explaining myself to myself (and
my wife) like an insane psychiatrist. No decision I ever made in my life
was so tough—at least no straight do-or-don't non-moral decision—
and all the other crossroad turnings came easy afterwards.

Curt Lang was in his element, being about eighteen then, and
furiously hungry to taste all experience as soon as possible and drink
every cup bone dry. Jim Polson, more a friend of Curt than myself, was
with us because he'd actually been talked into it by his friend. Polson's
character was phlegmatic, notably unenthusiastic about anything that I

ever noticed. I believe knowing Curt supplied him some *élan vital*, and plugged him in on life.

. . . . .

We landed on the docks at La Havre, after a windy voyage I thought sure would sink the creaky old *Ascania*, soon to be taken off the trans-Atlantic run. The ship had pitched and rolled like a drunken cowboy, decks covered with sawdust to soak up the green vomit.

La Havre was bright with sunshine, but it was raining in Paris when the express got there around nine p.m. The three of us booked a room on the Left Bank. Then we ordered beer and sat down to speculate about the curious ceramic creation, like a drinking fountain for midgets, which was the room's most prominent object. "It's to wash your feet in," Curt contributed. It was our first sight of the bidet, invented by some Frenchman held forever dear to the hearts of loving women.

Next day we set out to find a friend from Vancouver, the painter Richard Culdesac. That isn't his real name but it'll have to do unless I want to get sued for libel. When Curt introduced me to him in Vancouver, Culdesac was reading Proust in the original French. This impressed me a great deal, especially when he came up with: "Dear boy, the Scott-Moncrieff translation is simply mah-vellous, but really you know, one shouldn't speak to kings through an intermediary."

"Huh?" I said.

Culdesac raised his eyebrows and scornfully said nothing more. I felt so uncultured I might just as well have been born in Ontario.

But Richard was a damn good painter, and he worked at it like a pro whenever he wasn't talking about Proust. His work impressed some Vancouver patron enough to unloose the official purse strings that are reserved for those with genuine talent. Culdesac got a painting scholarship and went to Europe. The address we had for him was also on the Left Bank, but when we found the right number the concierge said Culdesac had gone to Chemery, a little village in central France.

After the three of us got tired of wandering around Paris on foot, emitting little cries of ecstasy in Le Louvre at Delacroix and Gauguin; drinking wine along the Seine and rummaging through the open air bookstalls, gawking at Notre Dame—we decided to visit Richard at Chemery. A certain callousness to Culdesac's own wishes could be noted in this decision, but he wasn't around to be asked.

. . . . .

Each of us left Paris on a different day, Curt having a girl he wanted to pursue a hair's length further, Polson being occupied with architecture and myself with wine. I started south from Paris trying to hitch-hike, first taking a bus to the suburbs before sticking out my thumb. I stood at the side of the road for two hours, without getting more than a disdainful stare from the beautiful girls driving by.

Saddened with the state of French womanhood, I took a bus south, then another and another, flailing my arms at bus drivers and accentuating every spoken syllable but the right one. I ended up north of Paris instead of south. So I caught a train. It was nightfall before we entered Blois. I decided to stay there and recuperate from my semantic struggles until morning.

It was at Blois where I learned some French toilets are not like Canadian toilets. Feeling the need, I entered the little three-foot-square room in the hotel. Suspended over my head was an ominous box making discontented gurgling noises. And from this box dangled a long chain. Instead of the usual ceramic affair we have in North America—which the French must have decided was too complicated—was a simple and undeniably functional hole in the floor.

No fol-de-rol, just a hole. In front of it, two footprints in stone, on which one balanced precariously for as short a time as possible. A very short time in my case. But when I unwisely pulled the chain while still in a state of *déshabille*, water plunged down from above with the volume of Noah's flood. I made my getaway with all speed, spirits slightly dampened.

After that experience I acquired a certain respect for French institutions, such as the bidet, and the musical pissoire adorning the streets of Paris. They undoubtedly influence the national character. In other countries too, students will find lavatory studies a fascinating subject. Village hotels in Turkey, for instance, where bathrooms have no doors.

. . . . .

It was the following evening before I reached Chemery, a tiny village of not more than a thousand or so people. My stomach kept turning over sickeningly every hour on the half hour while traveling, from the effects of the French water, making toilet facilities mandatory at all times. I drank wine instead of water from then on, but this gave French towns and villages a blurred look and made the swinging doors of pubs behave oddly.

I stayed that night in Chemery. Next morning I hired a cab, arriving at the ruined tenth century church where Culdesac was domiciled at about ten a.m. No true artist ever rises that early, except to paint the dawn or take a leak. Culdesac appeared in the raw golden air swathed in a blanket, visible only as a hunched shoulder surmounted by his long gaunt face, his one visible eyebrow raised questioningly. He extended a limp hand in greeting, the measure of his enthusiasm for visitors at that hour, or perhaps reluctance to expose more of himself than necessary to the chill air.

The church was a rundown, shabby looking place outside, but the interior was white and dazzling. At one end of the huge vaulted room was a cross, from which hung a plaster Christ in obvious agony. The other end of the church was used to store the excellent local wine, which turned out to be quite handy. And of course paintings, paintings, paintings all over the place.

Once inside, Michel, Culdesac's boyfriend, materialized at my elbow and grinned intimately. Richard immediately began the first of his many expositions concerning the loose morals of Michel. "That boy," he said, his eyebrows resuming their familiar escalation, "that boy is not to be trusted out of my sight. Actually Proustian, that's what he is. You no doubt remember Charlot in the master's *Cities of the Plain?*" I nodded, giving him a vacant non-committal look to signify attention. "That boy, I've actually caught him in the toilets of Le Louvre with Americans, doing his dirty business with them for money." Culdesac's eyebrows rose triumphantly above their normal elevation to a height which signified extreme moral abhorrence.

Beside me Michel grinned on without understanding. "Uh, Richard," I said, "it's been two days since I started out from Paris. Is there any place where I can flake out for a couple of hours?"

In the evening Culdesac was at the schoolhouse across the road, painting a portrait of the teacher. Before going, he warned me again about Michel. "That boy will make up to you if you so much as smile at him. Always look the other way if you feel his eyes are on you." Richard's own deep-sunk eyes and haggard face stared at me earnestly. "You'll come to thank me for warning you. There are no depths of depravity unknown to Michel. Absolutely Proustian. I've been able to do nothing for him." Culdesac hunched his bowed shoulders together and stalked away like a large black bird.

Richard's favourite descriptive epithet was "Proustian," and it came to signify a whole climate and geography of decadent wisdom. Huysman's *A rebours* was a grade-school simplification of Proust, and Mirabeau's *Torture Garden* not to be mentioned in the same breath. De Sade was being name-dropped more and more frequently, and Henry

Miller—their dictums and pronouncements fell like gentle rain from Richard's lips; and I dared not contradict or even comment on his opinions, backed as they were by the authority of Proust, De Sade, Wilde, and Miller. If not outflanked by Culdesac himself, I was outnumbered by the living and the dead surrounding even casual conversation like parentheses.

· · · · ·

But I admired Richard tremendously, let there be no doubt of that. He once said to me, "I'd spend all the money I had on a half ounce of perfume for a beautiful woman, even if it cost fifty thousand dollars." I must have looked blank, for he waved his long graceful fingers and said, "It's the meaningful gesture, the important triviality. In this Proustian age we are surrounded by the cheap and meretricious, in which an attitude is more important than a passion—" He stared at me as if I were a hopeless idiot, "Do you see?"

I suppose I didn't then, but I have a glimmering now; and it ties in with Richard painting furiously night after night at the same time for a week, just before the sun went down, trying to get a particular texture of colour and sky-shading into the painting. Richard outside the tenth century church, bending over his easel, glancing swiftly back and forth at sky and canvas, concentration absolute inside his own solitude. He was not, perhaps, a great painter, but at the very least he sensed the attributes of greatness, felt them hovering near him—and when you look at his paintings you can see an amalgam of Van Gogh, Rembrandt and Titian. He himself was also that amalgam, his conversation a mixture of Proust, De Sade, Gide, and Miller. Perhaps the ghost of himself never dared walk in that company.

Richard was a very old man at 28, just as I was a very young man at 35. By his differences from myself I knew him, and I learned a great deal from him, though at the time I understood very little.

· · · · ·

I left the church that evening, and went for a walk in the French countryside for exercise and contemplation. Richard was otherwise occupied; Michel was wherever he was. I walked vigorously along the rural roads, a different moon now silvering the sky, throwing the farmhouses and trees into an unreality that made their shadows more black-real than substance. The kind of evening and situation that makes you say, "What the hell am I doing here?" To which the only answer is, "I don't know." The entire moonlit landscape before my eyes seemed complete fantasy. There were no lights in the houses, no sound but my own footsteps.

I turned back because it was getting late, and in the complete silence heard other footsteps. They became louder, and we were moving towards each other in the night. I stopped and listened, but the other steps continued. Richard's warning again whispered to me from the schoolhouse: "That boy is not to be trusted." Proust's Charlot capered obscenely among the shadows. I didn't believe a word of the whole scene. It was too damn silly. On the other hand, I wanted a measure of choice whether I decided to become a homosexual, if one ever makes such a decision apart from the exigencies of the event.

Of course the footsteps were Michel's. He accompanied me on the long walk back to the church. He smiled (in the moonlight), I smiled (in the shadow). It was like the meeting of dogs too unfamiliar even to sniff. When Richard greeted us at the church his raised eyebrows indicated the innate delicacy that forbade him asking what revolting orgies had been consummated on the moonlit country roads of France.

．　．　．　．　．

A few days later Curt Lang and Polson joined us at the church, Polson having been ill on the way south from Paris. Shortly after their arrival Culdesac decided to abandon the church-studio and returned to Paris with Michel. I went too, helping to carry the dozens of paintings tied together with binder twine and sticky with new oil paint. Curt and Polson went further south to the Riviera. I didn't see them again in Europe.

In the City of Light I found a hotel room, again on the Left Bank. Culdesac and Michel went back to their rooms on the Rue de l'Ancienne Comédie—a name I loved. The three of us ate dinner in one of those eating places that looked like an abandoned tenement.

Richard spoke French to Michel and English to me, saying, I have no doubt, the nastiest things about each of us to the other. After the onion soup he leaped to his feet, staring wildly around the restaurant crowded with French businessmen: "I can't stand it any longer! That boy is making eyes at everyone in the place!" "Huh?" I said. "You don't see it because you don't know the language they use, the little signs and gestures they have. He's betraying me every time he turns his head, and I won't stand for it any longer—" Richard threw down some franc notes and literally ran for the door and disappeared. Michel and I stared at each other. I shrugged my shoulders; he made the equivalent French gesture; and we kept eating.

Fleas were racing around my midriff just above the beltline, clockwise and widdershins, in my hotel near the Odeon, where I kept trying to decide if the fleas were real or I was real. Then Culdesac decided to move to London. "That boy is making my life a misery," he said. "The situation is neo-Proustian. I thought I could help him to a better life, an understanding of himself. But I can't do it. He's just evil, evil, evil..." He looked at me like a hungry bird. "Can you loan me ten thousand francs till the end of next week?"

I was tired of tramping around Paris by this time, so I helped Culdesac transport his paintings to London. At the Piccadilly tube station I left him waiting while I went inside to get cigarettes. And didn't come back. By this time he was into me for fifty thousand francs.

London was such a huge rabbit warren of a place I kept getting lost, but managed to find my way to the theatre one night to see Rex Harrison in *Bell, Book and Candle*. Then I went on to Liverpool where I'd been sending American science-fiction magazines to a bookstore there. These couldn't be imported new into England, therefore used copies were in hot demand by science-fiction fans. In return for all the thousands (literally thousands) of magazines I'd sent, I received British books, and took my remaining credit in cash, some 150 pounds.

With this magazine windfall I bought a ticket for New York on the liner *Britannic*, and went to Scotland for a week before the ship sailed from Liverpool. At Iona, the island St. Columba reached in a wicker boat bringing Christianity to Scotland, I met an Englishman who carried his kidneys around in a shopping bag. A plastic tube ran from his pants, and the requisite part of his anatomy, into the shopping bag. This so intrigued me that I paid as much attention to the shopping bag as to the graveyards of the ninth- and tenth-century Ionian kings. And not far from their tombs lies the body of a drowned German sailor, washed up during a storm in the last war. Always after, I have thought of Pincher Martin in William Golding's novel in connection with that German sailor. Before Martin drowned, the events of an entire novel took place in his mind: when his body was found later, he hadn't had time to throw off his sea-boots before drowning. It was a cheerful holiday.

. . . . .

Homesickness was the conscious reason I gave myself for returning after only two months away. And I was homesick, missed my family and friends, the drunken booksellers of Vancouver, streets where I knew what was around the next corner. Also, I felt out of my element, the break too sudden after having my life arranged and adjusted by the tyranny of the time-clock.

The liner *Britannic* took four days to reach New York, where I wandered up Broadway, bought a copy of Jean Paul Sartre's plays, *No Exit*, and a ticket to Vancouver by Greyhound bus. I got home early Sunday morning. Having passed all customs inspections, I was able to remove the copies of De Sade's *120 Days of Sodom* and Henry Miller's *Tropic of Capricorn* from under my shirt, the book titles printed sweatily on my chest like a literary tattoo.

Back where I started from in the first place, Vancouver seemed viewed at several removes, its familiarity tinctured by a restless indifference now I was there. My wife and I both wanted to depart the evergreen playground. We loaded a five-year accumulation of junk into the red '52 Chev, rented the house and drove east.

We landed in Montreal quarrelling violently as usual, and rented an apartment on Linton Avenue in the Côte des Neiges district. My wife got herself a job with the CPR, in order to support me while I demonstrated my genius, and I settled down to write plays for the CBC, and poems for the breathless waiting world.

CHAPTER NINE

· · · · · · · ·

THE BAD TIMES

It's strange to be talking about things that were momentous and important for you, occasionally even life and death for you. And when you get them down as words on paper, they sound commonplace. Or is it that after a bad time is over, you'll never duplicate such things on a typewriter? But I'm not trying to do that. I just want to remind myself of something. I don't know what it is. But when I come to it, I'll remember.

· · · · ·

My wife and I had been living in Montreal for a year that ended in the summer of 1957. I was writing radio and television plays for the Canadian Broadcasting Corporation, with nearly a minimum of success. (I had to write eight or ten of them to get one accepted by the hard-boiled CBC producers.) Eurithe worked as a secretary with the CP Railway for that period, sometimes showing symptoms of discontent with our situation.

We made a few friends in Montreal, mostly literary people: Frank Scott and Marian, Ron Everson and Lorna, Irving Layton and his wife Betty, Louis Dudek, Milton Acorn, Ingrid Lewis, Henry Ballon and Annette, and a few others.

There were parties. Doug Kaye (whom I had known while working at the same factory in Vancouver), Henry Ballon and I made beer in an oak whiskey barrel. We produced fifteen gallons every five or six days, much more than we could drink. There was talk for a while of our home-brewery becoming a commercial proposition.

And we met some painters. Marian Scott, Frank's wife, was a very good artist. Louise Scott, no relation, whose work I thought impressive. A sort of bohemian art colony in Montreal, gradually becoming surer of its own abilities, or at least pretending to be sure.

We all made noises of genius of course: with the exception of Frank Scott, whose character made it unnecessary for him to brag. Louis Dudek had a direct pipeline to the one true God, Ezra Pound—and Louis was a carbon epiphany. William Carlos Williams also ranked high in Dudek's pantheon; but I was never able to appreciate him.

Irving Layton was the Montreal magnet for me: a man with a word for everything; never in the time of my knowing him did he appear to be at a loss. Irving seemed to hypnotize himself with his own voice, feeding on echoes of his own opinions. But warm, with a feeling for other people. And the warmth made the rest bearable. I felt about him as I had not about any other Canadian writer, a kind of awe and surprise that such magical things should pour from an egotistic clown, a charismatic poseur. And I forgive myself for saying those things, which are both true and not true.

. . . . .

By the spring of 1957 it was obvious that I wouldn't make a fortune writing plays for CBC, although Alice Frick had given all sorts of valuable advice and had accepted two or three plays. (One of those was an adaptation of Thornton Wilder's *Woman of Andros*, a novel that shivered itself into my backbone.

My mother in Ontario was 79, and not in the best of health, she needed looking after. Therefore, Eurithe and I and our twelve-year-old son, Jim, moved into the old brick house in Trenton. It was a town of some ten thousand people. Eurithe's own parents were in Belleville, not far distant. She and I were both resolved to find a house, a plot of land, something of our own, after the feeling of having to rent the air itself in Montreal.

We were not entirely comfortable living with my mother. Eleanor Louisa Purdy: she had outlived the world of her youth and middle age. Coal oil lamps for house lighting were replaced by electricity. Automobiles had nearly taken over from horse-drawn buggies and wagons. The roads around us were swiftly becoming paved. The people even *looked* different. Everyone seemed younger.

Her friends were mostly dead. Only God remained constant. He was the same. And she went to church three or four times a week, surprised to find the church locked tight on weekdays. Even her son, myself, was almost a stranger. And the streets kept changing without warning; after a while she'd get lost on her way to church, and had to be brought home by the town police.

The children next door, they were always shouting at her when she went downtown. She would smile and often give them pennies. But pennies would buy little in 1957; they wanted more. And the sun was so hot when she forgot to wear something on her head. Work around the house was hard, climbing the stairs so tiring . . . Alfred and his wife, they weren't much help. Off somewhere else in that red car . . . looking for something, always looking for something . . . She was alone, except for God; she was alone.

. . . . .

The old red Chevy we had driven from Vancouver to Belleville and Montreal the year before made protesting noises but chugged on mufflerless. Eurithe and I explored the area within a thirty mile radius of Trenton, looking for land, looking for anything, a place to end this displaced feeling. This belonging nowhere and anywhere sickness.

Of course we didn't say that, even in the silence of our minds. The ostensible reason was more mundane: just a place to live within our financial means, which was around $1,200. (I had sold three plays in Montreal.) We wanted cheap land, a cheap house. There was an element of desperation about the search. But I was a blustering sort of person, and would rarely admit such childish fears.

The south shore of Roblin Lake, a mile or so from the village of Ameliasburgh, in Prince Edward County. The place met most of our desired standards. Our lot bordered the lake shoreline, a teacup of water nearly two miles long. Dimensions of the lot were 100 feet wide by 265 long, with nobody else living within a few hundred yards. The lot cost $800. We paid $300 down to farmer Harry Gibson, who owned the entire lake shore. The other payments were to follow in two instalments.

Eurithe's father, Jim Parkhurst (my one-time partner in the failed taxi business), lived in nearby Belleville. He suggested that we build our own house. He would supply know-how, and even some of the necessary carpenter tools. Obviously we needed a place. Co-habitation with my mother in Trenton was like living in the proverbial goldfish bowl: very little privacy.

There's a kind of good will ethos among some people. They'll do "anything for you," as the saying goes. In the country north of Belleville, especially in the fringe-quality farm land area, this so-called ethos is fairly common. People had very little money during the twenties and "Hungry Thirties," but they helped each other at harvest time, made survival possible during bad periods, loaned and borrowed from each other as if everyone was their blood relative. I think it's one of the most admirable qualities of human beings.

Jim Parkhurst was part of this northern ethos, which of course is not confined to the north. (In selfish contrast, I've always had a strong feeling about ownership, the privacy of things, the inviolate object attached umbilically as a logical right.) Reactions to him by other people were not, however, always flattering. My own feelings about him were ambiguous. He was a puzzle to me at that time. My own somewhat sheltered life had not equipped me to deal with anyone like Jim Parkhurst.

At the same time, these admirable qualities were only the visible tip of the Parkhurst iceberg. In many ways he was quite unscrupulous, and completely unaware of the dark side of his own nature. "I've never done anything in my life that I was ashamed of," he once told me. I interpret such a claim as the self-righteous quality some people have—of making either good or evil the same in one's own moral judgment. It means: if I did a thing or said it, then it's okay.

A large building complex was in process of being torn down in Belleville at the time. We paid $500 for a pile of used lumber, concrete blocks, studdings, beaverboard and the like. Two of Jim's sons helped us dismantle the stuff and transport it to Roblin Lake.

At that time, if I had permitted myself to think of such things, it would have been to label myself as a failure. Despite the 1955 production of my first play, A Gathering of Days, by CBC in Toronto, and several other plays later, I couldn't sell enough to make a living. But I refused to stop writing—not that anyone had asked me to stop. Eurithe didn't. I believe we both thought I might write a sexy best-seller one of these days; then we could retire from everything.

In the meantime, we stood on the shores of Roblin Lake, sombrely regarding this great pile of crap—I mean scrap; that is, reclaimed building materials. There was no shelter at the lake. We had to drive back and forth to Trenton every day. There was a shithouse, a small shed which I had adapted to this honourable usage. But the sunlit scene of lacustral splendour was a bit grim in our eyes. Eurithe and I regarded each other that way too.

Our personal relations were somewhat wary and careful. Volcanic quarrels would be succeeded by armed truce, or a disguised tenderness.

Sexual relations were always nocturnal, occasionally resembled combat in their hostile preliminaries. But—let us say—there was love, although I avoided such words. If not, how could we possibly have tolerated each other?

> Lying side by side
> >naked in darkness
> bodies stiff with anger
> . . .
>
> Mad as hell in a bedroom
> >in Ameliasberg Township!
> Even as in the councils of the great
> >(my darling)
> and the consultations of the kings of earth
> a small quarrel like ours can't be solved:
> >and while that white body protrudes
> >over on my side of the bed
> >pride is damn difficult . . .

—from *The Quarrel* (1962)

Roblin Lake was turquoise and dazzling blue in mid-summer. Orioles, robins, sparrows, swallows and goldfinches thronged our living space, which was also *their* living space. One morning on first arrival I saw a great blue heron stalking the shore, an ungainly native. And we saw muskrats. They pushed a wave ahead of them with their noses while swimming. It was idyllic. I looked at the delightful Eden landscape and longed for the grimy streets of Montreal. I was not a country guy, but a sallow-complexioned cigar-puffing expatriate banished from the big city. It must have showed in my permanently dismayed expression at Ameliasburgh—I hate beautiful trees. Eurithe interrupted my contemplation of them: "Get to work!" The tone was imperative.

To build a house! My own carpentering skills were nearly minimal (I could saw a board more or less straight, and pound a nail without always bending it); Eurithe's were non-existent. We'd come across some architect's plans in a *House Beautiful* magazine that appealed to both of us, a small A-frame structure with adjoining kitchen and bath. It didn't look like every other house around Roblin Lake. But in order to build on our lot, we had to prepare the land: it was a jungle of willows. So I became a temporary lumberjack, chopping, sawing and burning.

When negotiations had been under way to buy land, the lot adjoining ours appealed to us; it had a shoreline that projected out into Roblin Lake. But Harry Gibson charged by the foot for the entire winding length of that shoreline, instead of the straight-across footage that would have cost much less. Therefore we opted for the nearby straight-across and more affordable lot. Later on we intended to build our own handmade peninsula, by wheelbarrow and muscle. (After ten years we had extended our small kingdom out into the lake by about forty feet.)

After pondering, lucubration and cogitation, we enlarged the house-plan foundation to thirty feet long and seventeen wide. The A-frame section was eighteen feet high, measuring from the floor to gable. It was erected on four-foot walls. And a twelve-foot square kitchen-bathroom was planned for one side. The finished house at that point was entirely in our heads, of course. And I've come more and more to realize: without Jim Parkhurst's help, it could never have been done.

His character was phlegmatic and almost unbearably calm; mine excitable and ever mercurial. I'd come to him sometimes, despairing and despondent with an insoluble problem. The difficulty would melt away and seem never to have existed; do this and do that in the ordinary course of building. It was almost possible for me to think I'd solved the puzzle myself; but not quite. He'd drive to the lake from Belleville once or twice a week, listen to our woeful account of difficulties. Our troubles simply disappeared in the face of his unchanging calm.

As will be obvious, I pondered the man. His mind worked on a different level than mine; he wasn't self-aware in quite the same way. To say that he was concrete and I abstract wouldn't explain it: he could at least imagine what our house should be, shadowy in his own pragmatic mind, ordinary as a bent nail. Whereas I thought the projected house was something marvellous, a factual dream of solidity. I think, therefore I am: I think a house and ergo the house am?

There was always a reserve about him, a foreignness even; some kind of dirt-poor grass roots aristocracy, a northern nobility I couldn't quite conceive. And of course I'm embroidering a bit here, searching for something about the man that may not exist at all. But I must forgive myself for doing it, since I'm saying as much about myself as about him.

Early summer, 1957. Eurithe and I stand near the shores of Roblin Lake. We measure the supposedly equal sides of our house-footing with diagonal lines. That is, we stretch a cord kitty-corner from and to opposite ends of our wooden forms. Then we switch sides and do the opposite. This in order that all angles, lengths and widths should match and measure true. All this time, orioles and robins plunge the sun-bright air around us. They build their nest-houses in playful joy and love without measuring a damn thing; ourselves in worry and suspense and labour. I grin at the thought, promptly messing up our diagonal measurements, forgetting to keep the lines taut.

Sometimes all the studding, fibreboard, planks and nails danced in my head, like those ephemeral little flies that dance in bright sunlight. A dance of nothingness it seemed to me. And I felt dubious about the house ever being built. And I must do the things I do for their own sake, their own worthwhileness. Anything else was illusory. The poems I wrote must live in themselves, exist as entities and dance in their own sunlight. Without an audience, minus acclaim, even from a few. Thinking such things is treading gingerly close to a fifty thousand gallon tank of bullshit, teetering even. I wallow and rejoice in self-pity, my stiff upper lip is a dirty dishrag. In short, we built a house.

．　．　．　．　．

A mile away from our building site across Roblin Lake, the village of Ameliasburgh. Owen Roblin, an early settler, was largely responsible for its growth and development. He built a grist mill there in 1842, on the lip of a little green valley above a tiny lake. Water was conveyed from Roblin Lake to his mill wheel via a deep trench. The four-storey mill was over a hundred feet long; its walls were three feet thick. For its time and setting, the mill was a marvel.

When the stress of house-building lessened a little, I explored Ameliasburgh, once called Roblin Mills. As a writer, you made use of the materials composing your own surroundings. My thinking went that way when I thought about it at all. Montreal and the Layton-Dudek-Scott-Everson friends were far away. I couldn't afford them at that distance.

Ameliasburgh had a post office and grocery. Fat, good-humoured Norman Sword was the postmaster, the person I saw most of in my yearning for city friends. The one main street stretched for nearly a mile. Its architecture was commonplace, gables, board siding and brick, with one stone house. And dogs. When I walked the mile or so to Ameliasburgh, they trailed me, and sometimes barred the road completely. Not little yapping curs. Cannibal dogs, seemingly hungry for human flesh. It was like facing nemesis or personal destiny, something you can't over-dramatize. And it was also a game of bluff. But you couldn't be quite sure of that. It was possible to lose two pounds of your own steak at a price you couldn't afford. I'd bend down, pick up stones from the road, make throwing motions and hope. It worked sometimes: but when a dog faces you from six feet away, snarling at you with dripping teeth, it tends to ruin your sense of humour.

Harry Gibson, the farmer at the end of our lane, owned a monster that hated me especially. Gibson was cutting the hay in his big field by the township highway one day, the dog attending him. I was coming home, made the turn into our lane, and the dog recognized who was driving this particular car. He cut across the field behind the car before I reached the house, and started chewing at the wheels. It must have been difficult for him, since the wheels were moving. I stopped, reversed gears and tried to run over the dog backwards, feeling a killing urge in myself. Of course I couldn't hit the animal. While Harry Gibson watched, his mouth hanging open.

That 1842 grist mill was the village's main attraction for me. I explored it from top to bottom, careful to avoid dangerous black holes in the floor. And marvelled at the 24-inch-wide pine boards from the county's vanished forest. And carved wooden cog wheels, millstones and rotting silk from the flour-sifting apparatus . . . Some dirty flour, unmilled grain . . .

I had the sense that those nineteenth-century people had just stepped out on some errand or other, and would be back soon. I could see the sunlit wagons, loaded with grain for milling, pulled up outside. At harvest time several wagons: the pioneer farmers joking with each other, their wives comparing recipes. Illusion based on an old reality. You realize you stand at the head of a long procession, the rear part of which is invisible, and those ahead of you do not yet exist, except as creatures of the flashing sunbeams. I talked to the old men about the village's beginnings. An ancient named Doug Redner supplied some details; a family name file supplied additional info; the village black-smith also filling in some gaps. It was like hearing names, then having bits of knowledge about them piled on other bits of knowledge, until finally even their faces wavered through the dusk towards you. People existed there in the past, people with ambitions, anger and jealousies, achievements and failures . . .

Owen Roblin, a United Empire Loyalist descendent, had settled as a young man with his family in the county's southern part early in the nineteenth century. Riding his horse one day he happened on Roblin Lake (of course not named that at the time), and the settlement's few

houses. There was already a mill, built and owned by one John Way.
Roblin bought land overlooking the millpond below the hill. He built
his own mill, married and had sons and daughters.

I've seen Roblin's picture, taken when he was a very old man. I
think I would have disliked him. Clean-shaven at this century's turn,
with the look of a martinet, a domestic sergeant-major, pioneer
become village artifact with an uneasy smile. He was the oldest
postmaster in Canada when the photographer took that picture.
Shake hands with Owen Roblin, our living fossil, the man who made
this village go, the kindly boss of everything, a dead man whose
name is alive on county maps.

Below the highway and ruined mill, where the hill plunged down a
hundred feet or so, there were still traces of that nineteenth-century
village. Foundations of Sprague's carriage factory and several houses
lay blurred in the long grass; a graveyard, some of whose markers
reiterated village names; the millpond itself, black water sprinkled with
dead tree stumps, like an eye peering forward and backwards; garbage
scattered down the hillside, a kitchen midden and repository of broken
worn-out things. Some village Babylon . . .

> And the story about the grist mill
> rented in 1914 to a man named Taylor
> by the last of the Roblin family
> who demanded a share of the profits
> that poured golden thru the flume
> because the new miller knew his business:
>   & the lighting alters
>   here and now changes
> to then and you can see
>   how a bald man stood
> sturdily indignant
>   and spat on the floor
> and stamped away so hard the flour
> dust floated out from his clothes
> like a white ghostly nimbus
> around the red scorn
> and the mill closed down—

—from *Roblin's Mills* (1965)

. . . . .

162

Once a week Eurithe and I drove to Trenton to visit my mother, a distance of eighteen miles. Her health, physical and mental, was fragile. She had made a last will and testament with the Victoria & Grey Trust Company. The will left me the interest on her money, while the principal remained with the trust company. At my behest, she made another will which gave me the principal. Some friends visiting us from British Columbia, Doug Kaye and his wife, witnessed this new will. But for the present, we had scarcely any money at all.

At our worst times, even food was scarce. When our new neighbours, the Eleys, ran over a rabbit, we made a stew with it. Eurithe's brother, Alvin, had the contract for removing garbage from an A&P supermarket in Belleville. Much edible food was buried in that rotting mess, and it was saved for us. Mrs. Cannon, an old lady in her seventies at the beginning of our lane, gave us the use of her garden to grow vegetables (I remember her with strong affection). Our sub-teenage son, Jim, fished the lake for bass and pike. Once he caught a huge eel which thrashed in the rowboat like a sea serpent. And once I shot a duck, and nearly threw up from the stink while cleaning it.

Among the most awful clichés that litter your mind: "It was the best of times, it was the worst of times"—But yeah, it was. Both. The house became a ragged cobweb against the sky. We moved in long before it was finished; and really, it was never finished; still isn't. Eurithe and I poured concrete for the footings with a non-musical throb of cement mixer pounding our nerves. And we quarrelled. About damn near everything. Name something we didn't quarrel over, and I still can't be sure we didn't.

But the house was important. We never thought of it that way, but it was. Our lives were involved and wrapped up in that silly house. Survival. When food gets scarce, that word survival lurks in the near periphery. Sure, Eurithe could have left me and taken safe refuge with her family in Belleville. But what kind of disgraceful defeat is that? You live, this is the way it is; make a fuss if you don't like it; scream at the world a little, exaggerate everything like I'm doing now. (Am I really?)

Alf Eley, our new neighbour, worked on the roads for the township. Mrs. Eley (I omit her first name, because she was always Mrs. Eley to me), talked all the time. They erected their pre-fab house in the spring of 1958. Mrs. Eley began talking the first time I met her. When I stumbled away, deaf and blind with the beauty of her wisdom, she visited Eurithe with scarcely a comma between past, present and future. And brought us a dish of food, having surmised we might need it. And recurring echoes of Mrs. Eley have remained with me ever since.

Our half-built house was erected on low-lying land; after heavy rain the ground was flooded for a day or two. Jim Parkhurst and a helper were excavating a cellar in Belleville with jack hammer and pick and shovel at that time. It was suggested that I raise our front lawn's altitude with the contents of that Belleville cellar. So I drove an old truck back and forth several times a day, loaded with limestone strata, dumping and returning for more. Our front yard became visibly higher.

And a box car load of scrap lumber became available from CP Railway, courtesy of Gordon Parkhurst, now a CP employee. I spent a week hauling the stuff to Roblin Lake, and additional days cutting it to stove-length on an old belt-driven saw machine.

In Vancouver, and later in Montreal, I had always been a beer-drinker. Not a souse, someone who sits in a pub hour after hour and day after day soaking it up. But a few convivial beers with friends had always seemed a sociable way to spend eternity. But here I had no friends as such, only endless brothers-in-law and relatives by marriage. Here I had very good health and strength, but no money. However, an abundant crop of wild grapes grew on countryside fences all around. For several weeks in the fall of 1957 our cottage industry was picking wild grapes and brewing home-made wine.

You could say that making wild grape wine was labour intensive. A bushel of grapes took six or eight hours to clean in addition to the original harvesting on farmers' fences. Ten-gallon plastic garbage cans replaced wooden barrels: pour them half full of cleaned grapes, plus fifteen pounds of sugar, add water to within six inches of the top. After a couple of days they sing a purple song, as if a whole hive of bees was contemplating marriage. Then scrunch the grapes to mush in your hands. And presto, some invisible alchemist goes noisily to work on purple nectar that, if not divine, is certainly earthly.

During my top production period I had some twenty-five dozen 25-ounce bottles ready to drink after a decent period of maturity. "Maturity" being when it was still working if I got thirsty. A night club near Belleville provided empty whiskey bottles, which it wasn't necessary to wash because of the previous alcohol content. From October to Christmas at Roblin lake the house throbbed softly, an omnipresent alcoholic sound, a dreamy music that reached high C at about eleven percent proof and sang to me in my sleep.

My mental condition was sometimes turbulent. I was sour and jubilant, depressed and ebullient by turns. Being broke continually was getting to me. As well, nobody noticed the poems I wrote. As much as I tried to tell myself that reward was in creation itself, my spirits sank at the complete silence that greeted my efforts.

However, I still believe it: if you don't enjoy feeling your own mind explore and create, if you must have continual outside stimulation, then you shouldn't be writing at all. And that is both true and not true; it's bullshit to some extent. One writes in a silent vacuum, and needs some small encouragement at least. But talking about writing makes me despair of saying anything relevant and authentic. So much is said, and nearly all of it worthless.

But those awful depressions I went through, sometimes lasting for several weeks! Poverty is like that. Reading Orwell's *Down and Out in Paris and London* and Norman Levine's *Canada Made Me* is depressing and exhilarating. To endure such experiences is to be transformed into a socialist or a nihilist. I was neither, but suicide sometimes did enter my mind. As something to think about, as a trapdoor if all else failed, as an ending for the unendurable present.

We ground it out, the time, the bad experiences, and poverty that seemed to have no ending. At a later date I wrote a poem in the Arctic, on Baffin Island, one that seemed to say something about those bad days. It concerned the desolate sound of old squaw ducks, so mournful it's like a dirge for humanity. I was spending the night on an island in Cumberland Sound, inside a sleeping bag. The Eskimo hunter I was with knew no English. I felt terrible. And those ducks were singing Mozart's *Requiem Mass* for Salieri in an eighteenth century crazy house. My line was: "I think to the other side of that sound . . . " Which is really a lie, because on the other side of "that sound" is death, as it was for Mozart.

But what do you do, how do you stand it: poverty, failure, all the rest? There is no answer. You go on, or you don't.

My son Jim went to the country school at Ameliasburgh (and wasn't very happy about it either, which I didn't know at the time). Eurithe had her own kind of fortitude, which wasn't communicable to me. We talked, but not at the spiritual nails-on-the-blackboard level. I regarded her as a strong woman, myself as a not particularly strong man. I grumbled, made noises of protest and discontent in a kind of catharsis; she was mostly silent.

But we did reach each other on some unidentifiable level of feeling. It was not the ideal one hears about, the twin-feeling of male-female oneness. I'm not sure that exists anyway, that it isn't a much-wished-for myth. You settle for things, you make do: which unenthusiastic description is regarded as terrible cynicism by lovers lost in each other's bodies and perhaps lost to reality.

Three or four miles distant at Mountainview there was a military airport. The three of us, Eurithe, Jim and I, scrounged its garbage dump for anything useful. It was amazing the good stuff we turned up. Boxes made of quarter-inch plywood; quarts and gallon cans of paint, sometimes only half used, black and red predominating; military emergency rations, instant coffee, different kinds of powdered milk and condensed soups, etc., all in little metallic envelopes for safe preservation. There were even small cans of vegetables.

This windfall of food joined our own meagre larder. The plywood was nailed to our living room floor, in a kind of jigsaw pattern because of its different sizes. We painted it red and black from the garbage dump paint. Hoping for an artistic effect, I suppose. It looked like a checkerboard with odd-size squares, oblongs, even triangles made necessary when the plywood had been damaged. It was a job we enjoyed doing, making something useful from other people's discards.

On the surface of existence—if not underneath—we were enjoying life at Roblin Lake. Eurithe had spent her childhood on a farm near McArthur's mills, some eighty miles north of Belleville. The second oldest of eleven brothers and sisters, she had a more or less normal childhood. And I'm really not very sure what that "more or less" means. Perhaps family affection, relatives nearby, berry picking and swimming in summer, dogs and cows—why don't I know more about her childhood? It seems inadequate.

Myself, I was a neurotic kid, and have a cousin's evidence on that point. Jean Woodsworth (née Ross) said, many years later, that I "was the most spoiled child she'd ever seen." It was probably my sole distinction. I was an only child, and driven back into myself for recreation and amusement. I played with other children, and also joined the Trenton Library and did a lot of indiscriminate reading. I seem to myself to have created my own world, inhabiting several levels of existence. In none of these was I entirely comfortable, unless perhaps in the world of my own imagination.

Jimmy, our son, a blond twelve-year-old, was also very much self-contained. When he was at an early age, his mother had made it plain that she intended to "raise" him in her own manner and method, without interference from me. Our relationship was sometimes explosive enough without me tempting fate unnecessarily. But the result was that Jimmy and I had very little communication. If he needed anything, whether advice or encouragement, he went to his mother. I was an intimate stranger, perhaps a person who stole time away from him with her that he thought should have been his time. Not an attractive picture, a recipe for disaster even.

But Roblin Lake in summer, planting seeds and watching things grow; doing a marathon swim across the lake while Eurithe accompanied me in a rowboat; working at the house, making it grow into something that nearly matched the structure already in your mind. Owls came by at night, whoo-whooing in a row of cedars above the house; blue herons stalked our shallows; muskrats splashed the shoreline; and I wrote poems. Mrs. Eley showed up, unsurprisingly, bringing the gift of an inedible rhubarb pie, so sour it couldn't be eaten.

And Mrs. Cannon who lived down the long lane at the county highway. In her late seventies, with a no-nonsense voice old ladies achieve to hide fear. She lived with a male ancient in his late eighties, "for companionship," she said. The old man could scarcely walk, staggering down our laneway with a cane to watch the house-building, complaining about his infirmities and fear of dying. But Mrs. Cannon was sprightly, chirpy and bird-like; she was generous with her garden that first year at Roblin Lake. I remember her with affection.

Norman Sword, the village postmaster, was very fat; he must have weighed 250 pounds, and had a bad heart. Norman was genial. We got on well together. I'd stay talking with him until arriving customers made more talk impossible. Harry Gibson, the farmer from whom we had bought the lake property, would have been difficult to know. Irascible and reclusive, he once charged down on me when I left the party line phone off the hook. His face very red, he charged me with crimes worse than murder in a shrill high voice. I wasn't very polite to him with my own response.

The house was still a skeleton without flesh in the autumn of 1957: flesh being insulation, siding, paint and other amenities. An old cookstove in the A-frame living room supplied heat. We had scrounged coal oil lamps for light (there was no electricity). Three of those lamps, clustered together, if you read a book, meant your eyes wouldn't fall out of your head. But they were a smoky dangerous fire hazard right out of the nineteenth century. When winter came like a lion, tiger and tyrannosaurus combined, the lake we used for water became armoured with ice—ice three-foot plus thick in March.

I chopped through it with an axe all that first winter. In March, you had to chop a four or five-foot circle in the ice, narrowing at the bottom to produce a huge funnel, from which water leaped upward in a reverse cataract at the final downward blow. I'd be sweating profusely as the work proceeded in fairly mild winter weather, discarding pieces of clothing one by one. At the end I'd often be stripped down to shorts. Mrs. Eley, observing me from her kitchen window, said I was "Mr. Tarzan." This flattered me inordinately.

The surface of our lives was tolerable, bearable, even enjoyable and producing occasional laughter at times. We were healthy, all three of us were, and a damn good thing too. Our original Montreal grubstake of some twelve hundred bucks had melted away, leaving a few measly dollars hoarded against emergencies. But ours was a permanent emergency.

A small chapbook of my poems was published that year by Fred Cogswell at the University of New Brunswick. He probably felt sorry for me; and I now think that little book was simply bad. (Alden Nowlan produced a much-superior first book of his own the following year.) And I did a lot of writing in 1957. But poems about this traumatic period for me didn't appear until much later, during the early 1960s.

Winter, 1957. The county forests turned a brilliant scarlet and gold; the sky of autumn filled with hundreds and thousands of migrating Canada geese, squawking ceaselessly. And winter appeared without transition, Indian summer directly to frozen lake and miles of snow. We had to wake up at three-hour intervals through the night to stoke the cookstove, when the temperature plunged far below zero. A few feet from the stove, wind whistled through openings I had neglected to caulk. My deficiencies as a house-builder were very obvious.

Outside was white-magic: trees clothed in wedding gowns of snow, or a rattling armour of ice after freezing rain. When the lake had been in process of freezing, partly covered with sheets of ice, wind lifted the ice at intervals, producing a sound like extra-terrestrial animals wanting to return home. In deep winter and sinking temperatures, ice cracked with a terrifying noise, as if a god were scourging the earth.

In the morning, when you emerged bleary-eyed from many-times interrupted sleep to piss: the white damask was scrolled with a delicate tracery of art work—animal footprints, bird hieroglyphics, your own deep yellow calligraphy. Empty by day, the cold world was populated by rabbits, stray cats and dogs, squirrels and chipmunks by night.

But even in winter, the weather sometimes turned suddenly warm. I remember one occasion like a spring evening, except that flakes of snow were drifting down softly as dandelion parachutes, and there was a luminous quality about the lighting. As if the white blanket was internally glowing, and a convention of white fireflies had decided that here was the place they wanted to sleep.

I was getting ready for bed, had removed all my clothes. Then, on a whim, I put on my shoes and went outside into the falling world. It was like being caressed by little white sparks, the touch no more than a ghostly awareness of touching. The feeling of having once had wings, or an additional sense beyond the ordinary five which enabled the possessor to be part of things instead of separate from them. But after five minutes or so the cold attacked my naked body, a thickening of perception and slowing down of movement. Retreating into the house, I felt as if I had glimpsed a human faculty we had lost when life was "nasty, brutish and short," but you could speak to snowflakes in their own language . . .

Money was an absent guest, a necessity we didn't have. We were short of food, the car was empty of gasoline. Eurithe and I talked it over. "I'll have to hitch-hike to Montreal and get a job," I said. "Maybe," she said, "But not now, not when it's so cold."

So I delayed my departure until it got warmer. But it didn't get warmer. After a bleak Christmas in which there were no gifts but good wishes that didn't cost money, January was a continual Ice Age. I refused to think of how cold it was. Eurithe said don't go. I went, bundled up in scarf and overcoat; but no gloves; I had none.

It was Sunday. There were friends in Montreal with whom I expected to find temporary refuge. The sun shone like steel; cold cut like a knife. I got a ride to Belleville. Another to Shannonville on #2 Highway. Then a long wait, and another twenty mile hop eastward. One kindly motorist, noticing I had nothing on my hands in this bitter weather, gave me a pair of gloves. I was almost weepily sentimental thanking him. And I reached Kingston by noon of that January Sunday, while people went to church and prayed to the God of their fathers . . . I stood by the roadside with thumb extended, wondering if it would help to pray a little. And decided it wouldn't.

Another ride to Gananoque, twenty miles east of Kingston. And there I stalled. Standing on the side of the road for an hour, for an hour and a half, for two hours, I lost track of time. Cold bored into my body; I jumped up and down to relieve numbness in feet and legs; I tried to think good thoughts and thoughts of food. I had eaten the sandwich lunch in my pocket, but food-thoughts made me hungry again.

After how long a time at Gananoque I don't know, and after no motorist even slowing down to examine me curiously, I switched sides of the road and attempted to hitch-hike back the way I had come. At that point I was feeling desperate and despairing, very, very sorry for myself. The switch worked. I got a ride right away, and another after that. I walked the last six miles home. And entered the house ashamed. I suppose that amusing anecdote was my low point.

I'm bound to over-dramatize it, of course. But it's difficult to do that with the nadir, and what's lower than low?—foolish grandiloquent writer reduced to penury, crying in his beer if he had beer. "Corpse discovered near Gananoque on #2 Highway?" Whaddaya think, Eurithe? "Would you like some hot soup, dear?"

Spring came, the birds returned, dandelions bloomed, frogs sang on the shores of Roblin Lake. The mating season, flashes of colour in the air, green and yellow on the ground, the sky blue and grey with sun and rain. Our financial situation was no better, but we survived.

· · · · ·

During my year of exile from cities I renewed acquaintance with my cousin, Don Ross, whose father used to bring us apples at Christmas. Don now ran the orchard farm between Wellington and Bloomfield in Prince Edward County. He'd spent most of the war in the Canadian army, the latter part of it plodding north on the Italian peninsula in pursuit of Germans. Emerging from the war an alcoholic, neurotic and often quarrelsome, his marriage broke up and everything fell to pieces for him.

Don's situation made me think how lucky I was by comparison. There had been a sympathy between us as children and teenagers. Some of it still remained. We drank beer when I had the money for it. I listened to him about the horrors of the Italian campaign, which were indeed horrible. He visited us at Roblin Lake, sampling my wild grape wine, amiable to a degree. But his manner seemed rigid; I felt his nerves were liable to fly apart at any time. He talked jerkily, not so much to me as to himself, his eyes focused elsewhere.

He ate diner with Eurithe and I one Sunday, leaving a little drunken in early evening. On the way to his car I saw him stagger climbing a rise of land. I dashed out to help, make sure he didn't take a bad tumble. He turned, hearing me coming, fists rising and ready to strike. I stopped, bawled him out in as scathing terms as I could think of: and he went.

Later on I heard his girlfriend had been killed by a train, whose rail line bisected the middle of his farm. It was a curious story. The Prince Edward County railway spur was a "Toonerville Trolley" kind of train.

It made only two trips a day between Picton and Trenton. Don's girlfriend, said to be his best friend's wife, had been sitting on the railway tracks when she was killed. Very odd! Something had been left out of the story that would make it more understandable.

Two years later Don was thrown from a horse, landed on his head and was taken to hospital. He had been drinking at the time. I was about to visit him at Kingston General Hospital, when I heard he was dead. His sister, Jean, said to me that she thought life had been wasted on him. I don't know. I remember our childhood friendship, and think of him now with strong affection.

.   .   .   .   .

My father-in-law, Jim Parkhurst, disliked bosses. I shared the feeling, although it provided no special bond between us. I am a verbal and rational sort of person—the latter to some degree anyway. Jim was instinctual, his speech slow and spoken after much apparent deliberation. When our house-building had been carried as far towards completion as it could be, given our low-ebb financial plight, Jim and I went on scrap iron-hunting expeditions.

He was an impressive physical specimen, and possessed enormous strength. When I joined him for one of these expeditions, the lids of steel drums had to be cut out in circular fashion with an axe. He sliced out the sheet steel almost casually with one arm, his expression never changing. I was little more than half his age; but I couldn't do that with both arms.

He drove an old stake truck, the same one I had used to transport gravel fill for our front yard and CPR waste lumber for winter fuel. We ranged all over the county in search of scrap metal, calling at any house whose backyard disclosed a derelict car rusting among the weeds. He knocked on doors or I did, asking householders if they'd like to get rid of that worthless hunk of iron which undoubtedly spoiled the view of their outhouse. If they did, we'd take it off their hands, free of charge.

My own view of the world and time and human existence during that period was largely the angle visible from Jim Parkhurst's truck, limited and narrow. I've sometimes thought you can divide people into at least two camps because of their attitudes to life, whether buoyant and hopeful or depressed and on-looking. I was one of the world's losers at that time. I always expected the worst, despite a secret opinion that I was a pretty good writer. (No one at all shared that opinion.)

Among the more interesting questions that I now pose to myself: why and how did I change? Because I am no longer a defeatist, no longer a loser: I've expected to triumph at almost anything I do for years. "Hooray for me," my psyche says to itself (if I needed to say it, which I don't). How did I change? Why did I change?

I hasten to amend and clarify any erroneous impression of my character resulting from the above passages. I think there is no way you (meaning me) can conduct your life over the long term that will not reveal exactly what you are. In other words, the way I screw myself up and lose track of my own thought in this sentence gives the possible reader an unprofound insight into me (unless of course I revise the sentence later).

I think it is possible that if I were to act and speak in a particular way, it would endear me to women; people would shower money on me in large golden quantities; and I would be popular in all areas of society. All of us, we human beings, could act in such a way that we would be both rich and extremely popular. *If we just knew what way.*

But I would bore myself to death very quickly in such case. Having sometimes started a conversation resolved to keep my temper and patience in check, I nearly always forgot myself and lost both. Despite elementary politeness and manners, I yam what I yam, in the quite unsuitable language of Popeye the Sailor. But somewhere in the past I changed from being a loser to someone expecting not to lose. At least not in the areas which I think important, and if I'm not successful it wasn't very important anyway. How and why did I change?

Among the Parkhurst/Purdy expeditions were a couple to the Bancroft-Maynooth area with apples to sell. Despite its distance of only a hundred miles from Belleville, people there regard it as the true north. And certainly, those northern people are different from those of more populous sections. They're much less prosperous for one thing, and perhaps a little more cordial. Jim regarded the north as something special, where nearly everyone knew him, and those that did loved him personally. He felt romantic about it, and knew many people there. He had left to join the army when very young, and every return seemed like a homecoming for him. People in the south were more or less anonymous, he felt; in the north they were human, with special remembered quirks and idiosyncrasies.

On Highway 62 the palaeolithic chin of the Canadian Shield pokes south to within forty miles of Belleville. (In the limestone county of Prince Edward there is, surprisingly, a small protrusion of the same Shield.) At century's turn the Ottawa government financed and built a colonization road through northern Hasting's County, called "The Opeongo Trail." The road was probably a mistake at the time, responsible for hardship and early death. The reason? Land there was only occasionally fertile enough to support farms; when thick forests were cut down, marginal grazing land was often the only result. But people rushed in to settle the cheap land, and once arrived were never able to accumulate enough money to escape again. It was a rural trap, a grassy ghetto.

Eurithe and I both worked at Jay Sprague's Mountainview canning factory in 1958. She peeled tomatoes. I operated a machine which capped the 28-ounce cans. Earlier, I had picked tomatoes in county fields; but my back couldn't stand the continual bending.

My mother died that year. Since building our house the year before, we had driven the eighteen miles to Trenton every week to see how she was getting along. Her sense of time was becoming mixed-up; Sunday became any day of the week; her "Redeemer" was a non-paying boarder in the nineteenth century brick house where I grew up. There was a little framed motto on the wall: "Christ is the head of this house, the unseen listener to every conversation." It made me very uncomfortable before my religious beliefs vanished.

This unseen guest seemed to have taken over the household. And my mother's health was worsening. Eurithe and I discussed things, wondering what to do.

But the possibility of doing anything was taken out of our hands late in 1957. My mother stumbled and fell in the upstairs bedroom. She remained on the floor unconscious for more than twenty-four hours. The neighbours noticed her non-appearance at windows and called police. She was taken to Trenton Hospital. That long period on the bedroom floor had caused pressure sores. Eurithe and I arrived shortly after she was taken to hospital.

Three weeks later at age eighty, after removal to a nursing home, she was dead. If we had been able to live with her in Trenton, I don't think it would have happened. As it was, my guilty feelings were pretty overwhelming. Understanding between us had always been incomplete. It seemed she had lived her life, at least the latter years, for my sake alone. It seemed also that she wanted many things from me, the chiefest of which was love. I sometimes felt beleaguered as a result, as if love could be doled out like a weekly money allowance. But that's a mean way to express it, since love is freely given or else takes the form of coercion.

Anyway, the United Church minister called on Eurithe and I at

Trenton prior to the funeral. We talked briefly about very little, then I made a bad mistake: said I wasn't a very religious person. If I'd been watching closely, I'd probably have seen the man's face change expression. When he delivered the eulogy for my mother at the funeral chapel, his words were aimed directly at unbelievers, specifically me. And he knew I knew. I could tell from the look on his face, the eyes that sometimes looked directly into mine while he was speaking.

Relatives and friends of my mother had gathered in that chapel: the smell of flowers, the smell of people's Sunday best, the smell of the dead. I was very angry at that preacher. My face was hot with it. But I was trapped by circumstance, as if I'd been tied hand and foot. There was no escape. And thought: if this is the sort of god and his representative on earth that my mother loved, that god is for her alone. In the unlikely event such a god actually existed, I'd mount an armed expedition to the Heavenly Gates to rescue my mother from his clutches.

I received a thousand dollars from a Canada Council grant in the spring of 1960. I bought a train ticket to Vancouver; at the same time Eurithe got a job with Parke-Davis and was sent to Brockville, Ontario. During the tenure of my short-term grant, I planned to revisit the places where I'd been stationed during the war, at Woodcock in the Hazelton area of northern BC.

Driving an old 1948 Pontiac from a Vancouver used car lot, I drove north, sleeping in the car. In fact I lived in that car for nearly twenty-four hours a day. Parked on a side road in the Hazelton wilderness area, I set up literary shop. My idea was to write about Indians and whites, loggers and miners and trappers.

I drank beer with them in the local pubs, talked to everyone, from Mounties to railway workers. And wrote poems. Once I interviewed an Indian while drinking beer with him, asking questions about his life style, education (which seemed fairly extensive), and ambitions in life. His expression while I asked my questions was most peculiar. It turned out he was the son of the Chinese Canadian hotel owner in Hazelton village.

It was a savage place. There were giant mountains towering in every direction. Again I saw "Rocher de Boule," shaped like a huge loaf of stone bread. The Skeena River roared, twisted, lisped and foamed past, much the same as it had during my wartime exile here. When I drove back to my side road haven one evening, a horde of dogs appeared on the road. At least a dozen dogs of all sizes. They headed straight for the car, their leader a handsome white animal. I was certain they'd slow down and swerve aside before reaching the car. They did, all but one, a white Samoyed. He broke his neck slamming into the fender and bumper.

I turned into a service station farther down the highway, informing its operator about the accident. He owned the dog, and seemed unsurprised at its fate. At my side road camping spot, I had rigged some pots and wires as an alarm system while I slept in the old Pontiac. There had been no sound in the night. But wandering around next morning, I stumbled on the Samoyed's body in a nearby ditch. It gave me a jolt, this ghost dog I had killed seeking out its murderer. Of course the service station operator had simply thrown the dog's body there, as a handy method of disposal.

On my return trip east the American states slipped past slowly. Montana seemed to last forever at forty miles an hour. The Pontiac had a throttle, a gimmick you pull out, and the car keeps a steady speed as a result. I slid back in the seat, almost dreaming, thinking about poems. Those I had written in Hazelton seemed nothing special, but how can you ever tell about your own poems? And caught myself up: of course you can tell; if you can't, what's the use of writing at all? In this case, the poems were ordinary. I knew it, and didn't want to admit it. Or maybe they weren't so bad, repeating in my head the title of my 1959 chapbook, *The Crafte So Longe to Lerne.*

· · · · ·

The big job that summer at Roblin Lake was getting electricity into the house. Jim Parkhurst had wired the place, using cheap second-hand electric stuff, with me helping as best I could. And the Picton Hydro was scheduled to run a line into the house from the lane two hundred feet away. But first I had to get a hydro pole on site, ready for the electric people.

A tall cedar near the house supplied a pole. I dug a hole some eighteen inches deep to receive the pole. At that depth I encountered—solid limestone. What to do? I talked to village people who'd used dynamite in their own work, and bought some myself. I rigged a fuse long enough to give me plenty of time to escape the blast. I lit it and ran, taking cover behind a breast-high pile of stones.

I waited and waited, but nothing happened. And felt extremely nervous. Maybe the stuff would explode the instant I got close to it, and stayed behind my protective stone barrier. After a few more minutes I began to feel quite foolish, but alive and intending to stay that way. I didn't dare climb down into the shallow hole I'd dug for my hydro pole; but sat on the edge and thought about the problem. The fuse had gotten extinguished somehow, and maybe it could be lit again. But not down in that hole, not by me . . .

Newspapers? Maybe that would do it. I gathered an armload of them, scrunching them up and twisting as if I intended to light a fire. Which I did intend, to light a fire. When the dynamite hole was filled with crumpled newspaper, I threw in a match and ran like a rabbit before they got well ignited.

This time the results were more satisfactory. After a few moments the earth made a low baritone *crump* sound, as if in bad humour about something. Dirt and stones flew into the air. I started to breathe with less difficulty. And resolved to have nothing to do with dynamite in future. I've already forgotten how I crimped that fuse into place, in case anybody should ask me to do the same again. I won't. Cowardice is sometimes necessary for survival.

It took six years to get my mother's will settled. Over that entire length of time Eurithe and I had been expecting our poverty to be lessened, even a season of mild prosperity. We had no idea how much money was involved. But apparently the Victoria & Grey Trust Company didn't intend to let me have it, whatever the amount.

During most of those six years, I had been driving the eighteen miles between Roblin Lake and Trenton once a week. My lawyer there kept making encouraging noises. Things were going well, he'd say: just a few months more, be patient a little longer . . . That sort of thing. The Trenton lawyer's only advantage was that I didn't have to pay him any money until the will was actually probated. But I had very little anyway.

Over those six years since 1958, I published several small chap-books. My style of writing had taken a ninety-degree turn in the direction of—what?—modernism? I don't like these labels anyway. Whatever the terminology, the change in me was radical. My reading had become omnivorous and carnivorous. As well as poems, I also wrote radio plays at the rate of at least one a month, sometimes more. On one memorable occasion I wrote an entire hour-long radio play overnight, finishing off a couple of bottles of my home-made wine in the process. It was a very bad play.

The image of myself I see reflected from then to now is not particu-larly attractive. Our small family was poverty-stricken. My own moods alternated between exaltation and depression. But I was writing excitedly and ferociously; it was a fever, an obsession, almost an illness. And I was probably neurotic as hell, a psychiatric mess.

That Trenton lawyer was useless: my impatience with him during interviews badly concealed. I couldn't look in his mind, but I wish that had been possible. I boiled and simmered in his waiting room; I chewed silent nails when I talked to him.

Visiting Frank Scott in Montreal, I asked him for advice and the name of a good lawyer in Toronto. Scott mentioned Andrew Brewin. But shortly after that Brewin was elected to parliament. He handed over this small probate job to a young lawyer in his office, Ian Scott. It was an excellent choice. After a trip to Belleville by Scott and a session with Judge Anderson, my mother's will was probated in 1964.

A dozen radio plays of mine were produced during this approximate six-year period. Alice Frick and Doris Hedges at CBC Toronto were largely responsible for any small success I had with play-writing. They sent me scripts for adjudication as well; and to read bad plays and contrast them with good ones is a way of improving your own writing. I had so far to go that I couldn't help improve.

I published *Poems for All the Annettes* in 1962. And regard this book as a watershed in my own development. But I don't like the word development, which sounds like a boxer or pole vaulter prepping for a big athletic meet. However, I admit to being almost fully aware of the changes taking place in my own mental equipment, changes that were partly the result of discontent with nearly everything about myself. The previous six-year period was one of turmoil and radical change, as I've intimated.

And some interesting questions might be raised here: why and how does one change? Writing itself was part of the reason for my own small movements from what I was to what I am. Scribbling poems is supposed to be an occupation for the eternal amateur, even if the poet makes money at it and is regarded as highly accomplished. One might say the poem researches an adjacent universe for truth and beauty. And those last two words sound a bit ridiculous in this day and age. My own idea is that writing poems is a mental discipline that stretches the mind; although I don't regard myself as a very disciplined person. "Inspiration" is another word I dislike; but there is a mind-cloistered condition in which the physical world is extinguished like a match, thoughts float free like small clouds inside infinite space of the human skull . . .

But enough maundering. *Poems for All the Annettes* caused some small comment in Toronto literary circles. Deciding that the timing was right, I submitted the manuscript of *The Cariboo Horses* to McClelland

& Stewart in 1963. It was published two years later, winning the Governor General's Award. I borrowed a suit from my brother-in-law for a trip to Ottawa and the ceremony.

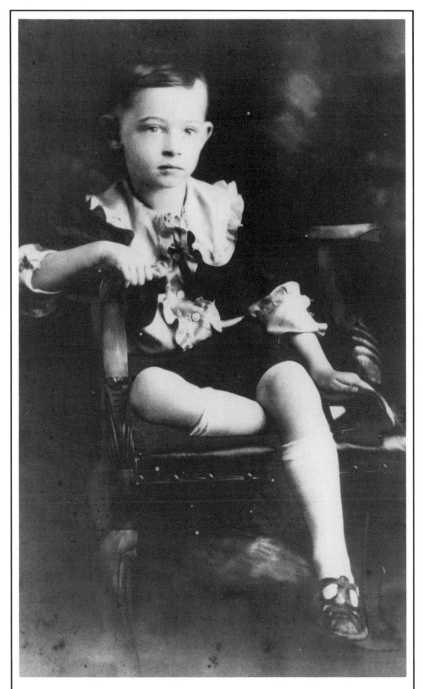

*My first memory, Trenton, 1921. I got out of that Lord Fauntleroy suit
damn quick in case other kids should see me.*

My father and I, 1920. I've just bitten his finger.

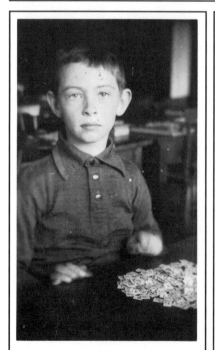

At Dufferin School in Trenton, around 1925. I've been playing with letters ever since.

My mother, at about the age of 60. She's probably wondering where I've gotten to.

1935, age 17. This was just before I rode the freights to Vancouver, and found the world didn't appreciate me enough.

*Kitsilano Beach, 1954. With Curt Lang, Doug and Toni Kaye, and a
guy who attached himself to us.*

With Earle Birney near Stanley Park, late 1960s, letting our egos show.

At the Trentonian, *1963, right in the middle of "the bad times."*

1966, my first GG. I was wearing my brother-in-law's suit, which was much too large for me. The GG explained one of my poems to me.

With Mike Ondaatje, early 1970s. We are wondering whether to bite the hand that feeds us.

With Margaret Laurence, deciding whether St. Paul was a misogynist.

With Ron Everson, pretending to be sensitive.

With Eurithe at Ameliasburgh; she long-suffering as usual.

At Machu Picchu, 1973. Earle Birney told me he once climbed that mountain in the background. The town bridge at Trenton was high enough for me.

Accepting the GG award from GG Sauvé in 1987. She seemed unaccountably nervous when talking with me, as if my fly was open.

At the Milton Acorn Festival, 1992. Milton thought he was a raven, then an Indian. I've marvelled about him since our first meeting, around 1956.

CHAPTER TEN

. . . .

ANECDOTAGE

There's a demarcation or bench mark in my life at the years 1965–66. Before that my wife and I managed to survive poverty; and we built a house together (thanks largely to Jim Parkhurst) in a kind of desperation. Life became very different after *The Cariboo Horses*.

My own character changed as well. As if everything that happened before 1965 was an apprenticeship, an uncertain testing of my footing, a mysterious waiting period. And I do not mean to imply that after 1965 my writing program would produce nothing but masterpieces. It's just that the changes inside myself were so obvious, at least to me. And I was growing even more interested in and curious about other people. I was also fascinated by myself, a navel-watcher, narcissistic as hell.

Curiosity seems to me my most salient characteristic. I'd like the use of it for a few years more. I want to go on exploring my own limitations and boundaries. And in all my writing, there's a shadow self I'm trying to get in touch with, the other self who lives in all of us, friend, foe or neutral judge. A doppelganger of the soul, that absurd word designating someone who doesn't exist. Therefore I invent him.

. . . . .

Before 1965 my actions had been largely determined by economic necessity. In my mind there was always an over-riding master whose servant I was, a continual awareness that nearly everything I did must have an economic advantage.

Quitting that job in Vancouver in 1955, was a start. I was beginning to discover myself. How and why does one change? The uncertainty about one's personal self, that does not entirely disappear. For many people there seems no real purpose to existence, and generally we must invent or discover our own. Our brief lives provide no easy answers to the great question of being and nothingness. And it is probable that our own guess work has as much to recommend it as the long cogitations of the great philosophers.

Time and space are still mysteries, despite a multitude of theories. Deity in this doubting century seems to me ludicrous. But I add one proviso to that last opinion—that religion among the poverty-stricken in very poor nations is still necessary in order to give them hope for a better future. However, my belief is that we fashion our gods in our own best human image, and therefore we worship ourselves.

A very few of us escape our human limitations. It is perhaps a small index to my own character that I admire two of these escapees, without any hope that I could emulate them myself. I mention George Woodcock and Andrei Sakarov as examples of something I don't know how to define, but nevertheless venerate. And hasten to add, not in any religious sense.

From 1965 on, life opened up for me. At that time it became entirely feasible for me to go anywhere on earth and to write about it. I was also confident that I would write "well": and I hope that doesn't sound overweeningly sure of myself. But despite all uncertainties, I *was* fairly sure of myself, even if my innards sometimes quivered a little. And the last twenty-five years have not really been dominated by riding freight trains, unemployment, military servitude or the taxi business. I've been on my own, entirely responsible for what I was and am, nobody to praise or blame but my inescapable self.

. . . . . .

Baffin Island in 1965 was a beginning. Leaving Montreal in early June, flying over Ungava and Hudson Straits to Frobisher Bay and snow-splashed hills of Baffin like recumbent Jersey cows—that was exciting. I rushed from one side of the Nordair aircraft to the other, feeling delighted with myself that I had chosen to come here; nursing a big bottle of booze under my HBC parka in case of shortages; the strangeness and probably discomfort ahead all part of my fascination. No other poet I knew of had ever gone to the Arctic (except Robert Service, and he didn't count), it was virgin territory for me, untouched except for the mundane prose of explorers and scientists.

And the apparent harshness of the landscape masked over many small things. At Pangnirtung, where I stayed for the first few weeks, were no great fields of flowers, no forests dominated the horizon. But tiny flowers were tucked away here and there, patches of them in wind-sheltered places; and ground willows hugged the land and were nurtured by the land. All this life, hovering just a few inches above death. Death in the shape of permafrost, omni-present, permanent ice just beneath the little coloured flags on the surface.

I looked at everything for the first, second and third time, and kept looking. I was insatiably curious. Of course the government Northern Affairs people at Pang probably thought I was nuts. But they arranged accommodation for me at the Inuit kids' hostel, where children lived during schooldays in winter. Wayne Morrison, the regional administrator, looked after everything. And I explored Pangnirtung from end to end, even climbed one of the mountains surrounding the fiord—at least I got halfway up. And talked to everybody, and wrote poems.

Then I decided that Pang wasn't the last frontier on Baffin after all. Wayne Morrison made arrangements for me to go along with an Inuit family to their island home in Cumberland Sound. Despite looking at the map, I was disoriented, had very little idea where I was or what distances were involved. And neither Jonesee or Leah, nor any of their kids, spoke a word of English. The youngsters could not be identified by runny noses and big grins; all Inuit looked more or less the same to me.

Jonesee the hunter was a young brown-faced medium-sized man, with a little scar on his cheek. But he was a notably serious man in comparison to the youngsters. And seemed to know the water hazards well as we crept along the tall cliffs of Pangnirtung Fiord, past icebergs that towered over us half as high as the dark cliffs. Our journey took hours and hours; white spray so cold it felt like molten metal splashed over me at my seat in the bow every now and then; and I grinned like a fool in lieu of words whenever I looked at Jonesee and Leah. At nightfall we stopped at an island, one that didn't fit the description of the Kikastan group which I'd been told about back at Pang. And I couldn't make polite enquiries as to our whereabouts.

Along the island's gravel beach were strewn severed seal flippers, rusty tin cans and other garbage. My job on landing seemed to be helping a blind husky bitch ashore from the boat. The dog had milky eyes, and was a family pet; it was accompanied by three or four pups who scrambled after us, making puppy noises. I had a sleeping bag and some sandwiches with me, and felt pretty self-sufficient. Still, my mind was full of questions it was useless to ask.

During the next two or three hours a half dozen other Inuit hunters along with Jonesee fired at seals from the island's high cliffs. It was at least two hundred feet down to the water where you could see the slightest ripple, the daylight ambience continuing into evening. From the little beach on which we'd landed, boats pulled out to retrieve dead seals when the cannonading stopped. I settled down to sleep around midnight, with a lullaby from Old Squaw ducks echoing eerily all around me.

Next morning Jonesee's expedition started out again, myself still in charge of the blind husky and her pups. You'd have thought that dog knew all about her condition; she didn't growl at me once. The island we'd just left had been only a firing platform for hunters, a one-night stand for Jonesee on his way home. I'm not sure how many seals he'd bagged, but at least a couple.

Jonesee's island, three or four miles long, had several more-or-less permanent lodges; a couple of larger boats were pulled up on shore. It was a stone landscape, all brown, everywhere you looked. And surrounding the tiny settlement, iceberg sentinels. I settled down, with tent, groceries and Coleman stove, intending the place to become home sweet home for about three weeks.

And the dogs. There must have been a couple of dozen of those huge brutes. They didn't move out of your way either, just stood in your path and looked back at you unwaveringly. Those dogs pissed all over my tent from outside. I'd see their shadows against the canvas walls, as if they were waiting for me to break down and run away in terror from our close encounters. I believe they knew I was afraid of them; but if I had run away, I'd have been even more terrified. Jonesee—he just waded in among them with a piece of two by four instead of going around. Me, I went around.

The landscape was vivid contrast, golden-brown rock, steel-blue water and bright blue sky; and icebergs so brilliantly white they hurt the eyes. Those bergs added a final touch of grandeur to the world. Waking late in the night, I'd hear a whisper of the receding tide, which often stranded house-high bergs in shallow water. And half-asleep, helpless in the sleeping bag, hear them collapsing on themselves when the sea's support was removed: with a noise like massed artillery letting go at thousands of plate glass windows.

The most scarifying experience was being followed by those huge dogs when you left the settlement because of natural necessity. That parliament of trailing dogs, it had a purposeful look; a town pooch would have fled them in squeaking terror. And indeed, they did have a purpose. Some chemical element was missing from their food, and they were continually in quest of dietary supplement in the form of human shit. Jonesee's kid threw stones at them on my behalf, otherwise vital anatomy sections might have gone missing. I rewarded the kid with nickels, which proves they still have some value even if insufficient for candy bars.

He cometh forth hurriedly from his tent
and looketh for a quiet sequestered vale
he carrieth a roll of violet toilet tissue
and a forerunner goeth ahead to do him honour
yclept a snotty-nosed Eskimo kid
He findeth a quiet glade among great stones
squatteth forthwith and undoeth trousers
Irrational Man by Wm. Barrett in hand
while the other dismisseth mosquitoes
and beginneth the most natural of natural functions
buttocks balanced above the boulders
Then
    dogs^1
       Dogs^3
          DOGS^{12}
             all shapes and sizes
all colours and religious persuasion
a plague of dogs rushing in
having been attracted by the philosophic climate
and being wishful to learn about existential dogs
and denial of the self with regard to bitches
But let's call a spade a shovel
therefore there I am I am I think that is
surrounded by a dozen dozen fierce Eskimo dogs
with an inexplicable (to me) appetite
for human excrement
        Dear Ann Landers
what would you do?
        Dear Galloping Gourmet
what would *you* do
        in a case like this?
Well I'll tell you

NOT A DAMN THING
You just squat there cursing hopelessly
while the kid throws stones
and tries to keep them off and out from under
as a big black husky dashes in
swift as an enemy submarine
white teeth snapping at the anus
I shriek
>   and shriek
>   (the kid laughs)
>   and hold onto my pants
>   sans dignity
>   sans intellect
>   sans Wm. Barrett
>   and damn near sans anus
Stand firm little Eskimo kid
it giveth candy if I had any
it giveth a dime in lieu of same
STAND FIRM
Oh avatar of Olympian excellence
noble Eskimo youth do your stuff
Zeus in the Arctic dog pound
Montcalm at Quebec
Horatius at the bridge
Leonidas at Thermopylae
Custer's last stand at the Little Big Horn
"KEEP THEM DAMN DOGS OFF
YOU MISERABLE LITTLE BRAT!"

Afterwards
Achilles retreateth without honour
unzippered and sullen
and sulketh in his tent till next time appointed
his anus shrinketh
he escheweth all forms of laxative and physick meanwhile
and prayeth for constipation
addresseth himself to the Eskimo brat miscalled
>   "Lo tho I walk thru the valley of
>   the shadowy kennels
>   in the land of permanent ice cream
>   I will fear no huskies

for thou art with me
and slingeth thy stones forever and ever
thou veritable David
Amen"

P.S. Next time I'm gonna take a gun

—When I Sat Down to Play the Piano (1967)

Sleeping in that cold tent I caught a chill after two weeks, and came down with a fever. I dosed myself with quinine and poured sweat for a couple of nights. When the fever broke one morning after restless sleep, I felt very lucky. There were no doctors on call. But I was lucky in many other ways. It felt so marvellous to be writing poems in the high Arctic; when the Inuit wives visited me, nursing their babies, I'd read them my new poems. Which, of course, they couldn't understand. And smile forgivingly, because I was too stupid to have learned their own language.

That summer on Baffin added new pages to my life, which occasionally return to me in dreams. They are all there, Jonesee and Leah and the kids. That blind husky licks my hand, the pups frolic, guns are cannonading from nearby islands. And Baffin itself, a huge island sprawled across my mind, its patches of summer flowers and drifting bergs like medieval galleons . . . Someday I will go back there.

. . . . .

Louis Dudek, Mike Gnarowski and I drove from Montreal to Stanley House in New Brunswick in the spring of 1965. At service stations along the way Dudek would inform the gas jockeys that I was the idiot son of an American millionaire for whom he had been hired to be nursemaid and guardian, and to make sure I didn't drown myself in a toilet bowl. I played along with this imposture, which gained more and more realistic detail as we neared the Quebec border. Finally I was staring at the mirror in service station toilets, looking for actual signs of mental imbalance. One or two people really did shudder back in my presence as they listened to Dudek. That may have been because I drooled a little.

E.J. Pratt, the well-known poet, had just died. The three of us, I who-knew-not-Pratt, Gnarowski and Dudek who apparently did, composed a singable dirge to mourn the absence of Pratt from our careening vehicle. Each of us supplied an alternate line, to the tune of the Scots lament, "The Bonny Earl of Moray," which I had picked up on Baffin Island. My own special line was: "Till the bull winds of Labrador come down from Newfoundland." Pratt, of course, was an expatriate New-foundlander.

Nearly everybody I knew was at Stanley House: Frank Scott, Arthur Smith, Doug Jones, Fred Cogswell, Seymour Mayne, George Johnston, Ron Everson, Earle Birney and several others. Stanley House itself, a big white-painted frame structure, had been a gift from Governor General Lord Stanley to the Canadian government, and thence to the Canada Council. Its function was to be a guest house for painters, politicians and the like; it overlooked Baie de Chaleur on the Gulf of St. Lawrence.

When Dudek, Gnarowski and I arrived, we sang our newly composed Pratt lament for the other writers' edification. Our rendition was greeted with a loud groan. After drinks all round we tried again, and received no better reception. More drinks, then the nearly unanimous decision: as a troubadour trio, D., G. and P. were lousy.

Evenings at Stanley House were set aside for poetry recitals. It's a measure of my huge ego that I can't remember anyone else's work but my own during those performances. I read "Wilderness Gothic" and "Home-Made Beer," and was slightly embarrassed by the reaction. There was complete silence after "Wilderness Gothic," a silence that continued for a few moments after I sat down. At first I thought the audience didn't like my stuff at all, then realized it was a kind of tribute. I was gratified, of course, and felt defensive about my own gratification. (I mean, how do you say this stuff about yourself?) Everyone's attitude toward me over the next couple of days was just slightly different than it had been; they seemed a little thoughtful and speculative when they looked at me. One really is aware of it when something like that happens. Next day Earle Birney asked for my "Home-Made Beer" for *Prism* magazine, which he was editing at UBC.

We spent one of our holiday evenings over a big driftwood fire on the beach. The French-speaking housekeeper prepared a picnic meal, complete with hot dogs, melted marshmallows on the fire and free-flowing beer. We sat around on driftwood logs, swigging beer and gossiping. Ron Everson fell off his log at one point, looking very owl-eyed lying horizontal in the sand. Arthur Smith rowed a dinghy out into the bay, and on returning couldn't propel it back onto the beach far enough so he wouldn't get wet when disembarking. I undertook to help, grabbing the bow in a showoff mood, and yanked so hard the not-en-tirely-sober Smith tumbled into the bottom of the boat.

When the learned Doctor of Literature was helped to his feet, I noticed that his mouth was bleeding and felt appalled at myself. It was hard to tell if this was a mortal wound in campfire light. Mike Gnarowski was the rescuer, helping Smith ashore and ministering to the minor scrape on his mouth. However, I've felt slightly guilty about that incident ever since.

My return journey to Ameliasburgh via Montreal was in company with Arthur Smith and Frank Scott in the latter's car. Frank decided we should stop over at a Quebec City hotel with two hundred miles still to drive. The three of us congregated in one room for drinks and talk before going to bed. It was an easy moment of talk, and mention was made of a very good-looking woman officiating at the hotel desk, perhaps more girl than woman. One of those faces that momentarily drives any other thought out of your own head: you just stand there a bit stunned, while the universe narrows and expands disconcertingly, and you forget what you intended to say.

I've forgotten the exact conversational context, but Arthur Smith said something I've always remembered. He said, "You could get a disease." Frank and I agreed with him, of course, nodding our heads solemnly like those time-announcing birds one sees on the balconies of cuckoo clocks. Then we roared with laughter. And went to bed comfortless.

I had such warm feelings toward Scott and Smith, and toward those other people at Stanley House as well. There are few ways of bridging our human aloneness; these quite indescribable feelings are one way.

Both Scott and Smith are dead now, of course. I don't believe in any religious or supernatural mumbo-jumbo, and never hope to see them again. But a verse by Euripides, quoted by Tiff Findley in one of his books, fits my own feelings here:

> And every seed,
> Earth-gendered back to earth shall pass,
> And back to heaven the seeds of sky;
> Seeing all things into all may range
> And, Sundering, show new shapes of change,
> But never that which is shall die.

In 1964 I went to Cuba, one of a dozen Canadians on that trip. We were guests of the Cuban government, which wanted people to look at the country unhampered by American prejudice. Fidel Castro had chased the previous dictator, Fulgencio Batista, into exile five years previously. Castro's long struggle from his mountain refuge in the Sierra Maestras against Batista had made him something of a hero, but a hero the United States disliked for his recently acquired communist politics.

In 1962 the US had financed and armed a counter-revolutionary military force which landed at the Bay of Pigs. Castro took personal command of the Cuban army and militia, defeating the invaders and taking many prisoners. (A short synopsis of some complicated events.)

My own trip to Cuba was more or less accidental. Some months before I had a reading at Ross Dowson's Trotskyist bookstore in Toronto. And since my politics are NDP/leftist, Dowson asked me if I'd be interested in going to Cuba. I was. In fact I was ecstatic about the trip. Visions of new poems flashed in my head; maybe even a prose narrative about Cuba.

I visited Michel Lambeth, a Toronto photographer, one of the dozen Canadians invited. His photographs and my prose would go well together in a book; at least that was my thinking. But Lambeth, a few days before departure, decided not to go. He was afraid of being blacklisted as a Communist. He mentioned to me that the days of McCarthy witch-hunting were fairly recent, only ten years previously.

An organization called "Fair Play For Cuba" was the up-front sponsor of this Canadian trip to Cuba. Lambeth was nervous about that too, since "Fair Play" had been linked with the assassination of US President John Kennedy a year earlier. (Ross Dowson was involved in that outfit as well.) Anyway, Lambeth was extremely jittery where the Red Menace was concerned. He was employed by Toronto newspapers, and thought blacklisting would destroy his livelihood. I had no such fears myself, not being gainfully employed anywhere. Besides, I think you take your chances when you feel adventurous and have enthusiasm for a project.

Travelling from Canada to Cuba couldn't be done in a straight line, across the US to Miami, say, then south to Havana. American hostility to Fidel Castro and his nation precluded such a simple trip. One had to book for Mexico City, then wait for a scheduled Cubana Airlines flight instead. And there was a feeling of danger about the whole thing. Rumour had it that everyone Cuba-bound was being photographed at the Mexico City airport; the CIA was said to lurk behind every pair of tourist sun glasses.

Edith Firth, a York University prof who'd spent her teenage years in Mexico, was visibly apprehensive. "I'm afraid they'll stop me," she said.

"Who?"

"You need a visa to leave Mexico for Cuba. Then you need another one for the return trip to Mexico City." And there was a film of perspiration (never sweat) on her forehead. She could not be reassured. Besides, she probably knew more about it than I did.

I stayed at a cheap hotel on Avenida Reforma, wandering around Mexico City on foot, excited about almost everything I saw. The market, especially the Orozco paintings in government buildings. The cheap Mexican beer. And hovering over the entire city a cloud of dark pollution; the air so heavy and permeated with human smells, the stink of garbage and automobile exhaust, that you could almost weigh and package it. And the poor, the wretched, ragged, miserable poor. Beggars on every street corner and some in the middle of the block. Cripples begging, Indians begging for pesos, and me thinking: is this the reward for being human, for our supposed superiority to the animals, for having invented a kindly and benign God?

But I was too excited for continued depression. And the flight to Havana was exhilarating. Over the Gulf of Mexico there was thunder and lightning cannonading on one side of the plane, a quiet rose and scarlet sunset on the other. The aircraft plunged and dipped; the sky splashed bright silver inside. It sounded like longshoremen were piling beer kegs in my ears. It was like my childhood times at Trenton during a storm: I'd spend hours on the veranda feeling that silvery silence in my bones when lightning struck somewhere else, a silence like the ringing of bells on the far-off moon.

Cuba was a revelation for me, in several ways. We were met at the airport, given drinks, had our hands shaken and were grinned at. Friendly. And we met Alicia, blonde, generally smiling, and simply "nice." She was our translator and sometimes guide.

Among the Canadian visitors, a union shop steward and his wife from Vancouver. Frank something. About thirty-five, but fresh faced and looking years younger than that. Six feet two inches, he was very handsome, and had a talent for stating the obvious in portentous tones.

Barbara Something was young and quite beautiful; she disliked me for some forgotten reason. Ralph was a union organizer and official, about fifty-five. When we visited a cigar factory, I was asked to speak to the workers, all being given a free moment from hand-rolling cigars. That embarrassed me. I didn't know what to say, and asked Ralph to speak instead. He spewed the usual communist clichés that would have made Karl Marx blush. The cigar rollers all banged metal spoons on their desks and made a big racket, although I'm sure few of them understood English.

Two Montreal lawyers were with our contingent, both French Canadian. One spoke very little. The other was lean-faced, middle height, and balding, his manner self-possessed and confident. During one long discussion I had with him he described his formula for Quebec's relations with the rest of the country. I was impressed but forgetful, and later asked him to repeat again some key portions of his thesis. He refused, and nothing more could be said on the subject. His name was Pierre Trudeau.

Trudeau made me very careful of what I said around him. I had the feeling he'd notice anything foolish immediately. He might not mention it, but I'd know he'd know I'd been stupid. You encounter a few people like that from time to time; they keep you on your toes. Once during our Cuban stay, the eleven Canadians were sitting in a country school room, cramped by those little hardwood desks they have, listening to a Communist official explain the *modus operandi* of things since the revolution. I raised my hand like a small boy, asking if they arrived at decisions by majority vote. There was a little stir behind me, and Pierre Trudeau's voice said, "Don't be naïve, Al!" I nearly blushed.

The Canadians attended a ballet performance before we left Havana for a motor tour of the island. The prima ballerina's name was Alicia Alonzo. She was rather long in the tooth, but a big favourite with the audience. Long before the show was over Pierre and I walked out of the theatre, as stealthily as possible for politeness' sake.

We spent much of that evening walking all the way across the city to the Habana Libre Hotel. Along the route we admired ancient churches, bought cider from restaurants, and talked. I recited a poem of mine, written shortly before, "Necropsy of Love," feeling flattered when he seemed interested. I didn't dare remind him of his formula for Quebec as part of the Canadian federation; that would have been asking for a verbal rebuff. And yes, I was impressed with the guy.

In the past, whenever I've been similarly impressed with anyone, I've gone to some trouble in order to meet them again. And when you do that, the onus is on you to be interesting to them in turn, and perhaps showing it in a way not flattering to yourself. You either remain silent, or else reveal enough of yourself to be thought a fool. And sometimes too, you can read other people's thoughts about you while they're talking, quite different from those they are verbalizing. Of course all this is conjecture, since a thought on someone's face is like a shadow on the sun: it vanishes before you can be sure it existed.

May Day in Cuba was a chance for everyone to dress in their Sunday best; for the Cuban leaders to brag endlessly about their accomplishments; for soldiers and their weapons to parade through downtown streets; while Marx and Lenin looked on approvingly from murals on the sides of tall buildings. Carnival. The equivalent anyway.

The foreign visitors from Canada sat in a concrete grandstand at one side of a monster city park. Visitors from other countries were placed nearby, including ladies from North Vietnam in diaphanous summer dresses, and no doubt others from the Soviet Union. The sun pressed against your head like a dull knife. We sat there, and sat there, for hours, while people filed into the meeting place, or marched, or rode in army vehicles.

In the row of seats below us, a man was moving like a small brown cloud among the foreign visitors. He stepped up to where the Canadians were seated. A short and stockily built man, wearing olive drab army fatigues and black beret. He had a short beard and smoked a cigar. "Who is it?" I whispered to Pierre Trudeau.

"Che Guevara."

There is something about meeting a legend! As if history resided in his handshake, as if, as if . . . Che Guevara! Fidel Castro's first lieutenant and comrade; the Argentine doctor who'd devoted his life to proletarian revolution, crouching with Castro in the Sierra Maestra Mountains, hunted daily by the Cuban dictator's soldiers. A small man, brown-eyed and unassuming, in his mid-thirties, not bad-looking either. Shaking my hand at that moment, I could even smell the good cigar. And he was gone. Down the line of visitors, a sudden giant among the tiny Vietnamese ladies.

Some people are perhaps not vulnerable to meeting legends. I was. Later on Guevara disappeared from Cuba. He was said to be leading uprisings against various South American governments. Which governments, which countries? The news media didn't know. But he finally turned up in Bolivia, one of the most backward countries in the southern continent. And leading a peasant army in the jungle, being shot at by the Bolivian army with CIA advisers lurking in the shadow background. Being killed. His body destroyed. But first they cut off his fingers for fingerprint identification, to prove that the dead man was Che Guevara.

Of course I didn't know all this when we were shaking hands during the May Day celebrations. But there was something about the man: it was like turning a page of history and seeing a shadowy photograph; someone who looked like you, also present briefly.

Castro spoke. And spoke, and spoke. The sun pressed down. Water poured downhill off my head. I manufactured a flimsy hat from newspaper, quite inadequate. Trudeau had a handkerchief around his head. At one point we looked at each other, then both made for the concrete bowels of the grandstand with a single mind, as if pleading "natural necessity." And it was natural necessity. Castro spoke on. The tanks and armoured gun carriers baked in the heat. The bullets nestled in gun belts; the bombs slept quiet.

The 1958 Cadillacs, in which we joy-rode around the island, were wearing out. Spare parts were unobtainable because of the American trade embargo. But there was a decadent luxury about those Caddys, a feeling that we were being favoured and visibly appreciated. Of course, it was all laid on for propaganda. That was understandable, with Uncle Sam frowning down on us from Miami ninety miles away. Alicia's blonde smile was for sweet propaganda's sake. And so was everything else, so was our driver's easy grin, and so on.

But the Cubans were very likable; their enthusiasm impressed me. And when we stopped for lunch at country restaurants, so did their beer. Make an impression on me, I mean. Half the Canadians in our party didn't drink beer, and I was pleased to help them out of their difficulty, their non-appreciation of Cuban beer. Of course, it wasn't very good beer, being cloudy with sediment, its taste indifferent. But it was alcoholic, undeniably. And the end of the lunch hours sometimes left me slightly sozzled.

At Playa Giron, more familiar to Canadians as "The Bay of Pigs," we toured the battle zones, as much as the swampy terrain would allow. Here the US-backed and advised invasion force landed, and was defeated in a couple of days furious fighting. An alligator farm was in operation there. And jokes were made among us, to the effect that alligators resemble counter-revolutionaries or vice-versa. Pretty feeble stuff.

Near the end of our three-week visit, we traveled by jeep across the Sierra Maestras, arriving at a coastal sugar mill that had been attacked by sea raiders two days before. The jeep ride was unnerving: clouds of red dust exploded behind us; pigs fled squealing from the careening vehicle; we caught a glimpse of shocked faces in our churning wake. When we disembarked, our hands, faces and clothes were covered with red pigment from the dusty mountain road.

The sugar mill town looked like a western movie set. Horses and riders clopped the main street; burros waited outside false front buildings; but no six-shooters were buckled around waists. Near the ruined mill, mountainous piles of raw sugar were still smoking from gunfire;

a black man clambered over the sugar grinning at us with gold teeth. But the only human casualty from the sea attack was a woman, struck in the buttocks by a stray bullet. The entire scene was unreal to me, living in rural Ontario all my life; now suddenly transported to a war zone. Because that's what it looked like, a war zone.

Among the tangle of Cuban impressions, some stand out. Like the Cuban women. There's really no way to avoid the subject of Cuban women. The thought of them makes my blood heat up a little, speeding in transit from capillaries to aorta, and begging swift admission to the heart. In absentia I languish for Cuban women.

A country boy from rural Canada might say, "Gee!" or even, "Haw!" at the sight of such gorgeous ladies—but they don't even wriggle an apostrophe if you do. The only way to get their attention is to hiss like an old-fashioned stage villain, and twirl your moustache, if you have one. (A Cuban custom.) But then they look at you as if there'd been some mistake, and pass sultrily onward.

When a female pedestrian walks down Yonge or St. Catherine Street, and a male heaves-to in front of her, said female pedestrian generally lowers her eyes to the grey and neuter sidewalk. Not so in Cuba. Cuban girls fix their eyes on you and hold them there until boiling blood begins to seep from under your fingernails.

To give you the idea—I ran out of cigarettes one night at the hotel, and walked down the block a short distance to get some. Not more than 100 feet from safety I was impaled by a sizzling dark glance. My right foot several inches up in the air at the time, about to take another step forward. But three seconds elapsed before I could lower that foot to the sidewalk! I returned to the hotel dazed and shaken, without cigarettes.

A different impression: I was riding in our '58 Cadillac limousine over a mountain road late at night. We encountered an army convoy. Moonlight glittered on camouflaged troop carriers and men; big guns trundling along behind trucks; tropical palms overhead. On reaching Havana, I saw anti-aircraft guns lined up near the waterfront, their snouts like open mouths. An American warship, the Oxford, could be seen vaguely in daylight just outside the twelve-mile limit, its spy apparatus focused on the now-Communist island. It becomes a nightmare world, a place for dead lovers . . .

I would never maintain you get to know a country in three weeks. But one can form a liking for some of the people. Over that time we saw palm-thatched huts, sheet iron shanties and modern apartment buildings. We traveled from one end of the country to the other, from Hemingway's Villa to Spanish-colonial style hotels. If there was any racism among the blacks and whites on this island it wasn't visible to me. Of course, we didn't see the prisons and camps for political detainees. The Cubans put their best foot forward as one would expect. A country dominated by the US for many years was slowly regaining its self-respect. And some would say, regaining it at a heavy cost.

My own outlook on the world changed as a result of visiting Cuba. Not to the extent that I became Communist, or ever expect to be more left than a socialist New Democrat in Canada. But I have an admiration and liking for the country and its people. They fume and froth around the edges when the USA is mentioned; the spy ship Oxford was a constant thistle in their pants; and Castro in 1964 was a kind of legendary god. As is Che Guevara still. And of course, José Martí, hero of their war of independence from Spain. He is their patron saint.

No longer is Cuba a backwater of history, as it was before Castro. Not that there's anything wrong with being a backwater of history. In fact, I think it's admirable, like being the quiet eye of a hurricane world. And certainly preferable to being ravaged by wars and poisoned by atomics. I prefer the Canadian backwater to being a world power with its consequent inevitable abuses of power—i.e. the US.

However, Cuba exchanged domination by one country, the US, for domination by another, the Soviet Union. Their pride blossomed nevertheless; their name is known in the world; they haven't laid down in the centre of the road waiting to be run over. One doesn't have to be a Communist to admire the Cuban people, standing on their defiant little Caribbean island waiting for the barbarians to arrive. Armed to the teeth and waiting.

. . . . .

The New Romans was published in 1968. It sold twenty-five thousand copies, about twenty-five times as much as the average book of poems. I'd met publisher Mel Hurtig at an Edmonton party a couple of years before that. A small man, brown-faced and sort of crackling with nervous energy, he operated a book store and had recently started to publish books himself. I was haranguing him morosely at that party, complaining about the mistreatment of Canada by the United States, mentioning border disputes from the Maine and New Brunswick boundaries in the east to the western San Juan Islands. And not neglecting the injustice we suffered in our trade dealings with the Americans. I was really fulminating, a little carried away.

Hurtig listened calmly, then said, "Why don't you do a book about it?"

I'd already thought of that, and asked Jack McClelland if he was interested. He wasn't. To Mel Hurtig I said, "Nobody would publish it."

"I would," he said.

The party stopped for me at that moment; all around us noise died down as we talked. I could see the structure of the book take shape in the smoky air, first a shining cobweb in our minds, then the solid foundation and walls looming over furniture in an Edmonton living room. Both Mel and I coming up with ideas, joining them to the literary hash. Both of us were getting enthusiastic. It was exhilarating, the kind of thing where you forget time and wake up six hours later surprised that it's the next day.

"It'll annoy some people," I said.

"Sure," Mel said. He grinned. We shook hands.

"What about a title?"

"*The New Romans*," I said.

It was arranged that I should edit the proposed book, asking writers and politicians for contributions—or just about anyone who had a vigorous opinion. And the subject of the book? Canadian opinions of the United States.

Contributors had absolute freedom, could say anything they liked. And did. And they didn't have to agree with Mel Hurtig and I, just say whatever they said well. The only criteria was good writing, that it should be interesting. Most of it was, I think. But when I asked anyone to send me something, whether prose or poem, I was obligated to accept it. That was awkward once or twice.

For the cover, Roy Peterson did a cartoon of an American business-man smoking a cigar, wearing shades and Roman armour. It was gorgeous.

Right from the beginning, my wife hadn't wanted me to do this book. I believe she thought it would make a lot of people mad at me. I thought, what the hell, let 'em be mad. Of course, it wasn't good form to say nasty things about the US, victor in the last war against the Nazis. The United States, champion of democracy, refuge for the poor and down-trodden, shining land of freedom and future hope of the world! Bullshit.

· · · · ·

Anyway, we went to Europe in November 1969, all because of *The New Romans* (and I mean the book). We rode the Hellas Express from Luxembourg to Greece, charging through half a dozen snow-covered countries and crossing the Greek border into pure magic—ripe oranges like little glowing lanterns hung on trees. And Athens! But we were more enthralled by ruins of the past than the present big modern city. And all the *now*-places we saw had *then* behind them like coloured shadows.

Of course, the Parthenon. You get this religious feeling about Greece, about broken stone, and all those dead Athenians who were so self-important they thought they were the centre of the world. And they were, but not for the same reasons the Athenians believed. This is where philosophy really began, where drama and poetry flourished, and the *polis*, which is another word for ignoble democracy.

So you get this feeling. All that ruined stone, once painted in garish colours which time has subdued to grey! The marketplace, the *agora*— and your eyes blur from the continual passage of dead men and women over thousands of years. You can almost see them in the *agora*, husbands buying a pound of hamburger for their wives. That's what you do at the market, although it was undoubtedly slaves who did the buying in the year 500 Before Christ.

In all this reverence for the past, something is missing. The paradox is that what's missing is still there in another form, another guise. Tenderness? Yes, I guess so, but it's much more than that. I mean the other half of life itself. And that is female. In the dead past all the living females are stone, as if the gender had been mutated in order to receive relative immortality with dead philosophers and dead playwrights. And became goddesses by virtue of stone. Goddesses?

Maybe I'm missing a point here. Can you separate all the best things from the female gender and express them in stone other than as belonging to goddesses? I mean, omit the special flesh and delete their special names, turn them all into other abstract names like Athena and Hera, et cetera. As opposed to Socrates and other once-living male personages in stone, as well as the masculine gods. But women, girls, the real ones, where are they in this stone pantheon? Did Hera and Athena ever do the dishes, formed as they were of the morning dew?

While we were living in Athens, Eurithe's health became a concern. She was losing too much blood during menstrual periods, her energy much decreased. We decided an English-speaking doctor would be best, and booked passage on a ship to Bari, Italy. We intended to visit Pompeii and Rome along the way, before proceeding overland to England.

That time is lost now, except for what it did inside my head. But Pompeii remains indelible. Eurithe and I were very nearly the only tourists at this winter season. Walking the streets, following wheel ruts in the ruined stone, we lived in another time and place, feeling very weird. Of course it's a dead city, whereas Athens and Rome are bustling life. I wrote poems in Rome, and we got a free meal from a salesman's banquet where they tried to sell us a Florida lot! (A Florida lot in Rome?)

We did the touristy things there. Watched mobs of hungry cats thronging near Victor Immanuel's marble monument that looks like an enormous grand piano. Visited the Trevi Fountain, and dead Caesars in the museums. Even looked for Keats' and Shelley's graves in the English Cemetery. At an English-language bookstore near the Spanish Steps, I found two books by Earle Birney and Purdy. I bought them both, thus depriving the Romans of Canadian culture.

Eurithe had an operation at a London hospital. During her convalescence, Margaret Laurence rescued us from a crummy room in Earl's Court, where we just about froze when we ran out of shillings for the gas meter. I had met ML in Ottawa when she received the GG Award for *A Jest of God* in 1967. In England, she was a rescuing angel, and would not hear of us remaining in that cold room.

We took the train to Penn, Bucks, when Eurithe was able to travel. Margaret met us at the station with a taxi, and we were installed in a comfortable bedroom at "Elm Cottage." The so-called cottage was fairly commodious, with a huge stone-floored kitchen heated by an old-fashioned monster iron stove. The children were David and Jocelyn, fourteen and seventeen, both attending school in 1970.

I suppose there was some awkwardness and a time of adjustment at Elm Cottage, but thinking back I can't remember any. Margaret made us most welcome, and if not quite gregarious was a fairly social person. And she liked a glass of wine. We did a lot of discussing and arguing back and forth, reminiscent of my sessions with Milton Acorn; although ML wasn't nearly as dogmatic as Milton. Basically she was religious, but not in any formal sense. And since I am a WASA (white anglo-saxon atheist), I made desultory efforts to unconvince her of God. Quite unsuccessfully. In some respects we had a good-humoured contest in our attempts to get the better of each other in these "discussions" . . . Margaret admired St. Paul rather excessively, I thought. And while my theological equipment is almost nil, I entered debating lists anyway.

Jocelyn told me later she was surprised that anyone should dare to disagree with her strong-willed mother. But it wasn't like that at all: our discussions were good-humoured and friendly. I remember we re-hashed all the speculative old chestnuts, like there has to be a first cause for everything and what caused God? And if an orchid blooms in the South American jungle, does anyone know about it? And if no one knows, does the orchid exist at all?

Friends came to visit. I've forgotten all their names, but two of them were a Canadian couple who had written songs about the people in ML's new novel, *The Diviners*. And they insisted on performing for me. I have to admit, reluctantly, I thought the songs were terrible. And here they were, looking at me expectantly, waiting for my appreciation. But the choristers were so full of themselves and Margaret so pleased, I hadn't the heart to be a killjoy, and employed a few badly-chosen words of praise. (And think, what a phony I was!)

Between chasing books at various small-town stores, I read the manuscript of Margaret's *A Bird in the House*. I thought these stories were very close to wonderful. With ML's permission I sat down at a spare typewriter with one of them, translating it directly from story into play on the machine. And felt so pleased with myself, that I had the dramatic expertise to do this! Then I went off to Guildford, Windsor and other towns by train and bus to hunt books. When I returned a couple of days later, Margaret had taken my crude first draft of a radio play and turned it into a finished manuscript so professional in its use of dramatic radio jargon that I was amazed.

When Eurithe was healthy and again took charge of our lives, it was decided that we should go back to Greece. I am, of course, writing long after these events. Margaret died of lung cancer in 1987. My own feeling when leaving Elm Cottage in 1970 and at Margaret's death much later—these two occasions get mixed in together. Your friends become part of your own life, and when they die it's as if little parts of you and your memory—which is you—are lopped off. What's left is a diminished self.

.　.　.　.　.

In late March we returned to Greece, on a package tour that took us to Delphi, Corinth in the Peloponnese, and half a dozen other places. The driver of our panel bus was a young guy working at this summer job to help pay his way through Oxford University. Or perhaps it was Cambridge. He visited us in Canada a few years later, as did two girls we met in Crete who worked for the BBC.

After a few days at Rhodes, renting a Volkswagen and driving around the island, we decided to go to Turkey. That country was vaguely visible across the narrow strait, and there was a regular ferry. Neither Eurithe nor I knew a word of Turkish, had no Turkish money, and took the trip almost entirely on impulse.

It was magical. We made our way with sign language and dumb show. And changed our money at a bank near the harbour of the unpronounceable town at which we landed. All that first day we rode mini-buses northward along the Mediterranean coast, all Volkswagens. On curves of narrow mountain roads the bus driver blew his horn continuously; at villages and towns the driver's helper yowled and screamed to solicit passengers. Yes, we decided, the Turks were a noisy nation. Every thirty or forty kilometres the bus reached its terminal, and continued no farther. Then we would have to search the town or village for another terminal entirely, from which a different bus continued north along that coast.

We were jammed into those buses with country people, the women shapeless in voluminous clothing; passengers included piglets and chickens, once even a goat riding just inside the sliding door. At day's end we stopped at a medium-sized town, feeling tired out and travel worn. Our hotel room cost three bucks in Canadian money; our bathroom down the hall had no door. Toilet facilities consisted of two raised footprints surmounting a small black hole in the concrete floor. A pull chain overhead enabled the floods to arrive, and you had to depart the premises quickly. I mounted guard when Eurithe was inside.

Nothing brought home the strangeness of the Middle East as much as seeing a funeral procession pass by while we were strolling through the town streets. The dear departed was laid-out on a rough wooden platform, about the size of a small mattress, covered only with a wool blanket. "Pallbearers" ran past us with the body, keeping quite a good pace, as if they were in a hurry to get the whole thing over with. Other "mourners" ran beside the corpse, all of them young else they'd collapse in exhaustion. I've wondered about that funeral ever since.

At Bodrum we found quite a modern motel, and completely empty of other guests. The hot water tap didn't work and there was no sink stopper. (I've since gotten into the habit of including a spare sink stopper in my toilet stuff while travelling: how's that for triviality?) Near the sea shore we visited a ruined Greek temple, with only a few upright columns standing.

Wading through deep grass where Eurithe was afraid of snakes, we found sculptured marble heads, about the size of very large pumpkins. No bodies, just heads. We felt like children discovering strange dolls, kept rushing around from one marble face to another, calling to each other delightedly when we uncovered a new one.

The whole experience of those heads brought the Greeks much closer to us, as wandering human beings building their doll houses everywhere. By comparison, visiting the revered Parthenon in Athens was a lot like going to church when I was a child, to bribe an invisible god with silver my mother gave me for the collection plate.

Near the ancient city of Ephesus is a modern Turkish town. We stayed at a hotel there in order to digest a complete helping of Greek ruins. Outside our third-floor windows, Byzantine columns of rough masonry, each with a stork's nest like a brush pile of sticks on top; and each with the angular-looking bird herself coming and going, but mostly staying since they had stork chicks to look after.

In early morning's first light, the mother storks would stand up and clash their beaks together noisily, as a salute to the rosy-fingered dawn I suppose. And just down the road a loudspeaker would chant something about Allah being great and the only god the record player knew about. A mechanical muezzin, I guess it was. And if you think sleep is possible with half a dozen storks and loudspeakers saluting the dawn all at once, you've never been there yourself.

Ephesus is the place where St. Paul did a lot of preaching; his "Epistle to the Ephesians" can still be used to induce sleep. The town has an interesting history. Founded around 1000 BC by Greeks from Athens, it was conquered by King Croesus of Lydia in the sixth century. This was the legendary Croesus mentioned in Herodotus, whose money helped build a temple to Artemis, called one of the "Seven Wonders of the World." Croesus was in turn overthrown by Persia and King Cyrus; and Persia was finally defeated by Alexander the Great on the River Granicus.

And that temple to Artemis: it was burned down in 356 BC by a man named Herostratus who wanted his name to be remembered after death. Obviously, it was remembered. That story has a very modern ring to it. Immortal arson.

It sits in the middle of enormous ploughed fields, Ephesus does. All around it ploughmen trace their parallel lines, encircling the dead city with growing things. From certain angles there, atop the huge theatre for instance, you can catch a glimpse of those ploughmen at their work, and wonder what they are thinking. Probably not much of anything. (In memory, when I'd been working hard myself, the brain empties itself out; or else it has thoughts like drifting clouds in the sky, occasionally moving into and out of your awareness . . .)

Eurithe and I were both enthralled by Ephesus, me imagining St. Paul telling Diana of the Ephesians to fuck off, and Eurithe being indignant about those stone penises on street corners pointing directions to the local whorehouse. Some buildings had many small stone compartments, said to be employed for immoral purposes by ladies of the evening. And the drunks, who surrendered themselves to sins of the flesh, wandering home in early morning after too much wine, too much everything, greeted by harsh words from spouse or mother-in-law. The drunks and whores and wives have long been dust. Mother-in-laws last a little longer.

A paved stone road once ran here between sea and harbour. But some time in the past the River Cayster grew choked with silt, removing access to the sea for several miles. Eurithe and I never went beyond the scarlet poppies that emerged everywhere from between stones on the harbour road. We were tired from walking these ancient streets, and felt almost as old at day's end. But the poppies, even in moonlight they glowed scarlet. I wonder: would they have lighted the way for a lost pedestrian at midnight, wondering where home was in this maze of look-alike stone.

We had started out on this romp through ancient history with the idea of proceeding north after taking the ferry from Rhodes, and hopefully reaching Homer's city of Troy near the Hellespont (now "The Dardanelles"). But Turkey in early May is an oven, and we sweltered. Taking a train up the coast to Izmir, a big modern city, we collapsed in an air-conditioned hotel room; both of us huddling close to the cold air vents. And flew home via England.

. . . . .

In 1984 we went back to Turkey, me with Homer's *Iliad* for guidebook to Troy; as it was for Heinrich Schliemann, who re-discovered the city of Helen and Agamemnon and Achilles. After a few days in Istanbul, visiting the Hagia Sophia, sampling local wines (not very good) and taking a hired car to the Black Sea coast, we headed for Cannakale. That's the nearest town of any size to Troy. Our hotel there directly overlooked the busy harbour.

From our third-floor window you could see the least smile or expression of irritation cross the faces of hucksters and their customers below. On the harbour front's wide concrete apron is a continual dramatic program, a permanent hubbub, the seething sound of life which is so different from the life of silent words.

Freighters and fishing boats docking below. And the customs station: their power cutters slicing outward into the straits on official errands, looking very important by contrast with the plodding freighters. Ferries disgorging motor traffic from the European side of the Hellespont, buses, big transports, pickups, private cars, campers, everything. And making a roar so continual and normal that you scarcely notice it.

Only in the mid-hours of night, if I got up to use the john, had the place grown quiet. But not very: a mile out in mid-channel the big freighters trundle by with lights blazing like Yonge and Bloor; sometimes a dark warship, its silhouette a visual password to hell. In fact, the name of Hellespont came from a girl named "Helles," who drowned there.

Just east of our hotel a long finger of land extends out into the Hellespont toward the European shore. Around 500 BC, the legend goes, a young man named Leander swam across the straits every night to visit his girl friend, Hero. This lady was a priestess of Apollo, sworn to chastity, and locked in a stone tower on the opposite shore. One night on his way to a rendezvous with his girl friend, Leander ran into a storm and drowned. His body was thrown up onto the rocky shore by wind and waves. Hero, finding her lover's corpse next morning, drowned herself as well.

In 1818 Lord Byron also swam the Hellespont, in the opposite direction, from Europe to Asia. Of course, this was in direct imitation of Leander. And Byron wrote a poem about it. In 1926 Richard Haliburton, a romantic travel writer, also swam the Hellespont from Europe to Asia, thus imitating both Leander and Byron. It's as if we're all under a spell from the past, condemned to repeat ourselves over and over . . .

Of course we visited Troy, maybe twenty miles from bustling Cannakale. I don't know the exact dimensions of this fabled city, sitting on its stone graves on a hill above the green countryside, but it *felt* very small to me. Like I was Gulliver in Lilliput, despite the phony wooden horse the Turks had installed at the city's entrance to intrigue tourists. *The Iliad* is a very big story, one that reverberates and resonates. You expect a world-stage for all those larger-than-life heroes.

Still, I forgot that expectation of bigness in the silence of stone. And we seemed to be the only *living* people here. Troy was a jumble of grey ruins. Nine different cities imposed and superimposed on each other. Signs labelled them Troy VI or Troy II or whatever, but it was difficult to make out transitions between different periods. Grey rock, grey walls, a small grey theatre, arrows leading you up and down a narrow path between ruins. But *ruins* is the wrong word: what you see and feel here is Time, time in your bones, time as air and breath and life, time as the opening you inhabit between yesterday and tomorrow. The child I was, the old man I am, which co-exist where the hourglass sand is clogged. Time as a great sea in which you can swim in any direction . . .

Troy VIIa is supposed to be the Troy of Priam, Paris, Hector and Helen, and of—Well, does it matter whom? I bend down, pick some wild flowers, imagining them in Helen's hands; and find some pottery fragments on the winding track, imagining them as part of amphorae that once furnished Priam's palace.

We met an elderly Swedish couple just when we thought to be entirely alone. They had driven overland from Sweden in a camper, both having a feeling that time was closing up on them, the illimitable sea of time foreshortening. We liked them; they liked us. And we drank Twining's Tea together in their camper for half an hour or so. They took our picture with our camera; we took their picture with theirs. One of those encounters that has no point, and yet you remember—which I suppose is exactly the point.

And Troy sits there with its phony wooden horse. Alexander the Great was fascinated by the place. He stripped off his armour, running naked and oiled around the tomb of Achilles here, before setting off to conquer the world. Mad Caracalla, the Roman emperor who actually thought he *was* Achilles, came here. And Xerxes, on his way to costly victory at Thermopylae and later costly defeat at Salamis and Plataea— Xerxes stopped here on the non-existent road to Greece.

His huge army, said to number a million men, ground to a halt. A black cloud of dust, obscuring the sun at times, settled over them as they camped uneasily on the Trojan plain, dreaming of ghosts . . . And slept badly that night.

·   ·   ·   ·   ·

"Time is a great sea in which you can swim in any direction," I said earlier (a little pretentiously). I am swimming backward now.

Irving Layton played a much larger role in my life than I've outlined thus far. A man with a personality like an attractive bulldozer: I think most people liked him on first meeting. Before my first European jaunt, I was peddling his early books in Vancouver, without much success. Then in the spring of 1956 Eurithe and I settled in Montreal for a couple of years. It was an intoxicating and euphoric period then to be a writer in Montreal. Layton has mentioned this to me since. There was a feeling in the air that anything was possible—Meaning that we were all young and confident and it was taken for granted that we'd succeed at anything we tried. We were all great writers, or would be soon. (Looking back, that attitude seems to me a bit ridiculous: nothing comes that easy.)

There were meetings, parties, gatherings at Ben's smoked meat restaurant, trips to Layton's cottage on Côte St. Luc, far out in the suburbs. Betty, sister of critic John Sutherland and now Layton's wife, was a wonderful hostess. A beautiful woman, she blossomed on these occasions, her dry wit refreshing in this atmosphere of hyperbole and exaggeration.

Louis Dudek's place was another focal point. He was tall and skinny with a large nose, and an engaging but sure-of-himself manner. During my first period in Montreal, Louis was having some serious disagreements with Layton, basic differences in their writing philosophies. And this after years in which both of them felt they were white knights riding forth in defence of Literature.

Dudek spoke slowly and judiciously, in the manner of a professor, which he was at McGill University. Layton was a listener much more than his friend, although when wound-up he would expound his ideas at great length. With him it was a matter of triggering some deep well of passionate words inside him; Dudek gave you the benefit of his wisdom without any trigger, a most uncomfortable feeling.

I have this weird memory of Dudek: at someone's party that was getting a little out of hand from the booze. Layton and I decided to arm wrestle. We were lying belly-down on the carpet, hands and forearms rigid with strain, jaws set hard, beer safely off to one side. I had the feeling I wanted to laugh. And became aware of a dark skeezix shadow bending over us, hearing Dudek say, "And these are sensitive poets!" Yes, we were. Well, weren't we?

At another time there was a contest to decide who had the most aesthetically pleasing balls, with Betty Layton the judge. Sure, it was juvenile, but also funny as hell when you noticed the expressions of people when the subject came up. Layton in his self-advertised role as a leading Jewish free spirit had to be first, especially with Betty as the judge. Dudek disapproved, and backed out altogether. I have to admit a thought occurred to me: what would my mother think? But that lady was far away in Trenton, Ontario, searching for her Redeemer, who was probably elsewhere.

Hugh MacLennan was an occasional guest at these parties. Tall, and I thought rather handsome, the title of his novel, *Two Solitudes*, had already entered the language in any discussion of relations between English-speaking Canadians and the Quebecois French. MacLennan had also known Norman Bethune, a Canadian doctor who had ministered to the wounded on battlefields in the Spanish Civil War, and later was active in China during the Chinese defence of their homeland against the Japanese invasion.

MacLennan's new novel, *The Watch That Ends the Night*, included a character much resembling Bethune, its publication scheduled for 1959. MacLennan had been a Rhodes Scholar, receiving a classical education which included Greek and Latin. Amazingly articulate, he would discuss and declaim on subjects of his interest, the USA and CIA, and their nefarious activities. (I do like that word "nefarious," and so did Hugh.) In measured tones he analyzed Canadian and world politics, and how the world was going to hell in a bucket. He was spellbinding, and I loved him too, listening without interruption as did everyone else.

You had the sense that here, in this room, among these boys who looked like men, the ultimate truth about the world's affairs was being unfolded. I was privileged to be an observer; and Milton Acorn was as well. But I don't think he was ever so impressed as me, or else he disguised it better. But then, Milton's obdurate belief in communism formed a protective shield against the invasion of alien ideas. These knee-jerk reactions of his would have been amusing to me, except they were so predictable.

We were a strange pair to become good friends, the friendship depending partly on mutual need and fellowship, but also because Milton was in process of changing into an exceptionally fine poet. I rather sensed this about him, although there was little evidence to support that feeling on my part. He'd published *In Love and Anger* at his own expense, shortly before I knew him. It was, in simple terms, a bad book. The language was cliché-ridden, the sentiments expressed were often sloppy, and his grammar was almost as bad as mine. But I emphasize his continuing metamorphosis into—if not a butterfly (how could Milton be a butterfly?—it boggles one to think of it), into a sturdy, honest and emotionally moving poet.

At this time I had gone beyond my imitations of Dylan Thomas, G.K. Chesterton, Oliver St. John Gogarty (the friend of Yeats), and others, but had not yet reached my ultimate mentor, D.H. Lawrence. Sure, Layton's blunt use of language was having its effect: I was taking shortcuts across vast fields of adjectives, and I was thinking about entirely deleting punctuation. But worst of all, I was imitating the English, the *worst* English poets. The kind of writer who leaves poems open to multiple interpretations in laborious fashion, who deliberately protect themselves with complicated varieties of syntax and prosody.

I refused to acknowledge it even to myself, but Milton's writing then was much better than mine. I'd visit the various crummy rooms he lived in, and be shown some of the stuff that appeared a little later in *Against a League of Liars* and *The Brain's the Target*, both 1958, and *Jawbreakers*, 1963. But how do you admit you're writing badly? I couldn't at that time, and it's only later that I'm able to acknowledge that Acorn was largely responsible for my own continuing changes.

Milton received a veteran's pension deriving from the second Great War, in which he'd received a serious head wound on the troopship sailing to England. But the pension didn't amount to much, and he often spent his monthly stipend too quickly, so that my wife and I had to feed him and sometimes have him sleep on a spare mattress we had in the apartment. He was an awkward guest, seldom if ever taking a bath.

Milton's mind worked differently from mine. When we were talking, his thoughts would slip away to something else, some otherwhere, and communication became difficult. I remember him reading a four-volume set of Freud I got for joining a book club, digesting it in scraps and pieces, then regurgitating it at me when I came home on the street car, worn out from work. At such times I felt desperate to defend myself against the Freudian flood yammering at my auditory extremities. In his own shabby rooms, the floor would often be knee-deep in manuscripts and paperback books, their subjects ranging from *Beowulf* to science fiction.

The magic thing about Acorn was this change in him—the continual becoming, his chrysalis splitting. But his everyday and every hour appearance remained exactly the same. The guy was a slob, and my own superiority in mentality, in manners and personal hygiene so obvious that I wouldn't acknowledge what was important in him at that time, only the slob part. But now I remember: that abstracted manner, the elsewhere he went to and lived "Sky's Poem For Christmas" before he'd even thought of it. The damaged brain in which white waves were washing against "The Island," its red earth turning water a dark maroon. It doesn't make me look very good to myself even now.

Does one look back and observe that other self far back at the beginning? As Loren Eiseley said, when did the brain start to grow? And I wonder, did all this happen to me as well? Because I've changed too, and look back on some of those earlier selves with disdain and even dislike.

Of course, I refused to abide by ordinary prosody, I mean the standard iambic stuff. If I could predict myself in any way, I'd discard it before the thing was written. But I'm anticipating. It wasn't until I got really involved with David Herbert Lawrence, the poor Lancashire collier's son, that I began to feel myself carried away, that I stopped "thinking" about writing and entered into the thing itself. This to the degree that I lost whoever I was for long enough to become an iguana or a blue-footed booby. When I could change my shape, when I could jump off the woodshed roof and fly far and away—or perhaps only think I did. The feeling must be much the same.

Layton's house in Côte St. Luc was a popular place. Visiting there you were almost sure of getting into an interesting discussion or argument—if not with Irving then with someone you didn't even know. Daryl Hine, a young poet from Vancouver, was also a guest at a party I attended there in the late 1960s. Hine was then receiving a good deal of attention from reviewers and critics. On this occasion he had a young lady with him, perhaps his girl friend. And Irving was prancing around the room chanting loudly: "And always at my heels I hear / Hine's winged chariot rumbling near," and getting a lot of enjoyment from his parody of Andrew Marvell.

That party was recalled to me with some force seven or eight years ago. One of my hobbies is getting books signed by their authors. I had five or six of Daryl Hine's, so I wrote to ask for his signatures, explaining who I was in the letter. Hine's reply said he'd sign them for me if I mailed them to him with return postage. And he asked me if I remembered the girl he was with at that Layton party. Then he went on to say that in the course of the long-ago evening at Irving Layton's, he got into a verbal fight with the young lady. And I had told him to leave her alone. In his letter he explained that I hadn't known the full circumstances of the situation, or else I wouldn't have interfered. Which left me with peculiar feelings, since I'd forgotten the incident entirely.

What happened, I mailed those books for Hine's inscription. Then time went by. And more time went by. I wrote Hine and hoped the books were delayed in the US-Canadian mails. He didn't reply. Of course he never will reply. The books and return postage are gone. And that is Hine's long-delayed revenge on me for telling him to stop fighting with the girl.

Several years ago at a Harbourfront reading in Toronto, Hine was a performer along with Stephen Spender. (I've forgotten the other readers.) Afterwards Hans Jewinski, a Toronto cop of literary leanings, asked Hine to sign his books. Jewinski's Hine-books had been carried in a plastic grocery bag; Hine refused to sign them for that reason. Stephen Spender leaped gallantly into the breach. "I'll be glad to sign my own books for you," he said.

Layton had many imitators and outright worshippers around him in Montreal. Some of them called themselves "disciples." There was Henry Moscovitch (who'd published a book called *The Serpent Ink*), Leonard Angel and K.V. Hertz, among those I remember. These worshippers of Layton often referred to other young poets they knew as their own disciples. When Milton and I started our little magazine, *Moment*, we asked Moscovitch for some of his poems. The embarrassing thing was that neither of us liked these poems; we had to return them to Layton's disciple.

For whatever reasons, none of these young poets ever came to anything, apart from work in mimeographed magazines they published themselves. I think they tried to take on all of Irving's colourations, the way he talked, his attitudes toward things, the rhythm of his writing, just about everything. All one can say is that such slavish imitation doesn't work.

For our *Moment* publishing venture, Milton had somehow liberated a mimeograph machine from the Montreal Communist party. It ended up dripping ink on the Purdy apartment floor, while we tried to figure out how to operate the fiendish device. And wrote away to anyone we admired, asking permission to publish their poems. We wrote to Wade Hemsworth, and published his "Squid-Jiggin Ground" and "Black Flies of North Ontario." And Phyllis Gotlieb's poems . . . (We also asked Phyllis to commit polygamy and marry us both.)

I had two separate stints in Montreal: the first 1956–57, and the second 1959–60. It was after the first period that Eurithe and I built the house at Roblin Lake, and afterwards had to go back to Montreal and earn enough money to finish it. I got a job at Johnston's Mattress Company on St. Germain St., Montreal East. My verse play of 1955, *A Gathering of Days*, had again been produced by John Reeves in Toronto. The CBC's six hundred buck payment came at just the right time, enabling us to eat, and buy some secondhand furniture. Eurithe and I feasted in jubilation at this unexpected windfall.

I have to mention here that all of the dates for these happenings are a bit jumbled in my mind. I have only an approximate time sense with which to locate most of them. My shortcomings have always been pretty obvious, even to strangers. As well as a poor memory for dates, I can't tell east from west or north from south in the sun's absence. I've even been completely lost around the corner from my own apartment. And several times after making telephone calls I've had to pick up the receiver again and ask the operator how to get out of the phone booth.

Anyway, during my first period in Montreal I wrote plays (one of them was eventually produced on stage at Toronto's Theatre in the Dell). During the second period I made box springs. That was "interesting," since it was the only job I couldn't do in a mattress factory. Not that I had been really accomplished at some of the others. But for box springs I had to start again at the beginning, assembling frame, springs, cotton felt and cloth cover like a jigsaw. The trouble was, I hadn't worked (apart from housebuilding) in four years, and my forty-year-old muscles were in terrible shape. I was also very depressed, since it seemed that Eurithe and I would never get any money ahead, and I was doomed to menial jobs forever. The future looked just as gloomy as the past, no hope anywhere.

When Dudek started his little magazine, *Delta*, he enlisted me to help with the mailing and addressing when I wasn't tired out from Johnston's. Louis thought I was a complete barbarian—well, almost. A very cultured and much-educated man himself, it was not an *original* culture, but something that had rubbed off onto him from sojourns in Europe and Mexico. He *thought* himself creative, in the manner of Pound and Williams. But actually, he was entirely derivative, a critic. Now, there's nothing wrong with being a critic, but in addition to that, Dudek was soured by the success of some of his close contemporaries. And by Layton's success especially.

But at the time I'm speaking of, I looked up to Louis Dudek, as a man of letters, as someone who had advanced the cause of literature in Canada. And not a poseur, because Dudek believes his own empty rhetoric. Since that time he has praised many lesser writers, and they have repaid him with commensurate homage. But praise for those others who have gone far beyond where he will ever go—those unsaid words turn sour and become bile.

In 1975, when I was finishing off a term as writer-in-rez at Loyola University in Montreal, Dudek came to speak to Elspeth Cameron's CanLit class. When his stint there was nearly finished, I came to the classroom to invite him for coffee. When he saw me, Dudek said to the students, "Purdy and I both write pure poetry; but I'm purer than he is."

At that point I think it became pretty clear to me. I said, "Pure, purer, and pur*ist*." Our relations since have not been good.

. . . . .

On the other hand, I loved Layton. He was, nevertheless, so full of shit he couldn't make up his mind from which end it would exit. And paradoxically, Layton was also genuine. He read his poems like a High Priest of the Ark of the Covenant, and a piece of the retractable carrying handle had somehow gotten lodged in his dentures. One faced this reverent atmosphere whether the poems he read were among his more trivial efforts or his best, although most of the time they were his best. And Layton praised himself in such glowing terms that the listener was often unable to decide whether to kneel in prayer, or make obeisance by knocking his own head on the floor. It was a dilemma I never resolved.

In 1959, coming back to Montreal from the west coast, I had arranged to meet Layton in a downtown pub. Both of us had written new poems, he a sonnet, and I a verse which I've completely forgotten now. Layton tore this poem of mine apart, with much more venom than I had expected (was I getting too big for my boots?), and I thought, unfairly. Of course I defended myself vigorously. In turn, Layton read his own sonnet, declaring that it would out-live Shakespeare. I disagreed with that opinion, some slight heat being generated in the discussion. It's surprising we didn't come to blows. Years later, I think we were both right in our unflattering opinions of the other person's poem.

Perhaps it was on that occasion he told me Malcolm Lowry had died in England. I felt desolated, and hadn't expected to feel that way. I was a mere acquaintance of Lowry's and he of mine. But he had touched me under the carapace we face the world with. His agony was genuine, even if sometimes a bit histrionic. In the same circumstances as Lowry's, I would have felt as he did, but perhaps also more aggressive and defiant. The gods of the Greeks never said we had to like what happens to us.

· · · · ·

In the late fifties I was still puzzling over my friend, Milton. I wanted to help him in any way possible, since he never had enough money to live more than adequately (and I wasn't a helluva lot better off myself). Physically he was unattractive, to phrase it in the kindest terms. Women were mostly repelled by him. And he was hungry for them. I'm sure he had fantasies that he would ramp and roar all over their bodies as if they were fields of daisies. If he ever got the chance.

Annette Ballon and I went to see Milton when he was still at one of those dirty near-slum rooms he lived in, the only kind he could afford. But it did have a toilet. And Annette did possess something besides an hourglass figure and a glance like a blowtorch in pitch darkness. (I'm too old to remember what she had besides that.) Anyway, she and I talked to Milton, a rather stilted conversation because he just wasn't used to women. Then I had to use the john as a result of previous imbibement. When I returned, Milton was crawling all over Annette, and she struggling to disentangle herself. What's the name of that Greek sculpture that looks like a mad octopus? Well, they did too. And I felt badly for Milton.

But we all composed ourselves and pretended it didn't happen. What else could you do? But our talk was even more stilted and awkward; we didn't stay long. (Years later, I think: poor Milton. And poor Annette, too, in her later metamorphoses.)

. . . . .

I remember a gathering at Frank Scott's—Dudek, Brian McCarthy, Gustafson, Leonard Cohen, etc. And Cohen was raving about Bob Dylan, how marvellous, how mellifluous, what a social influence on the American scene.

We listened, all of us, with a touch of skepticism. But Frank Scott paid attention, his slightly horse-like face infected by Cohen's enthusiasm. And Frank decided to go get a record then and there, making sure first there were plenty of drinks in his absence. Then we played Bob Dylan, as Cohen listened rapturously.

It sounded to me as if Dylan had a bad cold in the head, and could only sing through his nose. In fact, I thought it was rather like the honking of a large flock of Canada geese in concert. Looking at Gus and Dudek, they had an expression indicating they didn't quite know what to do or say.

"I can't stand this stuff," I told the musically inclined Cohen, (this was before he became a nightingale himself), and betook myself to the kitchen. It was a wise move; beer was immediately to hand. Two rooms away the faint drone of Bob Dylan could still be heard. I closed the open door and drank deeply.

. . . . .

Once Milton and I visited Leonard Cohen at the latter's Montreal apartment. Cohen had made a medium-sized splash with his first book, *Let Us Compare Mythologies*, a nice cozy title that allows all of us entrance to the learned societies. Three or four years later he would publish *The Spice-Box of Earth*, which impressed me a great deal. Something new had been added to the old neo-colonial mix of too-familiar voices. And beyond admiration, I felt a little jealous of Cohen, because I knew his mystic priestly attitudes were something foreign to my own character. I couldn't steal a damn thing from him.

These two men, Acorn and Cohen, were inexact opposites of each other. Cohen gave the impression of elegant aristocracy, wearing a fancy dressing gown to putter around the kitchen in, preparing coffee for his visitors. On that morning in the late 1950s, Cohen seemed to me perfectly self-aware, completely adjusted and comfortable in that just-short-of-luxurious milieu. So much so that he moved within a slight but perceptible aura of decadence. Not in the meaning of decline, just of standing aside in slight weariness, having been through life before and found it rather boring. (I think of George Sanders in the same way—he was the movie actor who killed himself from boredom.)

One gets the same feeling from some of Cohen's poems, excellent as they are. Even in "Suzanne," perhaps the best folksong lyric of its special kind ever written, there is an exotic and fateful sense of being on another level of consciousness than the mundane world of work and wages. It is a world that values the titillation of the senses more than money, although money is still very necessary. Huysmann's *Against the Grain* carries this attitude even further than Cohen.

I am sure that Cohen would know exactly what I'm talking about—as he strove self-consciously toward another level of being; and in the jargon you can't avoid, "A breakthrough onto another plane of existence." (Migawd!)

On this particular morning the languid and rather over-cultured Jewish aristocrat was foremost. By contrast, Acorn: a red fire hydrant in blue denims. One would almost think that one or the other of the two men had staged this meeting in order to feel more strongly and deeply the things that they already were. Acorn: slow in his impulsiveness, stutteringly inarticulate, the lava bed of his personality covered with shyness and the awkward aplomb of those who are self-righteously right, and recently escaped from the noble servitude of labour. He was a complete alien in Cohen's apartment, whose furnishings and decor seemed the result of a cultivated mind and personality.

After we drank espresso coffee the conversation got around to politics, a topic quite inevitable when Acorn is involved. And Cohen said, "Milton, if Communism is ever outlawed in Canada, and the Mounties round up all dangerous subversives, you'd be among the first arrested."

At the time I thought Cohen was right. But it has occurred to me since: wouldn't Acorn be too obviously and blatantly transparent a target? How could anyone imagine Milton Acorn as dangerous to the established order of things? He was always a comic-opera Communist, so tenderhearted he'd faint at the sight of blood, and pitied the beans he ate in greasy spoon restaurants.

Milton resembled litmus paper, the kind that changes colour on the least pretext. He was so sensitive he knew things before me, but his speech apparatus was too slow; I got around in front and always said them first. His face and body were those of a Neanderthal Man, the way you imagine that extinct humanoid. Now that he's dead, I think of Milton as a member of an advanced human species, not to be judged the way we judge those we meet every day at work or on the street. You couldn't judge him at all unless you knew him for some time.

In 1958 the Ryerson Press published Milton's *The Brain's the Target*. I had sent the manuscript to Lorne Pierce with a covering letter about Milton Acorn. However, the Ryerson general manager refused to believe that I wasn't Acorn myself, and that this wasn't just another gimmick to get a book published. My own *Pressed on Sand* had appeared in 1955, probably as a result of a poem of mine included in the earlier Carman-Pierce-Rhodenizer-edited anthology. And I had met Pierce around that time. He was a small and rather prissy man, but possessed his own kind of integrity. His opinion of me from this incident is obvious: I was not to be depended upon. As I recall, it was necessary to send the Ryerson manager a snapshot of Milton; and after seeing that, no one in his right mind could mistake Milton for me.

. . . . .

In 1960 I was having a difficult time at the mattress factory in Montreal East. I was forty-one years old, slightly fat and definitely out of shape. But I was large, weighing over 200 pounds, and this false front seemed a challenge to one of the French Canadians who worked downstairs in the two-storey factory. Beaudoin, the anti-Semitic upholsterer, had finally forced me to admit that lox, blintzes, bagels and kosher dill pickles were not my native fodder (I had pretended to be Jewish for his benefit). And Jacques, the downstairs worker, was good-naturedly annoyed by the presence of this large Anglo on what he regarded as his turf. He continually challenged me in his role as Bull of the Shop, to some kind of physical contest. Never overtly, but you can see what's in some people's minds.

Jacques was maybe twenty-five, weighed about 175, quite a bit lighter than me—but he walked like a jungle cat (am I building him up too much?). He'd come to my work table, lean on it and grin at me. I'd say hello in my best Anglo French, seeing into his mind and watching the little flashes of activity there. Beaudoin, perhaps still annoyed by my earlier imposture, would say meaningfully: "Jacques heap strong frog!"—mixing Hollywood Indian with Canuck slang.

Hymie Sloan was the foreman of that factory, and I thought him a good man. His uniform was always grey flannel pants, white shirt and bow tie. About forty, medium height and weight, kind of nondescript moustached, he was sometimes the target for Beaudoin's remarks about

Jews. But I thought Hymie ran that factory well: he was fair and impartial, he knew his job. And he played no favourites that I could see.

Mattress and box spring covers were assembled in the cutting room, on sewing machines operated by several women. Therese, the most beautiful girl in Montreal East, was a princess there. She blushed at the least suggestive word, when all the Johnston employees ate together in the tiny lunchroom provided. Tony, a fat little Sicilian, kept making unwelcome remarks to Therese; she turned her head the other way. Never having learned to keep my mouth shut, I told Tony to leave her alone. He cursed me in lurid Sicilian. Of course I didn't know what he was saying, although I could guess, and grinned at him in friendly fashion.

That weekend I went to see Milton Acorn at his pad near downtown Montreal. He wasn't home, so I went into a pool room on St. Lawrence Main hoping for a pickup game. There was a guy there who had no partner to play with. I noticed him aim a kick at a case of soft drink empties on the floor, but was too stupid to put two and two together. I tapped this guy on the shoulder to ask him to play a game of pool with me. The next thing I knew I was flat on my back.

He'd wound up with a full roundhouse swing when his own back was turned and I couldn't see what was coming, and landed a thundering right hand between my nose and forehead. The blow knocked all thought out of my head, leaving me with only feeble reflexes. I staggered to my feet, indignant and protesting. And scolded the guy, told him I had wanted to play a game of pool with him, called him down for hitting me. It seemed to have some effect. We played a game of snooker, while I tried not to bleed on the pool table when leaning over it. And sometimes felt quite dizzy. The management people left us strictly alone.

I've no idea what had gotten into the guy to make him swing on me like that. Perhaps he was drunk, on drugs, or his girl had left him. I don't know. I do realize I was a damn fool, and should have known better than to accost him like that without observing all the obvious signs of disturbance.

I took a cab to the apartment (Eurithe was away somewhere), staggered to a mirror and saw that my good looks and irresistible sex appeal were gone forever. The skin between forehead and nose was badly split and oozing blood slowly. I phoned a doctor I knew, luckily finding him at home. He told me to either come over and see him right away, or else leave the wound entirely alone and let it heal by itself. The latter course only if I didn't mind looking like a nearly dead battle casualty. I went to bed.

All this ungentlemanly activity was on a weekend. At work the following Monday, fat Tony the Sicilian looked at me in shocked wonder. I had a black eye that extended across the whole side of my face, one side looked like daylight, the other night. Tony thought his curses on me had taken full effect, something he hadn't really anticipated. Beaudoin grinned, asking what happened. "Ran into a door," I said. Of course nobody believed me, but that didn't matter. Therese, who was more beautiful than a straight seam, looked on me with shy wonder, as if I had fought for her honour and lost. We both looked away if either of us caught the other's eye.

Jacques was coming up to see me on the top floor at least twice a day. By this time I knew a gladiatorial contest was inevitable, and hoped Therese would attend the funeral. Jacques and I both could unravel what the other said to some extent, by dumb show and use of hands. Beaudoin would snigger occasionally to himself. He knew English perfectly, would say something to Jacques, then I think the opposite to me. They both would have that I-know-something-you-don't expression. I knew what they knew, but pretended complete ignorance. And Therese, I thought, would look at me with pity for what she knew was coming. Hymie, who knew everything, knew that I knew and therefore didn't have to warn me about Armageddon that was to come.

Jungle tom-toms wove their ominous music among the machines; the grapevine whispered that Anglo downfall was inevitable. I could see the pity with which everyone looked at me. Even I pitied me. I was much too old for this gladiator stuff. So how did I fall for it?

Jacques appeared one noon hour with his "Me Tarzan, you Jane" dialogue in *joual* Québécois. He wanted to arm wrestle. I thought what the hell, knowing this thing had to end somehow somewhere. And thought of charging admission, but the factory-arena milieu wasn't suited. I insisted that Jacques and I use our left arms, my own trusty left having defeated a score of RCAF pretenders to my non-existent title, during the Crimean War I think it was. Besides, my right arm was lame, which information I conveyed to Jacques in pantomime. Anyway, we arm wrestled; I won so quickly it was no contest. My victory being merely a matter of having more topside leverage derived from genetic inheritance.

Discontent furrowed the manly brow of the Bull of the Shop. He refused to understand how he'd been defeated so quickly, his wrist slapped down hard on the box spring assembly table not once but thrice. He suspected trickery. What did that Anglo have up his sleeve even if he didn't possess sleeves? And Jacques' prestige in Johnston's factory descended to the point where even little Tony dared grin at him when he dropped his luncheon sandwich. And Therese, whom I think he loved with dumb passion—Therese ignored him.

It was a predicament for him. And Jacques was not stupid, whatever impression I've given here. He was actually stronger than me in my forty-year-old state. I felt a little sorry for him, but not enough to cry surrender. That wouldn't have worked anyway. Jacques' own pride and prestige demanded that this Anglo must be humbled. Therefore battle was again joined during next day's lunch hour.

We clasped each other around the waist unlovingly. Jacques' arms felt like a dozen octopus tentacles, all trying to break my bones, and they very nearly did. I acted as I had once before, at that earlier mattress factory when a big eighteen-year-old was trying to cave in my chest: I let myself go, allowed myself to become completely limp. When the surprised Jacques swung me off my feet, I inserted one leg between his and managed to trip him. He thumped down onto the wooden floor with a bang that did my heart good. Maybe I even had a chance.

But I couldn't finish him off. Jacques leaped up like a youthful rubber ball among the machines, first one then the other having a brief advantage. But I was panting and nearly winded already. He was just too strong for me. If this thing continued more than six rounds nothing could save me but the referee—and we didn't have one.

Lunging and charging each other, we suddenly found ourselves in the men's john, and simultaneously each had the idea of trying to dunk the other's head in the toilet bowl. Summoning reserves of energy and endurance from a younger existence at this point, I wrestled the Bull to a standstill. And that's what it was, a standstill. Jacques had given up the idea that this Anglo was an easy mark, and I knew all along how lucky I was not to be defeated outright. So there we stood, hovering above that porcelain toilet bowl, clasped together unlovingly and sweatily . . . This was the *dénouement*, the climax of something or other, and we both knew it.

One of us started to laugh, or it may have been merely a chuckle. Then we both laughed. My own laugh by this time was from the conscious motive of putting a formal end to the contest. And we pointed at each other grinning, as if to say, "Look at you, what a silly damn fool I am and we are." Then I became conscious of a very strong odour—and it wasn't Chanel #5.

The battle was declared a draw. After that Jacques and I became, if not cordial, rather more wary of each other. I didn't intend to take another chance of getting my neck broken in that bastard's hands; and perhaps he wasn't quite so eager to break it. Perhaps there was some respect involved. His French and my English hadn't mingled, but our sweat certainly had.

Therese, whose beauty continued to be perfect as a straight seam, gazed on Jacques with favour. Her moon-pallor was sometimes tinged with an attractive pink, deriving from private thoughts. And while I do not recommend the confrontation of elephant bulls as an aid to *détente* between French and English, it worked for Jacques and I—up to a point anyway.

. . . . .

When I quit the mattress factory a few months later, Hymie Sloan shook hands. So did Beaudoin, despite a lingering dubiety as to my blood lines. Jacques, the necessary antagonist, came by to grin at me in memory of our Roman Games in the men's john. I suppose it's doubtful that we were friends exactly, but we sure as hell weren't enemies.

I surprised myself by quitting: the job had suddenly become unbearable to me. This seemed to happen all at once, one day I didn't feel it, the next day I did. There was a fever in my head to quit that factory. I returned to the house my wife and I had half-built in 1957, leaving her working at a nine-to-five job as a secretary in Montreal. I think she agreed that I had to get out of that factory. And Acorn came with me to Roblin Lake.

Several months before this I had applied for a small grant from the Canada Council, with Frank Scott and Layton supplying supporting letters. But that application was irrelevant to my quitting the job: something irrational had stirred in my brain. It said: stop wasting your life conventionally, waste it yourself, unconventionally. And I said: who are you to tell me what to do with my life? (You hafta treat these inner voice know-it-alls as if you have some rights too.) So I went.

The house at Roblin Lake still lacked most of the amenities—even the necessities—when Acorn and I arrived. It was late February, cold cold winter. An ancient wood stove created a small warm spot in the living room, and water would freeze at night a dozen feet from the stove. We went to the frozen lake for water, chopping a funnel-shaped hole in three and four-foot-thick ice, then scooping water out with a tin dipper. If it stormed between water expeditions, it was very difficult to locate the previous site. The lighting was still coal oil lamps; it's a wonder we didn't go blind.

My brother-in-law Gordon, who worked at the CPR sheds in Belleville, arranged for me to secure a couple boxcar loads of scrap lumber from the railway. I think that wood saved Milton and I from becoming frozen corpses. I managed to borrow an old truck, then Milton and I hauled wood to the lake. (Two boxcar loads!—such a huge quantity, it hung around the yard for several years. I used some of it for building a shed, which later became my workroom. We sawed some of our booty to woodstove size with a handsaw, lacking anything better; and just managed to cut enough to feed that ravenous stove and avoid freezing. Much of the wood was Douglas fir and gave an intense resinous heat.

During and between arguments about almost everything, Acorn and I worked at the house. All of Milton's opinions were red-hot gospel. In that cold half-built place—not merely gospel, but Communist Holy Writ direct from the mouth of Jesus-Karl Marx. I really didn't know a damn thing about Communism, but I was forced to learn very quickly. I couldn't let such dogmatism go unchallenged, and scraped the bottom of my brain, desperate for arguments and facts to refute Acorn.

Outside the frozen lake cracked from shore to shore with a sound like God's artillery; inside was nearly as noisy. The moment either Milton or I said anything at all, the other was bound to disagree. And to save my soul and spirit, I had to defend the most ridiculous theories and indefensible positions. What made things more difficult—Milton's arguments were getting to me. I was afraid he'd overwhelm my semantic defences, and I'd accept everything he said in total. I didn't care for that prospect.

But sometimes I was able to see where his skeins of thought were leading, then head him off at the cerebral pass. Though often he'd corner me with some obscure fact or astute bit of logic which I had entirely neglected. And the arguments continued, sometimes far into the night. The wild grape wine I had brewed in previous years declined noticeably in quantity.

I think Milton took himself more seriously than I took myself— which may have been a good thing, since no one else took either of us seriously. At the end of March there was a literary conference at Queen's University in Kingston, some fifty miles away. Milton wanted to go in order to escape me; I wanted him to go for the same personal reason. It was getting so we couldn't stand each other. He hitch-hiked to Kingston in near-zero weather.

I didn't hear from Milton for three days. I questioned him about it on his return. Too shy to attend the conference, he'd watched writers entering and leaving the university building; ate the sandwiches he'd taken with him; slept on a park bench near Lake Ontario and spoke to no one. He wouldn't actually mention his shyness as the reason he hadn't gone inside the conference building, but his face reddened when we talked about it.

I've seen Milton years later, when some of his shyness was gone, walking across the floor of a crowded room, quite oblivious to where he was and the other people around him. One could say he had spiritual qualities, which sounds ridiculous when you think of that red face and knotted body like an oak branch. But maybe not. Nobody ever thought I was very spiritual either.

· · · · ·

In 1962 Milton married Gwen MacEwen. She was very young, wrote poems herself, and appeared rather vulnerable to me. I stood up with them for the marriage at the old Toronto City Hall. After the ceremony they came down to stay with me at Roblin Lake.

This would be in early April 1962. Lake ice had melted along the shoreline, but remained unbroken a few feet away. You could see it under the water. Milton insisted he was going swimming in that cold lake; Gwen and I insisting that he remain on shore. We told him he'd freeze to death, and he damn near did. Wearing an old pair of swimming trunks and covered with goose pimples, Milton eased his body into the water inch by inch, knowing with every inch he shouldn't oughta done it.

But Milton had a point to make. He'd bragged about being a good swimmer and how healthful cold water was; and a real man from Prince Edward Island would not back away from a little zero water in Prince Edward County. Besides, his new wife was there to watch him being heroic—although he didn't mention that. Gwen and I watched the Acorn immersion fascinated, and to some extent enjoying Milton's discomfiture which he couldn't possibly escape by now.

"Warm water, Milt?" I enquired.

He looked at me miserably. "Go away," he said.

Mr. & Mrs. Acorn lived together on Toronto Island for a few months, then the marriage broke up. And Milton came to visit me for consolation. He was helping me with the installation of a television aerial on top of a shed roof near the house. We straddled the roof together, one foot on either side of the gable, holding the very heavy aerial at arms length above our heads. The plan was for both of us to walk slowly toward one end of the roof where the aerial was butted, raising the thing hand over hand, lifting it from horizontal to vertical.

At the moment of greatest strain Milton said, "Oh Al, I love her, I love her!" He started to drop the aerial, and it felt like I was holding up the sky alone.

"For god's sake! Milt, hold onto that fuckin aerial, or you'll kill us both!"

And Milton gave the matter some attention.

After a year or two of moping disconsolately between Toronto and Prince Edward Island, Acorn went to Vancouver. He stayed there several years. During that period Gwen MacEwen decided she wanted to get married again, but Milton wouldn't give her a divorce. Gwen asked me to help her, give an affidavit before a lawyer that—in the most delicate terms—her ex-husband had another girl friend. She told me that no one else would help her, that no one else *could* help her; and she felt desperate.

I pondered over that one long and hard. In the matter of marriage and divorce, I don't believe that either man or woman ought to hold onto the other if they don't want to be held. The feelings between people exist or do not exist, regardless of any law or religious mumbo-jumbo which have no real validity inside a human relationship.

However, my own role in the Acorn/MacEwen marriage break-up was ambiguous. I was a friend of both of them. In its crudest terms, to supply evidence against Milton resembled a doublecross so closely it made me acutely uncomfortable. But in the end I was responsible for enabling MacEwen to get her divorce.

. . . . .

My first meeting with Peggy Atwood remains vivid for me. She attacked me with a beer bottle and became somewhat emotional early in our encounter. Now I deplore this sort of thing in a social context, especially among young ladies. But she was very young at the time, and I forgave her.

The Atwood-Purdy incident occurred around 1963, when my wife and I visited Doug Jones at his summer cottage on Paudash Lake near Bancroft. We drove up there on a sunny summer day, in a rather carefree mood. But Doug wasn't home. His housekeeper told us he'd gone off to pick up his girl friend, who had just returned from England; they would be back shortly. So we waited.

When Doug and his lady drove into the yard, introductions were made and beer introduced into converse while we sat on the lake shore discussing Great Literature. Margaret Atwood was at this time a teaching assistant or junior prof at some university or other. A small girl, wearing horn-rimmed glasses for what I presumed was shortsightedness, she could have seemed mouselike. I hasten to add that she was not mouselike. Her personality was electric.

Doug Jones was as he always impressed me, resembling a tanned young athlete, and very likable with an unassuming manner. But somehow, while we sipped our beer and discussed great literature, Peggy A. received the mistaken idea that I was taunting her for being an academic. I deny this, of course. I *referred* to the condition only. However, this mistaken idea on her part caused a certain amount of hostility to enter our discussion about Shakespeare as a vaudeville comedian at the Mermaid Theatre.

As a result of this unwarranted assumption (that I was insulting her), Peggy grabbed her beer, shook it vigorously, then swizzled me with it. Full in the face.

Under these circumstances I felt retaliation on my part would be justified, but first appealed to Doug for arbitration in the matter. Even before he could deliver an impartial opinion I was nearly drowned. A great flood of beer, under strong muscular propulsion, struck my face and soaked my shirt, running down below the belt line.

The injustice of this treatment, the sheer failure of civilized reason, these things were shocking to one of my inoffensive nature. But I decided there was nothing for it and Ms. Atwood should suffer as well. I shook my own beer hard, and swizzled her with it. Surprise and outrage mingled on that lovely un-mouselike countenance—then battle was joined.

Peggy swizzled me when we met, jumping from the chair she sat in; time, you thief who love to get Beer into your lists, put that in!

It was a waste of good beer. But she kept doing it and I kept doing it. We ended up nearly drowned and very sticky from the stuff, wading in the shallows of Paudash Lake, filling our bottles with water to aid conservation (but it didn't swizzle worth a damn), holding each other clasped in an unloving embrace . . .

While Peggy stared at me with blazing academic eyes.

Eurithe and Doug Jones on the sidelines had watched our perform-ance with fascination—and with glazed expressions. "Glazed" in this case means they thought we were nuts.

In the early sixties the *Tish* group in Vancouver was making a small splash in Canadian literature. The group consisted of George Bowering, Frank Davey, Fred Wah, Robert Hogg, Jamie Reid and a few others, and the mimeographed *Tish* magazine was their literary outlet. Of those named, only George Bowering has grown much larger than he was then, far beyond his beginnings.

The kindest opinion would be to say that the *Tish* people were "influenced" by the Black Mountain movement in the US. The unkindest: they were slavish imitators. An American prof, Warren Tallman, who taught at UBC, conferred some legitimacy by writing an article about them called, "Wolf in the Snow." (It might be noted here, snow falls rarely in Vancouver.) A few years later, Tallman sat on the GG Award jury which selects their choice of the best book of poems published in Canada for that particular year. He never did get around to taking out Canadian citizenship.

Tallman organized a poetry festival at UBC in 1963, inviting many of the Black Mountain poets (the BMs also included the "beats" in Donald Allen's contemporary anthology), Robert Creeley, Robert Duncan, and several lesser lights—uh, I think "lights" would be a misnomer. The mentor and revered prophet of the so-called movement, Charles Olson, didn't show. The atmosphere of the time at UBC was redolent with rancid culture, I think mostly because of Tallman, the American prof.

I was visiting UBC then for a reading, my appearance being quite apart from the Black Mountain festival. George Bowering and I had been corresponding, and he was instrumental in securing my reading. Being very short of money, I was grateful, and gave him a copy of Irving Layton's first book (which I regretted later).

A *Tish* and BM party was in progress when I hit town. And here I should digress to say my ego was overweeningly high then, on a scale of one to ten, about six. My Contact Press book, *Poems for All the Annettes*, had just been published. I thought there'd been some kind of a breakthrough with that book, reaching another level of writing, with other levels still somewhere ahead. You must know when you've done something well, moved forward perhaps only an inch or so, allowing you to sight the far distance. You feel something surging inside you, this capability, this dragon, this incubus . . .

So back to the party. Everyone was sitting around on the floor of this bare room when I arrived, their backs against the wall. Booze was apparently in short supply, since the two bottles of rye I had unwisely brought evaporated quickly. Creeley was there, wearing his black eye patch, surrounded by worshippers. I thought that eye patch was pretty theatrical, but found out somewhat later it was necessary. Bowering came along about half an hour after my own arrival. The moment he entered the room Creeley sprang from the floor, attacking Bowering with both fists swinging. George fended him off easily, being a large and capable guy, but his feelings were badly hurt. You could see it in his face, since he rather idolized Creeley. And he left quickly.

Later in the evening, celebrations continued at Fred Wah's place on the UBC campus. Jammed into the car with others like bugs in a thimble, I asked Creeley unassumingly but rather insultingly why he didn't attack someone who didn't have quite as much respect for him as George Bowering. Creeley said placatingly that I didn't know the circumstances of all this—which was quite true.

At Wah's house (presumably rented from UBC for a minimal stipend to the promising poet), beer and booze flowed freely; I met everyone I hadn't met before; a record was played of the revered progenitor, Charles Olson, reading something that sounded like a laundry list. And Fred Wah asked me: didn't I think Olson was marvellous? (The question implied that Wah certainly thought Olson was marvellous.) Yeah, I said, he had a marvellous *voice*, my emphasis meaning that he read well but I didn't think much of his crummy poems.

Wah bristled and made immediate threatening gestures. Now generally I flee at about twenty miles an hour from menacing midgets, but this time I couldn't believe I was in any great danger. I said, in a disbelieving tone, "Are you gonna hit me, are you really gonna hit me?"

It was touch and go before he decided not to touch. We sat on the steps together, trying to decide our mutual intentions and basically held beliefs in God and the universe. But each watching the other from eyes' corner for hostile movement and sneak attack in ways we learned with our mothers' milk (I wonder: should "milk" be plural?).

I had to walk the several miles from UBC campus in Point Grey to the nearest bus-stop where I could get a ride back to town (there had been at Fred Wah's a noticeable disinclination to supply me with motor transport). I remember feeling some regret that I couldn't keep my well-justified opinions to myself, but as my wife has sometimes pointed out . . .

.　　.　　.　　.　　.

Again in the 1960s, Tallman organized another festival at UBC (the man was a real self-effacing demon for organizing things). And again the Olson clones who taught or had once taught at Black Mountain College in the US were the supernovas. Tallman published a tabloid periodical, advertising his festival in hushed religious terms, mentioning how marvellous it was we had these marvellous American writers mixing with their marvellous Canadian imitators. (Of course he didn't use the word "imitators.")

I nearly threw up after the second issue, using the first to clean up the mess. I wrote Tallman a letter, mentioning how wonderful he was, asking why he didn't arrange that these wonderful Canadian *Tish* poets get readings at wonderful American universities. I mean, why should Canada be the only beneficiaries of *Tish*. I went on to flatter Tallman inordinately, knowing that he would shyly welcome this well-deserved praise. To my regret I received no answer to these friendly overtures . . .

I read at UBC a year or two later; Marya Fiamengo arranged for my appearance. At the beginning of the reading I noticed Tallman among the standees in the aisle, no doubt there to count the house. I waved at him, but he didn't stay.

I'm sure all this sounds pretty silly. But don't let my lighthearted tone deceive anyone. I wasn't just a grouch making nasty remarks about Americans and their imitators who wanted to be noticed by a big league talent scout. And Tallman should never have been a member of the Canadian GG Award jury, without becoming a Canadian citizen. Olson himself I regard as a pretentious charlatan thrown up by his age; and such people appear in any age. Everyone is briefly impressed at the time, then inevitably bored and forgetful. They do their damage and disappear. The worst effect of the BM people was their quasi-religious overtones which made poetry sound like Holy Writ; and at the same time said, in effect, come and join the Chosen Ones, and you too can be a Great Poet. No work required. Now just say after me . . .

· · · · ·

Earle Birney and I were friends, despite the obvious differences in temperament and character. We got along well most of the time. Of course, there was a huge wall of reserve in him that you'd encounter if you pushed farther on some subjects than a tacitly agreed-on boundary. Birney was genial and expansive in the sense of a public man's expansive demeanour. And he growled at times. I think he did not suffer fools much, and could be very sarcastic. And was a "born teacher." I think he might well have instructed his own mother while he was still in the womb about her own pregnant behaviour, the way she should conduct herself in order to ensure a normal birth.

At times I felt awe of Birney, sometimes impatience, perhaps even a little fear, but always respect. He was obdurate, stubborn, combative and occasionally unfriendly; all these things to the degree that he resembles descriptions I have heard about myself when young: and denied vociferously. He was a friend.

(And here I must explain my use of the past tense: he suffered a stroke several years ago, and it's very unlikely he'll ever recover.)

Earle Birney took full responsibility for both himself and other people. He didn't shift blame that I ever heard of. I hate to say that he was a "father" to his students. It sounds awful, like a professional do-gooder, a glib never-tell-it-like-it-is politician. Earle was too outrightly mean and curmudgeonly miserable at times to be anything but a poet. Then he was human and generous, and you loved him. And sometimes we changed mental places, and both felt what the other was feeling, at the same exact moment . . .

I was visiting Vancouver in the early sixties (George Woodcock had got me a poetry reading at UBC, if I remember rightly), staying at a friend's apartment when the friend was off skiing. I was asleep, and heard this loud knocking while I was still at the edge of consciousness, and could have teetered either way. The night before, Peggy Atwood (she was teaching at UBC), a friend of hers and myself had visited a Main Street cabaret, and I'd arrived home very late. And now this awful noise that wouldn't stop!

It was Birney, of course. When I got myself together at the door, he told me about this young student of his who hadn't showed up for classes that morning, and Earle was concerned about her welfare. She was an exchange student from Japan. And the girl's husband, an engineering student also at UBC, was perhaps mistreating her? Their apartment was just down the street. Earle wanted me to go with him there, to ensure that nothing was seriously wrong. I got dressed hurriedly and accompanied him.

The lady's apartment door was locked, and repeated hammering evoked no response. Whereupon Earle rousted out the building superintendent across the road, impressing the man mightily with his credentials as professor and pillar of the community, doubtless also a crony of Vancouver's mayor. The super produced a master key, unlocking the apartment door, then disappeared.

Sadly, the door was still secured by an inside chain. That didn't stop Professor Birney. He talked coaxingly through the partly open door, as the sirens sang to Odysseus, as the nightingale sang to Keats and Fanny whatever-her-name-was. It worked too. The lady emerged first (she was a knockout) wearing a kimono; then the man, the husband, he in those ju jitsu-looking pyjamas that make you think the wearer is about to smash a concrete block with bare hands.

Birney talked softly and sweetly to the lady. The husband and I stood off to one side, in deference to seniority. And I felt, oh, otherworldly—is this really happening? As time passes, will I look back on this moment as something to marvel at? The husband, heavily built and slightly menacing in aspect, looked at me. Carefully benign, I glanced back at him; and shrugged. He shrugged too. (What does that mean—that we are men of the world?) And Earle talked on to the beautiful Japanese lady . . .

It was an incident you go back to, mentally examine its details, assess the significance of them. Probably the incident has no significance, but I was so much impressed by Earle at the time! Responsibility. Concern for other people. I have watched Earle ever since, as a friend and exemplar, knowing there's something in his make-up that will forever surprise me, the locked door that may or may not open if you have the proper latchkey.

. . . . .

There is probably a certain venom in my nature which I am not always able to keep under control in social relations. A case in point is David Bromige, whom I loathe wholeheartedly. In the late 1950s, when I published two chapbooks with Ryerson Press, Bromige reviewed them in *Canadian Literature*. He keel-hauled and flogged them in his review, infecting them with syphilis and gonorrhea; he bastinadoed them with poisonous verbs on the soles of their feet. One might even suspect he didn't like my writing. I think the principal reason was because I refused to make obeisance to the One True God of all the Black Mountain Boys, Charles Olson. (May he R.I.P.)

"Basta," I said to myself morosely, reading the Bromige review. "Je me souviens!"

Sure enough, I did remember. Many years later, a big batch of books arrived for me to review in *Queen's Quarterly*. To my great joy, there were two small books by David Bromige among them. Writing the review I explained my bias in the matter, then said, "These two books are fully as bad as I had hoped and expected." But I softened this reasonable and measured criticism by explaining that the books made mediocrity seem a virtue, and they weren't as bad as I had said. But nearly.

Paper moving at high velocities exploded in the editor's face at *Queen's Quarterly*. Several writers Bromige had once flattered wrote protesting letters from the US. There was talk of closing the undefended border. I got a letter from Bromige myself, informing me he wanted to start a dialogue, mentioning one poem in his book and asking pointedly if I had ever come close to writing such a great poem. I hadn't, and didn't want to start a dialogue with the bastard either. It might never end.

Earle Birney had received one of the Bromige howls of protest, and it was the only one that concerned me even slightly. Earle wasn't sure of my literary morality in this instance. I hadn't been much concerned with morality, enjoying my "fully as bad" description of Bromige too much. I pointed out Earle's own dislike of criticism, whether direct or implied, citing his listing the long string of rejections for his poem, "David," in the preface to his 1966 *Selected Poems*. He smiled at me, with a good nature that grows even more pleasant in retrospect.

In 1969 I edited Milton's book, *I've Tasted My Blood*, for Ryerson Press. It was, I thought, as did several other people, a strong candidate for the Governor General's Award. George Bowering got the GG instead. That wasn't exactly an injustice to Acorn; but Bowering was much younger than Milton, and was likely to have other opportunities to win the top Canadian literary award.

In 1970, therefore, some of Milton's friends got together and threw a testimonial dinner for him at Grossman's Tavern in Toronto. Milton sat at the head table with Layton, Atwood, Eli Mandel and a few others beside him. A large silver medal dangled from his neck on a purple ribbon. It bore the words, "Milton Acorn, The People's Poet." This medal approached the dimensions of a small-size dinner plate. In front of the ceremonial table swirled the usual clientele of Grossman's, ordinary beer-drinkers and bums, dead beats and free loaders, even a few genuine workers. And, of course, poets and invited guests.

The evening wore on, with newspaper reporters reporting, and CBC men, wearing that questing look of basset hounds, searching for someone who knew more than they did. Layton made a speech; Mandel made a speech; and so did Acorn. Milton displayed his medal with obvious pride; there was applause and beer. By ten o'clock Grossman's was so jammed that waiters had to hold beer trays high above their heads. The tavern seemed full of swaying yellow suns.

I was escorting a girl I knew through this dense human crush to the lady's john, when a guy hove in sight from the port side and said to me: "Fuck off!" It was obviously a case of mistaken identity.

Addressing him mildly I said, "Do I know you?"

Again he repeated the same instructions, of dubious benefit to myself, and I'm afraid he had something of a one-track mind. Of course, by this time a slight suspicion had entered my mind that this man had no friendly intentions. I pushed him in the chest, quite vigorously, propelling him into the laps of some seated beer-drinkers. They pushed him back toward me indignantly, thereby setting the stage for open hostilities.

Then a couple of waiters spotted the guy—having mistaken me for Mayor Dennison because they'd seen me swallow a microphone earlier between beers. And having some regard for the dignity of high municipal office—they threw the jerk out. My friend proceeded to the lady's john.

That party at Grossman's was half farce and half solemn event. In my mind the two were difficult to separate. Scores of friends paid tribute to Milton: CBC and newspaper reporters, the drunk with the two-word soundtrack, and beer-drinkers who had fallen in love at an early age with those swaying yellow suns.

Milton himself moved through the tavern like a one-man procession, a little swacked, happy about being "The People's Poet," medal dangling on that purple ribbon, soon to be stained with soup. Perhaps that was the strangest part of all in this boozy setting—the proud medal.

There are human differences I'll never fully understand: but Acorn's poems that night transcended such differences, and made Grossman's Tavern briefly only a roomful of listening people. I remember his lines about life itself being a gamble: "I play my mauled rainbeaten pack plus near three billion others, all to win." That night at Grossman's, Acorn won.

. . . . .

In the late 1960s my wife and I mounted a home-made camper on a pickup truck and drove to Newfoundland, picking wild raspberries along the road, stopping for the night in old gravel quarries, buying salmon and cod from fishermen, getting eaten ourselves by no-see-ums . . . The land seemed endless, despite the finitude of road maps. One is misled by maps into feeling that anything that can be crammed onto paper and seen there in its entirety can't be that impressive in actuality.

But you traverse a country foot by foot in shoe leather, and mile by mile with automobile tires. The elastic landscape stretches and stretches, the mind can't take it all in . . . When I wrote poems along the road, once again there was the feeling of mapping the country, giving it an additional persona and identity. Not ego in doing so, but in the naming of things there is a knowing, a forging of bonds between . . . I mean: you can get some feedback from a dog or cat or human, a word or growl or meow—but from the land there is nothing but a great silence, unless you build a word-bridge to help you understand a thing that may be beyond understanding . . .

At Port aux Basques, the ferry docking point in Newfoundland, a workers' strike was in progress. Eurithe drove our camper right into the mist of the strikers. She didn't know, I didn't know, we hadn't seen any signs until just before we almost killed some picketers. She stopped short of actually striking anyone, and we were thankful. But what the incident did, I had a point of rebuttal whenever Eurithe attacked me verbally for something I didn't admit to anyway, and I always had the second-last word.

After a stopover at small-town Deer Lake, we drove north over the dirt roads: three-car ferries across wide rivers, eating raspberries and salmon, drinking Newfie Screech in gravel quarries (just me), trying to understand the softspoken music of regional speech. Along our route on Newfoundland's west coast, nearly everyone spoke French; and there we spent some time exploring kitchen middens of animal bones left behind by the extinct Beothuk Indians.

One of the reasons for our Newfoundland trip was the Norse site at L'Anse aux Meadows, discovered by Norwegian explorer and writer Helge Ingstad. Along the road I was writing a review of Farley Mowat's *Westviking* for a literary magazine. When we arrived, Ingstad was amazingly still there, puttering around the Norse site with his archaeologist wife, Anne Stine. White-haired and bony looking, I thought Ingstad was. Lean with high cheekbones and ruddy complexion; both he and his wife cordial to these southern strangers.

The only physical traces of the ancient Norse, dating back to about 1000 AD, were outlines in the earth, from which overlying turf had been removed, exposing the stillness of one-time movement, places where people had once crossed and re-crossed. Such a strong absence that it felt like a presence. A Norse spindle whorl and some bog iron were discovered here, which Carbon 14 tests dated to the 11th century. Ingstad thought Leif the Lucky and his people had settled briefly here, and that this was "Vinland the Good."

How can one be sure? Farley Mowat said he thought Ingstad had "planted" the spindle whorl to authenticate his findings. And that the Norse site had been a whaling station, much later than Ingstad claimed. I wrote the explorer in Norway, asking about the possibility of whalers at L'Anse aux Meadows. His reply said the coastal waters were much too shallow for deep-bodied whaling ships to remain offshore while their crews constructed permanent settlements.

I don't know. Who could possibly know—despite the evidence either way? But I like to think that is the place where Leif the Lucky once stopped on his westward wanderings; and I was there too.

On our return trip back to Ontario, we stopped at St. John, New Brunswick. I wanted to visit this wonderful new poet, who was about to say things differently than anyone else, as you always expect a new guy to do. Nightingales and frogs will leap from his mouth; at least it occurs to you that they might.

Alden Nowlan. He was from rural New Brunswick, the country of his poems, which were often short lyrics about what a strange God there was, over or under his special earth. Greek tragedy in the poor-white hinterland of nowhere, here in the Maritimes. The stuff he wrote hit you, caused you to reverse his thoughts back to yourself. Nowlan's small chapbook was *The Rose and the Puritan*, a kind of paean to his own puzzlement at being alive, a puzzlement I shared.

Alden worked for the St. John daily newspaper. I phoned him there, arranging to visit him and his wife at their apartment (luckily he'd seen my own name in a magazine somewhere, and therefore knew I was some kind of writer). I had felt a stirring in me when I read Nowlan's poems. Like jealousy, like he was me, like he was my brother.

And we sat there in the Nowlan living room. Alden and his wife, my wife and myself. And we sat there. After initial greetings, Nowlan said scarcely anything at all; the silence hung and hovered. I'd speak and the sounds I made damn near echoed. Eurithe talked to Nowlan's wife; I did too, out of necessity.

He was a young guy, twenty-six or twenty-seven I guess; large, about my size but with an imposing presence I don't have. I kept feeling expectant of him, hoping for the marvels of intimate human converse; then I looked away, thinking I'd made him nervous. But if he wasn't, I was. It occurred to me: maybe he'd conceived an instant dislike for this visitor from the wilds of hogtown Toronto (but I ain't from Toronto). I don't know, I don't know. Mere simplistic shyness? No, that couldn't be. Not this marvellous lyric poet I had loved and was now beginning to hate for putting me through a torturous boring endless era prior to human speech.

But Alden recovered his voice when we left, and said goodbye. He must've thought I was a city slicker, and he a country boy from Hartland, New Brunswick. I had expected too much from him on the basis of his poems. We were both cordial, and that's enough.

Returning from the southern US in tandem with Ron Everson and his wife several years later, we stopped at Fredericton. This was principally to visit Nowlan, a poet much-admired by Everson. Before Nowlan and Alfred Bailey arrived at our hotel, we laid in a considerable supply of beer along with a tubful of ice to keep it cool. A little prior to this meeting I'd been reading a Nowlan column in the Atlantic Advocate. This column venerated Hollywood's John Wayne, the movie actor, describing him as an example for youth and an admirable specimen of American manhood.

Our guests arrived; we settled down for conversation and beer. (Yeah, Alden was in full verbal bloom by this time.) I raised the subject of John Wayne shortly after the amenities: asking Nowlan if the right-wing movie actor also made a good role model for Canadian kids. A slight heat was generated by Nowlan on behalf of John Wayne. I said, "But Alden, doesn't your favourite actor solve all problems, difficulties of any kind, with a sock on the jaw, a bullet or a kiss? The latter if it's a young lady or a horse. Do you really approve of such methods for settling disagreements?"

This was difficult to answer. For the next hour and a half or so, Nowlan confined his verbal sallies to Ron Everson or my wife. He responded to direct questions from me once or twice, but that was all. I became a mere spectator at my own party, although Alfred Bailey and I held small converse during the rare silences.

Nowlan had an operation for cancer a few years later, his voice becoming thickened and distorted as a result. I remember sitting at a lunch table with Nowlan and Milton Acorn at Blue Mountain near Collingwood. Acorn's voice was not a good example of faultless diction and bell-like clarity: his speech resembled a drunken tugboat in a bad storm. During consumption of food and consequent rather muffled speech, I attempted to translate Milton to Alden and vice-versa with limited success, sometimes having to improvise what I *thought* they said between dessert and coffee. The sound level of our table was high; I noticed other guests glancing at us curiously.

A few years later I had a series of readings in the Maritimes. Nowlan was writer-in-rez at the University of New Brunswick in Fredericton. Fred Cogswell and I met him in the restaurant there. It was a Sunday and you couldn't order drinks. But boy-scout Alden had a forty ounce bottle of rye concealed under the table close to his leg. We sampled it pretty freely, Alden perhaps a little more freely than Cogswell and I.

When an expensive coffee table book of poems and poet-portraits was projected by Monk Bretton in Toronto—a really fancy job, folio size on handmade paper—Doug Jones was editor and Morton Rosengarten did the portraits. When Morton came down to A-burg for my portrait we got along well; he stayed with me several days, claiming I was a difficult subject. We played some pool in Belleville, and the artist was a shark (which means expert in pool hall vernacular). Morton had already done the Nowlan portrait, and said Alden told him he didn't care how bad he looked as long as it was better than Al Purdy. I said that wouldn't be difficult, since all photographs made me look like a drunken hermit with a bad hangover.

Alden and I corresponded desultorily. I believe he may have regarded me as a rival, although I didn't feel that way myself (poems are not a four-minute mile or a thirty foot pole vault). We didn't talk freely, I felt there was always a guardedness. We were friendly, but not quite friends.

When he died—much too soon—and I reviewed his *Collected Poems* in *Books in Canada*, I said he was an excellent poet, but fell short of being the best in Canada. This review attracted several letters to the magazine critical of me for writing it. I found that a bit surprising.

I think Nowlan was, and is, unique, no one quite like him. His early stuff was marvellous; his later, written as much out of memory as from his immediate feelings, was less good. But he and Milton Acorn were the Maritimes' best by a long shot. Replacements? There are none.

· · · · ·

I have never learned to keep my mouth shut—as my wife has sometimes pointed out. This is a basic flaw in my character, and more than once has proved dangerous.

Some twenty years ago I gave a reading in Halifax, afterwards attending a party hosted by the sponsors. I was warned in advance that I might be buttonholed at the party by a pest my host called "the most boring man in Canada." Sure enough, I was and he was.

I can't remember what he looked like or his name, but after perhaps twenty minutes of listening to the guy's unending monologue I said in near-desperation, "You're the most boring man in the world!"

And that was the end of that.

Ten years ago I had another reading in Halifax, this time sponsored by one Andy Wainwright of the English Department at Dalhousie University. When I was at my hotel before the reading, a lady named Bonnie Purdy who did interviews for the local television station phoned me, and we talked about a Purdy genealogy. She told me the last two Purdy males in the family had been nabbed by the English on the Scottish border and hanged for sheep stealing.

"Well," I said, or something like that. It's encouraging to know your own criminal tendencies have roots in the past.

"And the two surviving Purdy sisters," Bonnie Purdy went on, "asked their husbands to take the name of Purdy so the family wouldn't die out. And that accounts for you and I being here today."

It also accounts for me being so wishy-washy—the Purdy blood was adulterated by two spineless husbands. But it's a good story.

I did the reading, and next day met Andy Wainwright at a pub as pre-arranged. From there we would drive to Halifax Airport, and I would fly back home. But it turned out Andy didn't have time, had to teach an English class or something. He'd arranged for someone else to take me instead. The "someone else" came by shortly, and we started out for the airport together. While we were passing one of those deep rock cuts in the highway my driver said: "Do you remember telling me I was the most boring man in the world?"

If I'd been driving, the car might have left the road. As it was, glancing at those rock walls, it occurred to me that the bones of ancient sea creatures had provided the ingredients for this limestone graveyard. I remained silent, the car's tires sounding abnormally loud. My driver looked at me inquiringly. I avoided his eyes, staring straight ahead.

"Well, perhaps —" I started out. Then: "Maybe I —" But that wasn't right either.

Silence *fell* like italics. And I mulled over the strong possibility that I might be making things worse than ever with these aborted beginnings. If the driver himself ever completed those two beginnings of sentences, "Perhaps" and "Maybe," would there be any hope of a long and happy existence for me? One thing though, at this point in time he wasn't boring me.

If anyone reading this brief anecdote can tell me what I should have said on that awkward occasion, I'll reward them with a valuable prize.

Perhaps. Maybe.

. . . . .

I forget dates. But once, while I was staying at Birney's Vancouver apartment in his absence, someone phoned the famous poet. A playwright, name of Beverly Simons, was reading one of her plays that night in the wilds of West Vancouver. And since Earle wasn't at home, I was invited to be the playwright's guest instead.

I thought it was very nice of Beverly Simons to invite me to her home. I'd been a bit claustrophobic and *agora*phobic in Earle's absence, so I accepted the invite to this cultural event. A lady with a car picked me up in Vancouver. We drove seemingly for many miles, over the Lion's Gate Bridge, through the rain forest and tall mountains—ending up I don't know where. But a party was in progress.

The playwright was young and attractive; her husband, a criminal lawyer, was cordial. They showed me around the house; I thought it was very close to palatial. At the party where I was introduced, there was some degree of social drinking going on, something of which I do not disapprove.

The playwright read her play, and read it very well. The lights had been turned down, while the audience sprawled on the carpeted floor or leaned against the nearest softness. I suppose my attention flagged a bit after the first hour. In any event, I was considering a stealthy exit to wherever they kept the beer. But that wasn't very feasible. I was hemmed in by many softnesses, arms and legs and torsos of unknown gender.

There was an intermission, during which I supplied myself with what I felt was sufficient beverages. Then Ms. Simons made an announcement: she planned to read another play, being a very productive lady. And a great feeling of injustice swept over me. I thought: this is not right, it's not infra dig or proper protocol or something. I mean, sure, the playwright had ability: but there'd been no warning beforehand that things would continue on and on . . . And wondered: would I ever do this myself, foist myself on an audience that couldn't escape? Virtuously, I decided that I would not do such a thing. Then lights dimmed, the first dramatic lines reached my ears . . .

Slightly overcome by my own sense of drama, I decided that my integrity was at stake. And wriggling past all the prone bodies I snuck out the back door so quickly that the old adage, "one for the road," slipped my mind. And sans beer, the road back to the bridge was black, no moon or stars that I could see above the dark forest. I suppose the time would be about ten p.m.

So I walked. And I walked. Through the mountains and rain forest; my only blessing was that it didn't rain. There were no streetlights, and only one car on the road, going the wrong way. I had to dive into the dark jungle to avoid being knocked down. But there were houses along the way, glimmers of porch lights deep in the forest, with dogs snarling death to strangers. One of the beasts even followed me a short distance, scaring the hell outa me while I thought of cougars.

It must have been two hours of hard slogging before I glimpsed the Lion's Gate lights. My feet hurt, my pride hurt on accounta being so stupid, and I had a generally low opinion of myself at this point. When a car travelling the right way came along, the driver must've assessed my physical condition of near-exhaustion by my crumpled look. Obviously of superior intellect and kindness, he stopped.

"Been to a party?" he inquired on our way over the bridge.

I mentioned Beverly Simons' play-reading party.

"Is she any good?" he said.

"Very fine writer," I assured him. And thought: to hell with integrity.

When we came back from Greece and Turkey in early spring of 1970, I had gathered together a fairly large collection of my old "love poems," to which I added several new ones. Irving Layton's anthology of Canadian love poems, entitled *Love Where the Nights are Long*, had appeared a couple of years before. It was a large-size book in white buckram, with drawings by Harold Town, very handsome. And I thought, what a good idea! Now if Town will just do some drawings for my own book! I sent the manuscript of love poems to McClelland & Stewart, and outlined my proposal to Jack McClelland in a letter.

Not long after that, Jack McClelland, his beautiful editor, ex-Hungarian Anna Szigethy (now Porter), and Harold Town came to visit me at Roblin Lake. They intended to discuss the proposed book. After drinks and dinner—which Eurithe managed extremely well on the front lawn—we settled down to talk. Both Town and Jack McC. had been enthusiastic about such a book in letters, but that was before they had read the poems. Now that they had, there was an odd atmosphere among my visitors. Jack's manner seemed a little embarrassed; but as yet nothing had come out into the open. And I wondered what they were trying to tell me without actually telling me anything.

After a long pause my revered publisher fixed me with cold blue eyes and said: "Your poems are hard-boiled. We had expected them to be romantic."

I was a bit stunned. But thinking it over quickly: my wife has the same complaint about me, although I hadn't expected Jack McC. to feel that.

"Uh, romantic?" I said falteringly. (At that moment, fifty mounted horsemen in the red desert rode their Barbary steeds to where their chieftain waited. Dismounting, they drew swords and swore fealty . . .)

"Romantic?" I said wonderingly.

"No, hard-boiled," Jack McC. said.

Harold Town nodded agreement. "You're just not romantic," he said, giving me a kind look and drawing his scarlet-lined cloak around him with a stylish flourish.

We had a few more drinks, then another proposal was unveiled: that I should edit a collection of twenty poets of my own choosing, with Town to supply portraits of each writer. In addition, I would write a critical and deeply analytical introduction for the book, which would contain all the academic qualities so deeply inherent in my own work.

This anthology job was apparently the best I could extract from my visitors. I did mention that it was a kind of sop, in order to keep me happy. This of course was denied. We had some more drinks. Town told a story of his snowmobile breaking down in a cold winter landscape, skiers swooping down on him much too close to the disabled vehicle, which he was working on to get started. The skiers annoyed him. He uncoiled a long black bullwhip he kept at hand for such emergencies, lashing them with it whenever they ventured within range.

I suppose Town told this story in order to demonstrate that he was a dangerous man and should not be tampered with. I think it was aimed at me. There was something cold and ominous in his demeanour in which, nevertheless, enjoyment of the skiers' discomfiture was evident. Later in the evening Jack McC. asked Town to sign my copy of *Love Where the Nights Are Long*, one of the unsigned review copies. Town refused, as he had earlier when I asked him.

"Oh, go on and sign it, Harold," Jack said. Town refused.

A few months passed. My book of love poems, *Love in a Burning Building*, came out sans Town, but with a preface intended to be amusing in which I described the incident. I did some desultory work on the anthology I was editing, becoming slowly aware of a great silence which emanated from Toronto. I did not like that silence, because it strongly indicated that something had gone wrong. And I had no contract from McStew for the new antho. But I knew that Town had been doing portraits. One of Earle Birney looked as if part of his face had rotted away. Another of Layton looked exactly like Golda Meir just after she'd delivered stern directives to the Israeli cabinet to wash their necks and clean their fingernails before making war on the Arabs.

I phoned an editor friend at McStew, John Newlove. He confirmed there was trouble re the Purdy-edited anthology, but wouldn't say more than that editorial integrity had to be maintained. Of course, I knew the trouble Newlove referred to was Town, but after Harold's earlier signing-refusals I couldn't fathom what new pitfalls he had designed for me.

I made an appointment with Jack McC. in that large and expensively appointed office which always slightly intimidates me. I had my audience. The crux of the matter, Jack said, his pale blue eyes fixing me intently, was that Town wanted seventy-five per cent of the take from the Purdy/Town anthology. I listened like a three-years child as Jack spoke reasonably, to the effect that Town was doing most of the work, these poet-drawings required onerous hours of toil and sweat and tears . . . Listening to McClelland, I felt much sympathy for that great artist who spent huge chunks of his time giving away genius to the waiting world. But not for free. For seventy-five per cent, at least in this case.

Like a gentleman, I forbore to point out that Harold Town was a friend of Jack's. But that's not like me either. I probably did point it out. Anyway, I said no, refusing Town three-quarters of whatever there was. Royalties had not been discussed during our historic meeting at Roblin Lake (money, in the process of executing great works of art, is always farthest from my own mind). These anthologies really don't sell worth a damn, and there wouldn't be much money involved anyway. But I had the distinct feeling that I was being pushed around, shuffled aside, as if what I thought wasn't very important. It probably wasn't, but I was annoyed: I refused to lie down and accept that kind of shit.

A friend gave me the name of a lawyer who was said to have some literary expertise. I went to see him and outlined the situation. Then my lawyer had a couple of lunches with Jack McC., during which they discussed the Purdy/Town situation amicably. I asked for a thousand bucks recompense for my work on the now-aborted anthology. Otherwise, I would find myself a new publisher: but that was probably understood, not stated openly. Jack offered $500. I said no. My lawyer had another lunch with Jack McC.—he said yes, this time I got my thousand bucks.

And I'd better explain all this a little. It's not that I am in any way important or "world-class"; but I *had* won the GG Award a few years before. And besides, it would look kinda bad for the publisher when I departed to Oxford Press (if they'd have me), or somebody else, sobbing bitterly and crying foul. So Jack paid off, like a gentleman, under protest of course. And my ambivalent feelings about him were subdued in respect. You pays your money and keeps your mouth shut, which would have been very difficult for me if I'd been him.

I asked my lawyer how much I owed him for his service. He said I owed nothing. I said, how come? He told me he liked my stuff, and therefore didn't want to charge. Well, that knocked me out a little. That doesn't sound like lawyer-behaviour at all. It's one of the nicer compliments I've received. And I can't remember that lawyer's name twenty years later. Obviously, he had marvellous literary taste.

Lights from the past continually flash back into your life now. Seemingly time is not a factor in remembering these incidents; they return to me all the way from 1921 and from yesterday. Ten or twelve years ago my wife and I were in Montreal. The original reason for that trip is forgotten, supplanted by the memory of a visit to Frank and Marian Scott's place in Westmount.

In Frank Scott's own long-ago past, he duelled with Premier Duplessis in Quebec courtrooms. Duplessis' Quebec government of the time was very hostile to the religious sect of Jehovah's Witnesses, often arresting them as they handed out their literature on street corners. Frank Roncarelli, a restaurant owner in Montreal, would sometimes supply bail for these jailed people of his own religious faith. On Premier Duplessis' explicit instructions, Roncarelli's liquor license was cancelled. And in Montreal it's nearly impossible to operate a prosperous restaurant without serving liquor.

Roncarelli got in touch with lawyers Frank Scott and Leo Stein. They fought the Quebec premier in the law courts, and won. Years later a television play appeared on CBC about the Roncarelli case. It featured, of course, Frank Scott. Eurithe and I were invited to Scott's place the night this play was produced.

Everyone was there; Roncarelli and his sons; and Leo Stein who had argued the case in court. And of course Marian and Frank Scott, the latter ebullient, almost smug, his justified reputation about to be verified by the idiot box.

I loved Frank Scott that night, and he loved himself too; it was a delight to see him enjoying himself so much. Of course you couldn't criticize the television play as a play, not in these circumstances. Frank's own comment: "Leo Stein won that case." Sure. But that night all of us were there to celebrate Frank Scott. He was too.

. . . . .

When Ryerson Press sold out to McGraw-Hill in 1969, having borrowed money from a Canadian bank to finance the transaction, I broke my contract with Ryerson and withdrew a book of mine they had. Jack McClelland, scenting golden publicity that might sell books, decided to publish *Fifteen Winds* himself. Peter Newman, an ardent Canadian nationalist, was editor of the *Toronto Star* at this time. Jack McC., masterminding the whole affair, arranged that I be smuggled stealthily into Newman's office, while sugarplum CIA agents danced in my head. I was rehearsed on what the story should be by Newman, a dark guy with huge eyebrows, then was passed on to a reporter for further interrogation.

Then I was stashed away in Anna Szigethy's apartment, in case

McGraw-Hill emissaries disguised as reporters should attempt to kid-nap me off to their dungeons under the old Don Jail. I snoozed through the hot afternoon on Anna's bed in the central Toronto suburbs—awak-ing to repeated knocks downstairs. Migawd, I thought, McGraw-Hill agents! Or the cops? I dunno what I thought; my brain buzzed with sleep and nervous terror induced by Jack McClelland. I snuck into the bedroom closet, hiding among Anna's silken underthings. (It was quite pleasant.) Eventually the disturbing noise stopped. It was probably the postman.

· · · · ·

Peter Newman. After the Ryerson sellout, I worked for him at *Mac-lean's*. An audience with him in that ten-acre office there—was like meeting an eastern potentate. For Peter was an exotic, those great overhanging bushy eyebrows like shutters over a harem. And yet he was shy. But it was a shyness that by an act of will he overcame. Forty years old then, author of best-selling political books, rich and famous, so patriotic he exuded maple syrup on the bed sheets at night. Able to say anything at all in print, insult or compliment all the great nonentities, and a nice guy too. But he couldn't prove it, couldn't let himself go, was never at ease amongst all us lesser beings. I admired him.

Newman gave me remunerative stuff to do when I needed the money, like work on a tourist brochure of Ontario; articles for *Maclean's*. The *Maclean's* articles were sometimes a lot of fun, riding a fishpacker through Juan de Fuca Strait off the southern tip of Vancouver Island in rough weather. Unused to the sea (I never did get used to it), I threw up my dinner in the Strait, threshing in my bunk so sick I wanted to die (there is nothing quite so awful as sea-sickness). It was very romantic.

And flying north from Port Renfrew, a little fishing town on the southern end of Vancouver Island. In a little Cessna aircraft. It was like clinging to a wooden two-by-four in mid-air. At Tofino, writing about the gill netters, the ass-ends of their boats tilted down and almost sinking with the weight of salmon; at Namu, clinging to the edge of mainland mountains: wandering the wooden catwalks, wandering among the trees to bunkhouses in the rain forests in deep silences . . .

I loved it. And felt I was mapping the country, long after those early cartographers, traversing the savage land Stan Rogers sang about. Not mapping it the way they did, but naming things, saying I was there, adding something personal to the map's cold nomenclature of heights and distances. I hope that doesn't sound silly or trivial. But we weave ourselves and our lives around such real and yet mythical places, strange multitudinous sounds in our ears seeping home into memory . . . Thinking about all this, I feel very privileged. And also feel a little defensive about the feeling itself.

. . . . .

There have been many trips to many countries, where I wrote poems. In Japan, around 1970, I stayed at Hiroshima for several weeks, feeling cut off from all human communication because of language. But that wasn't completely true: a little girl in a public park with her friends approached me daringly and asked what time it was. She wondered, of course, if the large barbarian would bite, but more than anything else she wanted to showoff for her small friends. In a way, this sequestered feeling I had was an advantage, since I lived with and in my own feelings as a result. It's rather uncanny to be a distinct oddity as I was, and yet be invisible from human company because of the inflections of sound.

. . . . .

In 1971 I went on a reading tour of the western Arctic, with stops at Inuvik, Hay River, Yellowknife and Fort Smith. At Inuvik, perched on the spongy Mackenzie delta area, all buildings sat on wooden stilts above the permafrost—I read at the town library. Maybe forty or fifty people showed up, among them a man named Ross. That is, of course, my mother's maiden name, and I was rather pleased at the prospect of meeting this possibly distant relative. Ross had written and published an article about me (he said), and that too was pleasing and a bit surprising. I preened a little, thinking gee whiz, maybe even the trappers and wilderness hunters have read "Home Made Beer" over their tea and caviar. Ross gave me a copy of the magazine containing his article, and obviously wanted to talk. I invited him to my hotel room next day.

Next morning I went for a stroll on the boardwalk, which winds through much of Inuvik above the permafrost. Along the way I met this lawyer from Yellowknife, a guy with the same name as mine. But a much taller man, about six foot six. Lawyer Purdy was in Yellowknife on legal business, had come to defend a service station employee in the courts for a criminal offence. (Since there were no roads leaving Inuvik, hence few service stations, that seemed a bit of an oddity.) But I had to read poems at the local high school that afternoon. I offered to change places with Lawyer Purdy: he'd read my poems and I'd defend his service station guy. (It seemed like a good idea.) However, I was not deemed to have sufficient court room experience, despite various incarcerations in the past.

I read the Ross article on Purdy just before its author showed up. That was quite a surprise. Ross hated me, it appeared. His article was a complete put-down, an exposure of my ineptitude and bad writing. Then what, I wondered amazedly, could the guy want with me now? I began to have some very strong suspicions on that point, and when Ross arrived I waited with intense interest to see whether my suspicions would be verified.

Ross didn't drink beer, which I had stocked in case the plumbing should freeze in this cold climate. I supplied him with an orange crush instead, listening with phony sympathy to the story he told about himself as a neglected writer, and one having much to offer people thirsty for Great Literature. I wouldn't mind meeting a few of those thirsty people myself, but in the meantime beer would have to suffice. And by this time, as previously surmised, I knew exactly what Ross wanted.

Over the next hour, in between jabbing him occasionally for his bad taste in literature, meaning me, I told him every way I knew to get money, where to publish his puerile drivel, and how to make out an application to the Canada Council . . .

He listened with a peculiar expression, somewhere between shame at asking a writer whose work he disliked for help, and pride that he could subdue his own pride long enough to do it. That whole thing with Ross was a humbling experience for me, as I certainly hope it was for him. I did my best to make it so in the latter case.

· · · · ·

At Loyola University in Montreal, where I was writer-in-rez for 1973–74, *Weekend* magazine proposed that I should write some articles for them. The magazine is now defunct, but for several years it was inserted into the Saturday editions of quite a number of Canadian newspapers. Editor Sheena Patterson was responsible for sending me to the Anahim Lake rodeo in BC; down the St. Lawrence River from the Welland Canal to Baie Comeau; west to interview an old cougar hunter and conservationist: Rod Haig-Brown; and talking to hockey players and fisherman from east to west.

Peter Newman, at *Maclean's*, sent me traipsing up the BC coast in fishing boats; Don Obe of the *Canadian* had me wandering the Cypress Hills and adjacent ranching country on the Saskatchewan-Alberta border; and later, leaving a Labrador coastal ship, the *William Carson*, visiting a Newfoundland outport called Harbour Deep. Eurithe and I lived at Harbour Deep for ten days or so, staying with a fisherman and his family, trying to decipher the strange sounds of almost-Elizabethan English in a province that voted to become Canadian because of the baby bonus. A year later, the CBC news reported that the *William Carson* had sunk along that northern coast. There were no casualties; crew and passengers had escaped over the ice floes.

In 1974 I went along on a Canadian Forces reconnaissance flight along the Atlantic coast, from Greenwood, Nova Scotia and far north to Nain, Labrador. Being inside that four-motored Argus aircraft was like being punished by an angry shouting father when you were a small child. Engine-noise was simply unimaginable. Everything blurred before your eyes because of the vibration. A crew member beside you had to shout in your ear in order to be understood; holding a glass of water in your hand, it had tidal waves.

Two Inuit hunters from Nain had been reported missing after they left home to trap foxes on a sub-arctic island. Tracks of their snowmobile ended at an open lead in ice-covered water. Our Canadian Forces flight was diverted to search for them. It was very exciting for me, and I was working on a poem at the same time as making notes for my article. It was rather more than exciting for the two Inuit, Jacko Onilak and Martin Senigak: it was life and death.

Over the ice floes we begin our dogleg sweeps, thirty miles in one direction and a parallel thirty miles in the other. Climbing down into the plastic nose cone, I am closer to the deathly ice than anyone else in that plane. I feel so alone that no human voice can speak to me, despite the ear phones on my head. I am suspended inside a clear bubble exuded from my body by a vestigial gland. Three hundred feet above the blinding white ice. Suspended there, like a newly invented spider. I was terrified. And exhilarated.

We never found them, Martin and Jacko. They are, of course, dead. In an odd way, I feel closer to them than many living people. I have thought and imagined them out of reality and made them a myth, taken them into my mind where they are not strangers.

.　.　.　.　.

I've been reading Hugh Garner books for many years, beginning with *Cabbagetown* in the 1950s and then his book of short stories, *The Yellow Sweater*, sometime later. And when I first started to do some radio and TV appearances after *The Cariboo Horses* won the Governor General's award, I ran into him a couple of times.

A short man with black moustache, receding black hair and a reputation for consuming an impressive amount of alcohol, Garner was in his late forties when I met him on the Bob Fulford show. Both of us were supposed to deliver piercing insights and mature wisdom on life and literature. Garner did, but I didn't. It was one of my first appearances on television: my throat siezed up, my brain froze and I could hardly say a word. He took in my condition immediately; he grinned at me, taking command of the talk show smoothly and even unobtrusively. I watched him weakly and with admiration. His opinions on that show I can't remember, but one of them was his great affection for the United States, a country about which I have mixed feelings.

But I liked Garner. One reason for this may have been that he, too, rode the freight trains, rode the boxcars and gondolas and reefers and flat cars during the Great Depression of the 1930s. I never talked with him about riding the freights, and always intended to. As for that Garner reputation about putting away gallons and jeroboams of booze, it was well-founded. He used to sign himself in to a private remedial sanitarium for a drying-out period of two or three weeks when he felt it was necessary; and it was necessary a couple of times a year.

Around 1975 my own acquaintance with Hugh became slightly more personal. A public exhibition of Canadian writers and their books was scheduled for Los Angeles in mid-summer, along with books and writers from other countries as well. Canada's Department of External Affairs was probably in charge of this country's exhibit.

In any case, McClelland & Stewart, my own publisher, organized the affair at this end, and appointed Jack Jensen, one of their more responsible employees, as major-domo of the Los Angeles expedition. Margaret Atwood, Irving Layton, Hugh Garner and myself were the Canadian writers.

(Many years later, I can't be absolutely sure that Atwood was with us, but if she wasn't, it's the first time anyone was ever uncertain about her presence.)

My equipment for this safari into the wilds of LA included my wife's electric coffee pot, some rather decorative plastic cups, and the ingredients for sandwiches. And I bought a bottle of booze at the airport duty-free shop. I thought it might be handy in case of snake bite.

At Toronto airport I arrived a bit early for the flight southward, and met Hugh Garner there. He said, "How about a drink," producing a half-full mickey of scotch from his hip pocket. The time was about mid-morning, and it occurred to me this was pretty early to start on the sauce, but Hugh and I retired to the john for a couple of snorts, and the bubbling music of the urinals kept us company.

Hugh and I seemed to like each other. He yakked away about

everything, which included a Garner comment about Margaret Atwood
which could have been construed as unflattering. Then I said the wrong
thing. Or rather, my tone of voice was wrong. "You don't like Peggy
Atwood?" I said disbelievingly.

Garner's hackles rose perceptibly. He suspected I was baiting him,
pushing him on to other comments about Atwood. And he was right.
After another drink I unwisely said the same thing, "You really don't
like Peggy Atwood?"

That did it. Garner's black eyes flashed dangerously. Drunk or sober,
he had an ear for comments that mocked or denigrated him even
slightly. His early liking for Purdy was annulled damn quick at that
point. He refused to talk to me anymore all the way to LA, keeping his
mouth shut except to guzzle at another mickey of scotch he produced
magically from the air around him. I went to another seat and talked to
Jack Jensen, feeling rather put-upon and having much more respect for
Garner than before.

The Canadians were domiciled at a nice downtown motel in the
movie metropolis. Our schedule had been a bit hectic, so I flopped down
on the bed for a brief siesta. The bed felt oddly uncomfortable. Something was digging into my back when I pressed down at a particular
spot. Lifting the mattress edge I discovered the reason. There was an
unopened 25-ounce bottle of Teacher's Highland Cream scotch whiskey between mattress and boxspring. Someone had stashed it there for
whatever purpose. The gods were smiling on me, at least temporarily.

Then Jack Jensen phoned that we were meeting in ten minutes on
the balcony to his room on the third floor. He cautioned me about
Garner. "Hugh looks half stoned already." I mentioned my wife's
coffee pot and sandwich wherewithal. "Would that help soak up the
booze?" Jack said it might, but sounded dubious.

The five of us sat around a card table on Jack Jensen's balcony in
bright California sunshine. Layton, Garner—and was it Margaret
Avison, not Peggy Atwood at all? But how could I mistake one for
the other, or did I drink more than I remember? Anyway, Hugh was
so stoned you could quarry him for marble by this time. His face red,
eyes half-closed, but managing to glare at me through the slits. He
looked malevolent.

"Have a sandwich, Hugh," I said, sliding the plate over to him.

With one imperial gesture he swept the sandwich, plate and all, off
the third floor balcony to the grass below. A white face looked up at us
with astonished eyes.

"That's okay, that's okay," I said in a flustered voice. Jack Jensen motioned urgently towards the coffee pot. "Have some coffee, Hugh," I burbled, and poured him a cup.

Garner reached out a long arm and cleared two of my wife's plastic cups off the table as well, not neglecting to include an empty beer bottle. "Glah!" said Hugh, deep in his throat. Or maybe it was "Grah." Then he left the table without further comment.

Jensen shrugged his shoulders. I thought: migawd, my wife's nice coffee cups! I dashed down the stairs to retrieve them, without waiting for the elevator. But somebody had already picked them up and disappeared. It occurred to me to look in the garbage; but thought it might be better to tell my wife they'd been stolen by an admirer of her good taste.

We went to the book exhibition that evening. The Canadian booth didn't get much attention, since Linda Lovelace, an actress who had starred in a pornographic movie called *Deep Throat*, was showing her wares next door. I think she'd written a book, or her ghost had, but the book was secondary to her other attractions. No one even asked a question about Canadian books and writers, and aren't Canadians just like Americans anyway? I did notice Norman Mailer nearby, talking to a lady in a low-cut gown, and thought of asking them to stand in front of the Canadian exhibit. But I felt shy about approaching him.

I roamed around LA for the next couple of days, visiting antiquarian book stores most of the time. And when our expedition boarded the plane for Toronto, Garner didn't show up. Jack Jensen stayed a few days longer, looking for him. Jack said later that when he finally caught up with him, Garner had made scotch whiskey in LA very hard to find. And had some vomit stains on his jacket.

After that I was very careful what I said to Hugh, whether in letters or in person. You have to be tactful sometimes, a lesson always difficult for me to learn. I really don't know what Garner had against Margaret Atwood, probably nothing serious. I corresponded with him for several years, then, suddenly, he was dead. I never did get to trade stories with him about riding the freights.

. . . . .

I was writer-in-rez at the University of Manitoba in 1975–76. Eurithe and I had quarrelled rather violently over whatever it was before I drove west in the late summer of '75. She didn't come with me.

I managed to rent an apartment near the university, one with a huge indoor garden of tropical trees and plants all jumbled together just beyond the lobby. At the time I encountered this lush profusion I thought, "Ain't that nice;" but later in the bitter man-killing Manitoba winter, when anyone on foot dies of frostbite within sixty seconds and corpses of polar bears and pedestrians are discovered under the melting snow every spring at Portage and Main—then I saw the reasons for this plenitude of green stuff.

Anyway, I got settled, renting one easy chair, one bed and a TV set. More or less camping in. David Williams, ex-football player, ex-lay preacher and current professor of English, was friendly. We got to know each other and didn't throw up. John Teunissen, the English Dept. chairman, did. In retrospect, it seems we disliked each other immediately. I misbehaved at a party in his apartment after drinking some rather potent Armagnac brandy. I have only vague memories of what happened, and have no wish for hypnotic aids to recollection. However, later on I felt I had to send Teunissen's lady, Evelyn Hinz, some roses to make amends to her.

Cold that winter was so extreme that in January, when I took a shortcut across an open field in deep snow to get to the university, I could feel my strength failing halfway across the field, and had to turn back. It was like wading through white molasses.

Some friends happened to be passing through Winnipeg by train. I visited them at the railway station; we drank some in their roomette. All the train windows were so frosted up, I don't think they ever saw the province of Manitoba. At night in the snow when I did some walking for exercise, the silence tingled and my feet made that strange crunch as if I was the only visitor to an empty planet. After that, I waggled my fingers outside the balcony window. If they fell off, I stayed inside.

In the middle of that Arctic winter a Canada Day celebration was scheduled at Brandon, a city of fifty thousand some 150 miles west of Winnipeg. I was invited to participate, and since my friend Craig Powell also lived in Brandon, he invited me to dinner after the day's festivities. Besides being a well-known poet, Craig was a doctor at the city's psychiatric hospital. We got along well together. I'd met him a year or two earlier, along with his red-haired wife, and one of those instant friendships ensued.

I took the bus from Winnipeg to Brandon. W.O. Mitchell was on the same bus, also invited to the Canada Day celebrations. We sat together and yakked enjoyably for the next three hours. I noticed at once that some of the elderly women in other seats were giving us peculiar looks, but decided that was because Mitchell and I were so obviously outlanders.

Bill Mitchell used to be an actor, and his voice carries as a result of his thespian training. I had done many readings; my own voice has been described as a foghorn in a phone booth. Mitchell and I had things in common. And we discussed everything, including the sexual proclivities of the Trobriand Islanders. W.O. also discoursed on the varieties of backhouse construction in our western provinces, and how this made it easy for boys from the local pub to overturn the one occupied by a minister of God.

Leaving the bus at Brandon, we received some pretty poisonous looks. One lady even had her mouth pursed up to spit at me, then remembered with regret that she was a lady.

The Brandon festivities contained nothing very memorable. Lloyd Robertson, the newscaster, was also one of the guests, and sat at the table with Mitchell, writer Bob Enright and I. Robertson impressed me as a very intelligent and personable guy. I was surprised he looked so small. Television changes the way everyone looks; I might even appear intelligent myself with a good cameraman.

I enjoyed meeting Craig and his really stunning wife, Jeanie, again. She's one of those redheads with a perfect milkwhite skin, and an unaffected cordiality if she knows you. On glimpsing her, you just stop and goggle, while the noise of television or traffic quietens down and becomes unimportant. She makes me think of one of my own lines:

> And women with such a glow
> it makes their background vanish—

Anyway, we had an enjoyable dinner, renewed acquaintance, etc. Afterwards, Sid Stephen, a captain in the Canadian Army, came by. He brought his book of poems about the Newfoundland Beothuks, a race of Indians now extinct. And this was not a coincidence. Craig had decided beforehand that the three of us would be giving a reading that evening. I hadn't expected to sing for my supper, and had left my books in Bob Enright's car for the return trip to Winnipeg. However, Craig supplied books; there appeared to be no escape. All three of us sat down on the living room floor, legs stuck out towards the room's epicentre in bohemian fashion, each reading a poem in turn.

Then a herd of elephants trampled onto the veranda and knocked at the door. It was the dozen or so psychiatrists and psychologists (I get the two kinds of shrink mixed up) from the Brandon Hospital, complete with wives, come to imbibe culture no matter what the cost. They were ushered to chairs in a half-circle around the three poets, and sat there staring at us with mad mad eyes.

Those eyes!—after a few iambs my own hard-won sanity tottered. I escaped to the kitchen after one go-round. Several other people were there too, including a couple of the psychiatrists' wives. Happily this was also the location of a big fridge jammed with beer. That supplied the wherewithal for a second party, and we sat around the kitchen table discussing Freud and listening to the PhDs in the living room discussing John Clare.

An especially beautiful girl, one of the wives, displayed all the classic symptoms of discontent by talking with me. I could understand this feeling, having just met her husband, and thoughtfully offered her a position as my live-in housekeeper in Winnipeg. Regrettably I couldn't give her tenure for the job because of prior commitments. But after a few hard-sell moments, I almost convinced her to leave her husband.

Then, accidentally, my elbow knocked a big salad bowl off the table. It made a loud crash. In the next room all the psychiatrists jumped; Sid Stephen stopped in the middle of a Beothuk poem; we drank some more beer. However, the incident of the salad bowl seemed to have an adverse effect on my relationship with the discontented wife.

Then Bob Enright and his girl friend called, with W.O. Mitchell as passenger, for the long drive to Winnipeg. Pulling out from the curb I looked at Craig Powell's house, seeing the curtains part slightly and the psychiatrist's wife's pale face peering out.

W.O. Mitchell sat with me on the back seat. At first we resumed the same conversation that had so entertained our fellow passengers on the bus. But Bill the actor quickly took over from W.O. the writer. Again he discoursed on how the boys had tipped over the backhouse in Laurel, Alberta, thereby unseating the minister of God inside. He told about winter overcoats and other apparel left at the church entrance being loaded with cowpads. We couldn't get him to stop.

Near Winnipeg Bob Enright and I both assured him that he wasn't really Mark Twain, no matter how excellent his imitations. Our words had little effect.

. . . . .

My wife and I were guests of the Soviet Union in 1977, along with Ralph "Gus" Gustafson and his wife. It was an odd pairing. Gus is so cultured, symphonies and cantatas sound in the street if he approaches a music store. Myself, I prefer the Russians and Team Canada playing hockey. On foreign turf he visits cathedrals and attends ballet; I sample the local beer and keep my options open. We are so different it's like

Martian meeting Venusian, and both are imaginary. He doesn't believe in me and I don't believe in him.

At Kiev, Mark Pinchevsky, a translator of English I liked, called him a gentle man, meaning he was different from Beau Brummell and macho types. That's true, but what a mess of opposites Gus is! Exceedingly ambitious for himself and his poems, yet rather self-effacing and soft-voiced. Also an idealist and romantic. Every day while we were in the Soviet Union, he wrote a poem. I believe he ended up with about eighteen, and I with a mere dozen.

At the end of our trip I said, "Gus, you out-poemed me nearly two to one. How about if you trade me ten of yours for one of mine? Would that be a fair trade?"

His answer was indecipherable.

Our Russian translator, Victor Pogostin, accompanied us all the way from Moscow to Tashkent and Samarkand, then back east again to Riga, Leningrad and Kiev. In Victor's case, I'd like to make the word "phlegmatic" become even more meaningful than it is. If he smiled, it was only about twenty-five percent of smile; the rest was a frown. Victor's English was almost non-inflected and neutral, expressing no personal feelings whatever. His high cheekbones reached nearly up to his temples. Short and heavily built, Asiatic about three bedrooms away. I suppose I thought of him as typical apparatchik bureaucrat. He wasn't, of course.

At Riga, Latvia there was a reception for the Canadians in the Writers Union building. Lalla, wife of one of the local scriveners, said to me as we were about to be introduced: "John Colombo is a better writer than you, Purdy. He wrote a poem just for me."

I had no ready answer to that one, and couldn't venture an opinion on Colombo's taste in the matter.

Having dinner with these Latvian writers was highly interesting. After black caviar and red caviar, vodka and Georgian wine, things got musical. We ended up singing every song we knew and some we certainly didn't. Peteris Peterson, a lanky stage director wearing big horn-rimmed glasses, sang like a locomotive. He sang "Deutschland Uber Alles," of all things. Of course, when he started that, we all joined in, even Victor. "Deutschland" is a German song of hate and their own superiority: and here were the Latvians rolling it out in the presence of Victor, our expressionless translator, symbol of their Russian overlords.

I felt caught in the middle of a melodramatic play, and yet not an actor myself. We sang "Lilli Marlene," about the soldier longing for his girl friend in the war that never ends, while I watched all the Latvian faces which by now had names in my mind. Cordiality towards the four

Canadians was immense and genuine (and I loved these people), but there was an undercurrent where Victor was concerned.

There were several more meetings together, and more good feelings. On an expedition beside the Baltic, Peteris Peterson got into a pair of swimming trunks and swam far out to sea, until everyone felt a little alarmed. Poets I'd never heard of appeared, as they had never heard of Gus and I, but with whom there was a warm conjoining. And we toured the mellow old buildings of Riga itself, buildings that seemed to partake of being human as much as bricks and mortar ever can . . .

At Leningrad, Eurithe and I left the others, visiting Dostoyevsky's pad, strolling by the Neva River, wandering Peter the Great's summer palace on the Baltic (Russians foist that word "great" on so many things!), getting my dark glasses shat on by a seagull. Meeting Voznesensky and his Osa at a restaurant, and many other Russian writers. And Samarkand, the blue city, where you merely dream you are living now; you are really living backward into the past. All that ceramic blue! It joins city to sky on cloudless days.

Back in Moscow we visit Lenin's tomb, the revered Vladimir's body embalmed inside a squarish red marble structure that manages to be both garish and conservative at the same time. The line-up waiting to see Lenin is about three kilometres long. The omnipresent cops order me to remove my hands from my pockets for some reason. Maybe they thought I intended to present Lenin with a lollipop. And he is a bald little man with sandy goatee, somebody you'd pass in the street without notice. But then, most poisons look harmless unless they're labelled for what they are.

In Moscow there's a place called the Dollar Shop, where visitors can buy expensive things with foreign currency. Russian bureaucrats were said to be the store's best customers. Anyway, costs of this Russian expedition were on the house for Gus and I; but our wives' expenses had to be paid off with western cash. Before we were scheduled to leave, Victor revealed unexpected tender feelings. He wanted to buy his wife, Natasha, a leather coat. And such scarce ladies wear was available only in the Dollar Shop.

So who did Victor go to when he wanted that leather coat for Natasha, and it would be illegal for him to go there himself? Not Gus. There's an air of honesty and incorruptibility about Gus that hovers over him like a halo. When Eurithe's travel bill was due, Victor came to me with the proposition that he pay her bill and I buy that leather coat for his wife at the foreigner's emporium where he was forbidden entry. I bought Natasha the coat, with some trepidation.

All the places I've visited, and all the people I've met, have left their impressions on me. You become, in however limited a sense, every place you've been and everyone you met. Some friendships remain at the same constant level, and endure; George Woodcock is one of these. Layton remains at a more distant remove, enthroned on his ego, which is to some extent justified. I was going to mention Louis Dudek—but you can't be a friend of Dudek's unless you allow him to teach you something. He's most obdurate on that point. Ron Everson, and that one has lasted to the end. Dennis Lee, whom I expect to astonish me at almost any moment. And Bill Percy, also dating from far back. I've been very lucky with friends, all of them writers, which of itself ought to say something about me.

A dozen or so years back, I was hunting books in Vancouver and ran into Peter Trower, Howie White and Curt Lang. They were distributing Howie's magazine, *Raincoast Chronicles*, at downtown stores and looked quite thirsty. Whereupon the four of us repaired to the Cecil Hotel for refreshment, then to the Marble Arch on cordial invitation from a couple of waiters at the Cecil.

At the pub I had a bright idea: why not buy some steaks, expand this enjoyable evening by cooking them, and stretch this boozy moment into eternity? I was staying at Earle Birney's apartment at the time, he being away somewhere delivering an address on Chaucer and the relation of Middle English to pub-jargon on Shaughnessy Heights. So why not surprise Earle's wife Esther with our pseudo-intellectual discourse and ten pounds of prime sirloin?

The idea was received with acclaim. We took a cab to Safeway, I bought the steaks, and we rang the doorbell of the Birney apartment. I began to have a few qualms at this point, in fact wondered if our move from the Marble Arch to here was entirely wise and judicious. Besides, I had forgotten to buy roses for Esther. And had I zipped my pants after that last visit to the john? *well,*— yes.

Anyway, Esther received us with some surprise and the greatest possible cordiality under those circumstances. And she cooked the steaks. While this was happening I noticed Trower was still wearing his cap in the house and gently removed it from his forehead, where poems were momently gestating and about to be born. But removing that cap was a mistake, for I noticed Peter's expression change, and a look of almost malevolence on his face. Then I remembered: the poet's few remaining hairs preferred to remain in decent privacy and gather their forces for re-growth in darkness. Sometimes I do stupid things, with beer often providing the impetus.

And Esther? The steak idea wasn't very brilliant either, but it was up to me to carry off the occasion with suavity and panache. Trouble is, I am not noted for those qualities. After the steaks I asked Peter to read a poem, the one about the last spar-tree on Elphinstone Mountain, which ends with the lines:

> Dream on in peace old tree,
> perhaps you're a truer monument to man
> than any rocktop crucifix in Rio de Janeiro.

It occurred to me then that I should have asked Peter to just gargle an earlier line, in order not to test Esther's finer sensibilities:

> excellent shits behind stumps with the wind fanning the
> stink away—

Esther's expression changed at that point.

· · · · ·

The Canadian Arctic was where I first took my ego in my hands and said to the Canada Council, I can write poems there. When you experience that blindingly white place of sunlight, vivid blue water and solitude that presses on you and surrounds you like air itself—you wonder at your own hubris and insolence in thinking you can write about it. And the Galapagos Islands, a place to shake you out of the complacency of being human, if you do feel that way. A world where people are quite extraneous, as if creation had ignored us entirely in that community of creatures without self-consciousness.

Eurithe and I went there in 1979, flew to Quito, Ecuador, and on to Guayaquil, a tropical city at the ocean's edge. We stood beside the city's great river as it swept westward to the sea, with twenty-foot floating islands of vegetation rushing past us; when the tide reversed itself, they came rushing back again in a continuous doomed effort to escape the river.

The Galapagos, (a Spanish word for tortoise), are very nearly perched on the equator, 300 miles west from Ecuador. It's the magic place where Charles Darwin dreamed of "the survival of the fittest"; and missing links and living fossils clambered through my own dreams. We got a room on inhabited Santa Cruz Island, spending much time watching the abundant animal citizens. Thinking of Darwin's theories, I'd look at them, glance elsewhere, then look back to see if they'd changed. That's an exaggeration, of course, but the thought does occur to you. Everything here is different, at least slightly, from their mainland relatives. And we, who are supposedly human, do we ever remember those other bodies we once had?

Santa Cruz Island, sparsely populated, is twenty-five miles wide. Its single town is like an old time western movie set, except for its location on the sea's edge. People clop around on burros and horses, wear spurs and cowboy hats, look kinda macho.

Our lodgings had a concrete apron fronting on a small arm of the sea. Black marine lizards lazed in the sun there, scuttling around your feet if you seemed about to step on them. Pelicans settled on the canvas awning above our heads, when they got tired of plunking into the sea in search of fish. Scarlet crabs dashed disconcertingly sideways among wet rocks, the only really shy creatures I noticed.

Darwin Research Station, a mile distant from our motel, swarmed with thousands of land tortoises, from thimble size to seven-hundred-pound monsters up to 160 years old. Subtract 160 from this year of 1979, it leaves you with 1819 Anno Domini. Which means that when Darwin arrived here on board the *Beagle* in 1835, some of these table-sized quadrupeds were already sixteen years old, and might have been patted on the head by the great man himself.

We visited several of the islands in the course of a ten-day visit, booking single trips on the luxurious yacht, *Delfin*, rather than the expensive group of excursions. We ate a lot of fruit and our electric coffee pot made sure the water was drinkable. Everything was spur-of-the moment with few things planned beforehand, and we felt exhilarated by the whole place. However, that summer was much hotter than usual, which caused both of us to leave a little excess poundage in South America.

One island was jammed with blue-footed boobies every few feet, their nests interspersed with the sunbathing preserves of yellowy-gold land iguanas. And everything was so fearless, innocent if you like; no animal or bird actually ran away from us for whatever reason. But there were a few prehistoric-looking frigate birds lurking in the shrubbery. These are the pirate birds who rob the harmless boobies of their fish. The frigate birds actually *looked* evil, although it may have been all in my head.

Some of the boobies were doing their mating dance when we arrived, flapping their wings like helicopter vanes, lifting themselves two or three feet into the air, then just hovering for the edification of female boobies. Those males were all showoffs. Being quite a large bird with wide wingspan, their performance stirred up a small hurricane of dust and dead leaves. Other boobies flapped their wings, but stayed on the ground. They actually pranced, parading back and forth in heroic poses, tilting the front of their feet upward, expecting their females to admire all that blueness. And whistled. Not the male human streetcorner kind of whistle, but like a small boy just learning how.

It was the only sound in that still island on the edge of nowhere. The people, all of us, were either invisible or inconsequential to those sexually minded birds. The booby antics made me think how ridiculous I must have looked myself at high school, playing football, sticking out my chest and walking tall, writing poems—all to attract female attention. Then not having enough nerve to do anything about it anyway. It's a bit humiliating to think that I was merely obeying a rule of nature; that's how the male gender acts in mating season, some males more subtly than others. And all my own high school posturing didn't work, young human females remained pointedly indifferent.

If one is theologically inclined, a good case could be made for divine order and plan on these animal-populous atolls (one of which is a hundred miles long) under a great blue emptiness. Or if an unbeliever, the values you can abstract from this place also seem valid. I mean the values of adjustments in nature, the conservation of something triggered by unknown causes a billion years ago and which will continue indefinitely, hermetically sealed by distance.

They are values of which the inhabitants of these island zoos are ignorant; but just the same, pelican, booby, iguana and the rest live by them. You can even, by an act of the imagination, see their bodily forms changing from what they were to what they are to what they might become. If you were God, some of your own creations would likely seem bewildering to you.

Among the poems I wrote in the tortoise islands is one about the blue-footed booby, which is perhaps the most slow-witted creature there. It's a not-completely-serious poem, which I thought might serve to lighten my customary philosophic solemnity. When "Birdwatching at the Equator" was published in a magazine, a Conservative Member of Parliament noticed it and read it aloud to the Liberal government in the House of Commons in Ottawa. His object was undoubtedly to embarrass the Liberals, to say, in effect: "Is this the kind of shit you people encourage through Canada Council grants?"

I was completely unaware of this cultural occasion in the legislative chambers. Its later repercussions also came as a surprise to me.

> The blue-footed booby
> stands on her tropic island
> in the Galapagos Group

stands all day long
shading her eggs from the sun
also protecting her blue feet
from too much ultraviolet
Sometimes the male booby
flaps his wings and dances
to entertain his mate
pointing his toes upward
so they can discuss blueness
which seems to them very beautiful
Their only real enemy
is the piratical frigate bird
floating on great black wings
above the mile-long island
Sometimes the frigate bird
robs them of their fish
whereupon the booby
is wont to say "Friggit"
and catches some more
When night comes all the boobies
sit down at once as if
God had given them a signal
or else one booby says
to the rest "Let's flop boys"
and they do

The booby's own capsule
comment about evolution:
if God won't do it for you
do it yourself:
stand up
sit down
make love
have some babies
catch fish
dance sometimes
admire your feet
friggit:
what else is there?

—*Birdwatching at the Equator* (1981)

. . . . .

A year later my wife and I spent a month in Victoria, BC. When the Superbowl football game was scheduled on television in January 1980, I went to my brother-in-law's apartment to watch, enjoy the company of other guests there and drink some beer. The Oakland Raiders and Philly Eagles of that year were deciding the American championship of the world at a game that was invented in Montreal or Kingston, Ontario, or so an old linebacker informs me.

There were seven or eight people at that apartment, including a guy named Gary, who is introduced to me as the manager of a dry-cleaning establishment. He wears casual clothes, shirt open at the neck, has an appearance of some prosperity. I sit opposite him on a high stool at the bar. And sip my beer slowly, anticipating companionship, good-natured badinage, an enjoyable football game. I could hardly have been more wrong.

Gary, it seems, has read a piece about me in the Victoria *Times-Colonist*, to the effect that a bad poem I wrote about the blue-footed booby has been subsidized by the Canada Council, hence also the Canadian taxpayer. And that means Gary personally.

As the football game proceeds, Gary compliments me in uncomplimentary terms for "ripping off" the taxpayer, saying that he would like to get away with such rip-offs himself. I am not sure if he's joking or not, and have my doubts. There is quite a barrage of these remarks from the dry-cleaning manager, to which I make mild rejoinder as is my wont, hoping to keep the peace.

Finally it gets on my nerves a little. I wonder, audibly, what it is he wants from me, an apology or a refund? "Why are you so insulting, Gary?" I want to know. "All of us have good feelings here, me at my brother-in-law's and among friends, just trying to get along."

"I'm not your friend," Gary says.

At this point I'm beginning to feel alarmed. And make a fast assessment of the physical capabilities of dry cleaning-managers—just in case. He is much younger than me, about thirty-five, and much lighter, about 160–165 pounds, and looks in pretty good shape. I shake my head at my own thoughts. It's just too fantastic that anyone should dislike a poem of mine enough to—enough to what? I didn't know, and didn't want to know.

The insults continued for about two hours. Oakland was far ahead of Philly for the Canadian champeenship. I'd consumed maybe three or four beers. Then a period of interregnum, during which Gary told a youngster present that the kid's other brother (not present) was double-crossing him. And there was a short discussion of that.

I was relieved, since my advanced age of over sixty ought to preclude the sort of juvenile violence that had seemed impending. Besides, my arthritic knees wouldn't hold up if I had to move quickly or rise from a prone position and forthwith flee to a place of safety. As well, I felt some respect was due my grey hairs. And therefore felt safe in commenting on something another person had said. Which was a mistake.

Gary told me quickly that my opinion was worthless, coming from (quote) "a piece of shit like you."

I hit the bastard. No delay, no thought, bugger all. As hard as I could. Quite hard, in fact, right at the end of the word "shit." And was about to leap atop his prone body on the floor, perhaps whomp his head a few times on the soft carpet. But my brother-in-law jumped in front before I could accomplish this fell design.

Gary is escorted to the bathroom to have blood washed from his face. Of course the football game is ruined for me, and nearly ended anyway. I ask one of my handy relatives to drive me home. Then Gary emerges from the bathroom, a little pale as I observe. We are invited to shake hands (that ritual whereby we pretend that we really love each other). I agree, thinking what the hell. Gary refuses (the clod).

I'm still all a-twitter when I get out of the car later. Nerves. I describe the incident for my wife and sister-in-law where we are staying. And ask Eurithe to walk around the block with me a few times until I calm down. She says, "No. I have to get supper. There isn't time." And that's my sweet understanding wife, administering to all my needs.

My description of these incidents may sound a bit lighthearted. At the time, it was not very lighthearted. And it all goes to prove that poetry can be dangerous to your health.

· · · · ·

Over the years I have valued friendship as something for which there is no financial or other tangible advantage to be derived from, but without which . . . Well, that sounds like something glib. Try again. Without friends you go strange and are liable to kill people; without women in your life, you cut yourself off from the most vital springs of existence . . . And I sound mawkish to myself. It's disgusting when you can't say something the way you want to!

After my first small CC grant in 1960, on which I went to Tsimsyan country in northern BC, I wrote George Woodcock about his play, *Maskerman*, which I had heard on CBC radio. That was the beginning of a thirty-year friendship, mostly via the postal service, although there have been a few meetings. Despite admiration expressed by both of us in print toward the other, I claim it is not a mutual admiration thing. On my own side, I admire Woodcock a great deal, as do many other people.

But admiration is scarcely adequate grounds for lasting friendship. I'm forced to confess, I don't know why said friendship exists, just pleased that it does. As has been said, George W. is a man-of-letters in the old fashioned sense. Before he returned to his Canadian birthplace, he knew all the writers in England, even if some were not yet born. And there's something about both George W. and wife Inge that is solid, reliable and trustworthy. He is a magistrate of literature in some odd way. (End of blurb.)

One of the friends I valued, I lost. It was at an anniversary party for *Books in Canada* in Toronto. I noticed and heard this guy talking in measured terms about things familiar to me. He had a drink in hand, was off to one side, was not part of the general hubbub. I have this habit of introducing myself to people who interest me. I say to myself on very short notice: I like that man, I want to know him.

In this case the target was Norman Levine. We seemed to get along well. Norman is not particularly shy, and I'm not either despite obvious reasons for it. He came down to the house at Roblin Lake a couple of times. My wife and I enjoyed their company, both Norman and his lady. George Galt, another friend who was present on one such occasion, liked them too. And I don't mean Damon and Pythias, Jonathan and whoever-that-was, just friendship.

Eurithe and I also visited Norman's and the lady's house in Toronto, and were cordially received. Dennis Lee, just back from a writer-in-rez year in Scotland, came around to say hello after his long absence. Small talk flourished. We moved from a front room through some French doors to another part of the house. I was greeted there by a small yapping dog about the size of a pint of milk. He went rah-rah-rower-rower! at my pants leg. So I did the same thing back at him. I went rower-rower-rah-rah! at the dog, and thought it was rather funny.

However, a certain silence prevailed among us after that. I mean after the lady of the house ushered her noisy pooch into a sequestered area, from which I could still make out some muffled unfriendly yapping. That dog was decidedly anti-poetry, or maybe just anti-Purdy? After we departed the premises, silence kept on prevailing from Norman, for several months. And has continued since.

I can imagine what the lady said to Norman Levine in my absence; at least some of the key words have been made known to me in a vision.

And I have thought since, friendship, ah friendship! Well, ya win some and ya lose some. And, love me, love my dog. Or else. Or else what?

. . . . .

I met John Newlove nearly thirty years ago, at Binky Marx's annual party in Vancouver. Binky was a short plump man with liver lips and a sort of overproof complexion, a well-loved character in lotusland for no reason I ever discovered. He worked at Duthie's bookstore, and seemed to know everybody and everything. Before joining Duthie's he ran a leftist bookstore near Hastings Street. Customers entering this place were said to be photographed by the RCMP, on the grounds that anyone entering such a crummy establishment must be Communist.

Anyway, Binky's party, and everyone who could rhyme moon/June or spell freeloader was there. I ran into Newlove just after memorizing where Binky had hidden the beer with commendable foresight. John was drinking rye and grumbling that he couldn't get any beer himself. I procured one for him, and with my usual tact and diplomacy knocked the rye glass out of his hand while handing him the desired brew. Newlove immediately tried to kick me in the balls, my evasive tactics narrowly successful. I could see that we were meant to be friends for life.

Without a place to sleep that night, Newlove invited me to occupy his quarters while he bunked with friends. It was a good arrangement, I thought, since the hour was late and I would've had to convince a hotel desk clerk of my complete sobriety.

However, the room was located right in the middle of a pottery factory—at least that's what it looked like to me. A kind of oasis, separate from all the dust and working clutter. And more, the place was directly under the Granville Street bridge. Traffic roar kept me awake for much of the night. I think the only reason Newlove was able to sleep there was he stayed sloshed most of the time. When I woke up early Sunday morning and opened the door to the factory proper, the first thing I saw was a torn-apart copy of *Slava Bohu*, a book about BC Doukhobors, on a nearby bench. It was a library copy. And I could see that John had a proper respect for literature.

Newlove showed up before noon, and dug out his poems for me to read. I thought they were pretty good, and also felt obligated because of the free room. I took the manuscript back east with me, giving it to Peter Miller at Contact Press. Later on, this manuscript was the basis for Newlove's book, *Moving In Alone*.

Over the years John has been a combative character. If we were friends part of the time, we were enemies for the rest. On one occasion at George Jonas's apartment in Toronto, we both had our fists cocked at the ready, confronting each other like over-age roosters. But John blinked first, on accounta he had to pick up a beer with the hand he generally used to throw a left hook. I can't remember what that one was all about.

Newlove was always broke or nearly so; conversely, he was always able to find money to buy booze. It has never been quite clear in my mind how we became friends, a relationship which he would deny vehemently.

One occasion with John and I drinking beer remains crystal clear in my mind and blurred at the same time. This contradiction calls for an explanation, since I'm confused about the incident myself. It was about twenty years ago. John was an editor at McClelland & Stewart then, and came to visit Eurithe and I at Ameliasburgh. Ron Everson and his wife Lorna were also guests at the time. And beer was available in some quantity, both John and I sampling it to the extent that only samples remained.

It was after midnight, that I do remember. We were in the kitchen, and everyone else had gone to bed, as sober and sensible people are wont to do. John and I were talking, of course, perhaps even arguing. My own sensitive nature generally precludes argument, but in this case the provocation was considerable. And a pause ensued, although I am not sure what it ensued after—I mean what event took place just before the pause. That event, whatever it was, resulted in John and I being washed toward the kitchen door, propelled there by a huge wave of water. I felt complete bewilderment at that instant. Danger of drowning wiped everything else out of my mind.

Of course we grabbed the doorsill while passing, and thus saved ourselves. Eurithe then emerged from the bedroom to ask in a sarcastic voice for the reason we were washing the floor at this time of night. An answer seemed uncalled for.

Next day I spent some time trying to figure out what happened, reconstructing the order of events in reverse. John and I had been standing by the kitchen sink, that much was certain. That sink had a sort of overhang built-in at floor level, enabling your feet to slide under and the dishwasher could stand close to the job. Since the water pump wasn't working, we had a ten-gallon plastic can of water placed nearby. We'd overturned it somehow. I think John must've had his feet trapped under that sink overhang, and when we fell had preceded me toward the floor, knocking over the water on his way down. But why did we fall in the first place?

I can't remember, and beyond the point of forgetfulness I don't much want to remember. But I am curious. Maybe I said something that annoyed Newlove. Maybe I said pleadingly, "I didn't mean to insult you, John. I apologize if I did." Maybe he punched me or I punched him. Cross-examination in a court of law might result in illumination, but enough said.

Next morning John had a sprained foot, and couldn't walk on it. Since we intended to visit our friends, Angus and Barbara Mowat, at Northport that afternoon, I was forced to become a beast of burden. Not without a few words of protest either. I slung the cripple over my shoulder, staggering around the backyard a few paces while Newlove screamed in my ear. John had started to eat heavily since achieving lucrative employment in Toronto, while continuing to drink just as much as ever. His disposition didn't improve either. He weighed nearly 200 pounds.

That ankle got more painful through the day, and finally I drove Newlove to Belleville hospital. I was getting pretty worn-out by this time anyway, whispering to Eurithe, "Don't give him anything more to eat; he's breaking my back already."

As it turned out, John had a broken ankle. He had to be fitted with a pair of crutches in order to get back to Toronto a couple of days later. The medicos in Toronto inserted a pin in his ankle-bone. And the moral of the lesson is—keep your temper. At least I think that's what it teaches.

I haven't seen Newlove for years. According to my information, John Metcalf's wife got him a job writing Mulroney's speeches in Ottawa (if it was me writing those speeches Mulroney would have been fired a lot sooner than he did). That job paid sixty-five thousand a year some time back, which probably ensures plenty of brew at John's right and left hands. And I've had a bad back ever since that visit by John Newlove.

· · · · ·

There's a Milton Acorn poem called "In This Game There Needs To Be No Losers," in which someone named "Ike Strange" (that name a pseudonym Acorn used, and I'll continue to use it here) is made into a hero for the poet's purposes. I ran into this "Ike Strange" while visiting Margaret Avison, so long ago that Mulroney was still a nasty child.

I had the strong impression this guy was going through Margaret's things in the empty apartment, the door of which was slightly ajar. I went in while he was doing it, which may have accounted for his furtive manner.

I asked Margaret about him later. She said he was a young poet without much money whom she was helping in any way she could, someone she was apparently fond of. Anyway, my suspicions may have been groundless. Sometimes I do leap to conclusions much too hastily. I let the matter drop.

Margaret herself impressed me as a fey sort of person, very religious, even otherworldly, and much of her time was devoted to caring for her aged mother. She was also a poet you'd never mistake for any other. I couldn't understand some of her stuff, but a few poems of hers would send the mind off in new directions, as if she'd opened up different areas of the brain which had suddenly started working because of her.

I sat with her on the porch steps one time; maybe it was just after rain. There were long stretches of silence between us which I can't explain. I felt a kind of awe for the lady, just sitting there in early evening with the street lights coming on while crickets began to resume their nightly comments. Margaret was so different from myself that she reduced me to silence, and I was able to join her at the edges of her mood without understanding at all what was in her mind. I suppose that is mystic, when you feel something but can't identify the feeling, only the source.

"Ike Strange"?—I was told later that he had gone to Spain with his wife, and abandoned her there, leaving her entirely without money. Later still, I ran into him on a corner of West 4th in Vancouver. He seemed to be just standing there, watching the traffic go by. His manner gave me the feeling that he was about to go off his rocker at any moment. He asked me to spend some time with him, I forget why. I said no, "No thanks." Acorn's poem which mentions the guy is one of his best, but leaves me still curious long afterwards.

Apart from a very few letters, I've had scarcely any contact with Margaret over the years. She was at the Gwen MacEwen memorial in Toronto three or four years ago, looking a bit frail. I shook her hand too vigorously, seeing an expression of pain on her face. Her hands had become arthritic and swollen; like a fool I didn't notice.

When Avison received the GG Award for the second time a year or so ago, I wrote congratulating her. Margaret replied, mentioning in her letter some difficulty in writing without the aid of beer to stimulate production.

Beer and Margaret Avison! What oddity on the human agenda may arrive next? A sudden vision of Margaret and I joining in the chorus of a lusty drinking song on her porch steps that long-ago evening. But the beer was consumed for health reasons. And the poems Margaret writes now seem to me quite understandable. But what was going on while my back was turned?

· · · · ·

John Glassco was an acquaintance rather more than a friend. I liked him; we corresponded desultorily, not very urgently. He looked at life rather differently than I did, and once paraphrased a well-known quotation: "It's better never to have lived at all." I disagreed with that, but he meant his judgment for humanity in general, although it also applied to himself. He made it after his own health was broken, his pleasure in being alive diminished, shrunken and limited. The comment made me feel sad for him.

Glassco left Canada for Paris, France in the 1920s. His ambition then was to lead a pleasure-seeking hedonistic literary life, and probably never return to Canada at all. In Paris, booze and sexual abandon had their textbook penalties: he contracted venereal disease and tuberculosis, with long periods of treatment in Montreal.

Glassco's Paris reminiscences, *Memoirs of Montparnasse*, was much more fascinating to me than most novels; in fact I regard it as actually that, a novel. All those conversations with US expatriates and Brit literary men, I can't believe they were verbatim quotes. But that doesn't matter anyway. I add *"Memoirs"* to my gallery of landmark Canadian books, in company with Buckler's *The Mountain and the Valley*, and Laurence's *The Stone Angel*.

Glassco's poems: I liked them but with reservations. Thinking of Housman and Jeffers with whom he has some parallels, Glassco's nostalgia and sadness are more human and less acid than either the Briton or American. He is different in degree of loud thump and hard bang inside his poems. The sorrow of "Corby the Trader" can't be likened to the different sorrow of Housman's "Could Man Be Drunk Forever" or Milton's mourning God in *Paradise Lost*.

In his youth Glassco had been boyishly handsome, the photographs in *"Memoirs"* are testimony to that. The long illness after France deprived him of both appearance and health. I felt a special sadness at his departure, as if more than one man had died. His writing had a uniqueness and special flavour in Canada.

I have another connection with Glassco, one not easily forgotten. In 1972 I was a member of the three-man committee that selected the Governor General's Award winner for poetry. The other two members were Ralph Gustafson and Wilfred Watson, the latter serving as "foreman" of our group. Two other committees made the selections for fiction and non-fiction. And the foreman of each of those three committees went on to be a member of the last three-man (or else male and female) committee, which made the final selection for all three categories of writing. The Canada Council was and is responsible for both the composition of those committees and the methods by which they arrived at their final decisions.

During the previous year there had been two books published which, in our three-man opinion, stood out over the others. These were John Glassco's *Selected Poems* and Irving Layton's *Collected Poems*. Watson placed Glassco first, but Gus and I favoured Layton. Despite the latter's much earlier "selected," *A Red Carpet for the Sun*, this huge collected chunk of Layton contained a great deal of new material. And while I felt Glassco's was a fine book, its excellence was less than that of the individual books from which it had been selected.

All three of us wanted our committee selection to be declared unanimous. Gus and I convinced Watson that Layton should be the winner, despite his rather obvious preference for Glassco. And besides, two out of three constituted a majority. Watson, the foreman, left us to become part of the final three-man committee. (I don't remember the identity of the other two members of this final committee.) During the deliberations of which, Watson reversed himself, and Glassco was chosen as the GG Award winner for poetry.

In the weeks that followed, Glassco wrote me, saying he knew I was responsible for him receiving the award, and thanking me warmly. I was very embarrassed by Glassco's letter, but thought it impossible to tell him his thanks were misplaced. That would have made things worse, or so I thought. And besides, it was not an unworthy award, Glassco had many fine poems in his *Selected*." But my own face remained red for several weeks.

I'm still annoyed over the whole thing: although not for my choice of Layton over Glassco and the latter's subsequent letter. I made my own selection on merit, and still believe it was the best choice. My irritation stems from the way Watson could so easily bypass the original committee which, presumably, was more knowledgeable about poetry than the fiction and non-fiction committees.

At the time I regarded Watson's double-cross to be a simple shirking of his responsibility, which was to vote in the way that had already been decided by the majority. And I'm annoyed by that three-committee method of selection, and the way that final committee could overturn the poetry committee decision. I think an injustice was done to Layton, and it still bothers me.

At this date (1992) selection methods for the GG Award have changed. There is only one decision-making committee for each writing category. Which is the way it should be. And think of John Glassco— the little stammer and hesitations of his speech, the milquetoast moustache, the pessimistic integrity: and these will not be repeated.

My *Piling Blood* appeared in 1984, George Orwell's year. It received good reviews, and I thought it my best book at that time. And trying to keep things in perspective, I still think so.

My wife and I drove west across Canada in the fall of 1986, just before my *Collected Poems* was published, settling into an apartment on Vining Street in Victoria. Eurithe had several brothers and sisters and their progeny in the city. We've been there several times previously, and yet I've always felt a little strange on the west coast. Vegetation there is lush and vivid green; the east is grey-green by comparison, almost a different breed of chlorophyll. The mind clings to its birth area.

Victoria is where aged English ex-colonels sit drinking tea with their girl friends at the Empress Hotel, dreaming of India. They will sit there forever, probably. While living on Vining Street I received a letter from Toronto. It hinted darkly about my leftist-leaning political views, mentioned secret agents and said I was under continual observation, but also absolved me temporarily from any penalty for being me. The letterhead said: "League of Right-Thinking Patriots"—or something like that.

"It's a joke," Eurithe said. "Sure," I said. And we forgot about it.

Then there was another letter, one that said I was being shadowed because of my "well-known" leftist views. "It's a joke," Eurithe said again. But her tone was a little dubious this time, as if repetition was making the letters seem more serious. "Don't you think it's a joke?" she asked me.

In late February of '87 I got a phone call that purported to come from Ontario. A woman's voice said, "Hello, Mr. Purdy. I'm in the office of the Minister for Civic Affairs at Queen's Park in Toronto. Congratulations!"

"Huh?" I said. And my mind flew back instantly to those two letters a few weeks before, which said I was under close observation. "Who's this again?"

The lady mentioned her name and identity, said I was being awarded some decoration or other, and what an honour it was, etc., etc.

"How do I know this isn't a joke?"

The government woman's voice sounded a little miffed and affronted now, as if I had questioned her sexual orientation or credit rating with God.

"I'll have you speak to the deputy minister," she said shortly. After a moment a male voice took over, piling his own congratulations on the heap of redundancy.

"Hold it," I said, and put my wife on the line. "See what you think of this guy. He sounds like a phony to me."

Eurithe talked to the guy, then came back and stared at me. "He said you've won something I've never heard of. Do you suppose the League of Right-Thinking Patriots has an office at Queen's Park?"

"I dunno. What else did he say?"

"They offered to fly us back east May 26th."

"Did you catch the name of the award?"

"The Order of Ontario."

"Never heard of it."

"Neither have I. You think it's the League of Right-Thinking Patriots again?"

"Probably. Or the Left-Turning Dildo."

"Let's pay no attention."

"Right. I mean left."

A couple of phone calls later, our obviously doubting attitudes were beginning to annoy the deputy minister of civic affairs, whatever his name was. I asked for a list of whoever was getting the award, as a means of authenticating it. Margaret Atwood's name wasn't on the list. That did it. The whole things was a phony, a joke, and I was getting annoyed.

"How come Atwood isn't on the list?"

"Because the selection committee didn't select her."

I thought that one over. Not select Atwood? The acme and shining pinnacle of pure Canadian womanhood, the *non pareil* of women's writing, the standard bearer for Canada against Philistines like Norman Mailer? Well!

"How come?" I said.

Anyway it turned out the award was actually legitimate, although I mourned the absence of Peggy Atwood.

· · · · ·

Milton Acorn died that winter. In late March there was a wake for him in Toronto, in which I was a participant. It was held at a little theatre on Ryerson Avenue, with Gwen MacEwen, Milton's brother and sister, Robert Priest, Fred Cogswell and several others. Hosted by one Cedric Smith. Milton's sister said he had been a little adult as a child, only in adulthood did he become a child again.

There was a lot of beer in the theatre basement, which made the time pass until I said my piece before the noisily appreciative audience upstairs. Fred Cogswell said Milton always made him feel uneasy; I said he always made me feel guilty because I wasn't nicer to him (much the same thing meant by Cogswell). I read my "House Guest" poem about Acorn. Cedric Smith read Acorn's "The Natural History of Elephants," and brought Milton back from the dead, right into the theatre with us.

I miss that red fire-hydrant face. I've often parked beside it.

Eurithe and I drove east in May '87, she doing most of the driving on accounta my blood pressure was acting up. In Toronto we discovered I had to wear dress clothes and black shoes for the Order of Ontario ceremony. That was a bit of a stunner, since I've never owned formal clothes. Eurithe supplies nearly all my clothes. We took an inventory of what I was wearing at the time; everything except underwear and socks came from thrift shops. We priced dress suit rentals at a tailor's place, and it cost too much money. Eurithe ruled that out completely. We bought a two-pair-of-pants outfit for two hundred bucks, also a pair of very tight black shoes from a thrift shop on Queen Street, the only pair we could find that were large enough.

At Queen's Park on May 26th, I felt like a clothes horse, and my feet hurt in those old shoes. But I met ex-premier Bill Davis (and got his autograph for my sister-in-law, Judy), asked him why he wasn't running for the federal Liberal Leadership. And I met John Polanyi, a recent Nobel Prize winner in physics (nice guy too); Celia Franca, who founded the National Ballet of Canada in Winnipeg, and I liked her too; Ben Johnson, who said hardly anything at all, a brooding slab of darkness.

Before, during and after the ceremony, Lieutenant-Governor Lincoln Alexander kept grinning, sometimes softening it to a smile. You'd think those ridges and lines of his face would affix themselves there permanently, a smile for the shaving mirror and a grin for the toilet seat.

In the legislative chambers, Bob Rae on the opposition side looked bored, and I swear there was a guy asleep in the back row. I met just about everybody, feeling a bit amazed they'd speak to me. At the top of a steep staircase I helped a teetering ancient black man down the steps, feeling rather noble. In the Queen's Park ballroom somebody standing next to me said, "Do you remember me?"

A middle-aged man, not handsome and not ugly, hair falling out in front like mine, kinda distinguished looking, very quiet voice. "Of course I remember you," I said. "You saved my life."

This was the guy in the lawyer Andrew Brewin's office who'd taken over the job of getting my mother's last will and testament settled in Belleville. I'd been going crazy over that for six years until 1964; it had had a very deleterious effect on my sex life.

"Ian Scott, I love you truly," I said to the Ontario Minister of Justice.

. . . . .

The 1987 Canadian Authors Association Award was presented in Halifax near the end of June. I remember it chiefly from June Callwood's condemning the entire masculine gender for their attitudes toward women. It preyed on our minds, Perry Bauchman and I, sitting quietly inoffensive at our table drinking beer while June raved on. "Perry," I whispered, "women scare me. I'd love to prey on them, but I can't. Did you ever chase them in a Spitfire?" (I'm trying to get Perry to write down his experiences flying Spitfires under bridges in the last war.)

"You're thinking of the Hurricane," Perry said. "That's a much slower aircraft, more suited to chasing human women."

"You mean Spitfires are to chase goddesses with?"

"Shh-hh-hh," someone hissed loudly. I hadn't collected my prize money cheque yet, so we did.

. . . . .

Gwen Hoover at the Canada Council phoned later that spring, informing me that I had won the GG Award for my *Collected Poems*. And on *Morningside*, Peter Gzowski asked me about all those flattering blurbs on the book's dust jacket, such as Atwood saying, "Purdy writes like a cross between Shakespeare and a vaudeville comedian (so did Shakespeare)." I said, "That's another guy she's talking about. I was only on stage but once, playing a drunk in *Mister Roberts*, and nobody mistook him for Shakespeare."

"Huh?" Peter Gzowski said.

Anyway, there was Alice Munro who got the fiction award, and they didn't mistake her for anyone else. Then Madame Governor General Jeanne Sauve gives me this book. It's my *Collected*, and it has a fossilized seal embryo glued to the front cover (which is more tasteful than the stylized antlers with which another bookbinder decorated *The Cariboo Horses*). After which I make obeisance to the GG and talk into a microphone. There's nothing I can think of bad enough to say about Mulroney, at least not in mixed company, so I brood and sigh at that microphone.

It was during the GG Award ceremony when Don Winkler and his

NFB film crew got serious over the epic they were making about me. Talking with friends I'd look up, and there was this electronic doughnut hovering near my tonsils. It was kinda inhibiting. I've been a private person all my life, despite a few platform appearances. I feel like anonymous, everyman most of the time. Sure, I know I'm not really, the way things have gone, but I *feel* that way. I'm me, and when I piss in the backyard at Roblin Lake it's private.

Not that there's any real danger of me becoming more than a village clown in my own ambience of obscurity. However: none of this crap in any way helps me to write, and doesn't mean anything at all in the land beyond next week. As I grow older, bones brittle over 70, rheumatic and arthritic, can't even masturbate any longer, my mind is on a few more poems, as many more as I can manage. Of course, more poems depend on living, living in its fullest sense, whatever that may mean.

. . . . .

When I wasn't writing many poems, I thought again about writing a novel. Maybe a children's novel? When I mentioned this to a lady bookdealer of my acquaintance in Victoria, she as much as scoffed at the idea politely, intimating that it wasn't so easy as it looked. I knew that anyway, having put off writing one for fifty years.

Thoughts of a novel brought on some memories of childhood, the burned and blasted foundations of a dynamite factory where I had played as a six-seven-and-eight year old. These were ruins right out of Grimm's fairy tales, and highly dramatic looking. A cousin, Jack Clegg, had played with me there sometimes. And the river, a green and blue, creosote-rainbowed serpent that flowed into me and around me as a child. The river would be part of it.

But a children's novel? No. I'm not a children's writer in any sense. My hero was me at age 16, but not all aspects of me, his basic character more enterprising, having suffered a river-change. My grandfather, yes, he had to be in there as well. Everyone I knew as a child, as a changeling, as the kid in high school yearning for Jean at the next desk, and giving her poems she probably never read. (Ah, that blonde hair and delicate quivering upper lip . . .) And sure, the dynamite factory, British Chemical, exploding its fireworks all night on Thanksgiving Day, 1918, forcing evacuation of the town of Trenton. And sure, include the Gilmour Lumber Company. All there, everything, right at the time I was being born myself.

I read John Melady's small book about the Trenton disaster, the only one ever written. Also the newspaper reports of that time in Trenton and Belleville libraries. And talked to a few old men who'd experienced the explosions at the British Chemical Company personally. I listened to a few first-hand stories of how people fled the town in absolute terror, piling their treasured possessions in anything with wheels, children's wagons, baby carriages, wheelbarrows, anything. They fled the town in every direction but south, blocked there by the Bay of Quinte. And holding their precious lives in both hands, almost as if they were prehistoric men fleeing a volcano, carrying the seeds of fire in a moss-lined basket to the next camp.

As mentioned earlier, I was present at the Trenton disaster mself, two and a half months before being born—listening and listening inside the nested flesh, the safe harbour of not-being.

But was my condition then really "not-being?" There's an odd sense in which I experienced everything, all the frantic hurrying and terror and courage, the solicitude for others and the very human selfishness. Sure, I heard that young girl singing a hymn and prayer to her unlistening god atop the mountain (as I described in my novel), the liquid sounds hovering over the refugee encampment, and leaving a quivering absence imprinted on the air.

That whole time seems like a single note of music to me, dying only when the last living people who experienced the Trenton disaster are dead themselves.

Every day for two years I sat at the typewriter and worked at my novel, in much the same way as I'm working over these memoirs. Three hours a day, more or less, including Sunday. I laboured at Ameliasburgh, Ontario, and Sidney, BC. I dreamed the people in that novel onto paper, I saw them inside my head and caused their paper birth. I shuttled back and forth between both realities of now and then; and twice visited the grass-grown ruins themselves. The ruins were a silent village lost in time, with present-day factories rising up among the burned remnants. You see the present and you see the past; both are real, but you can live yourself in only one of them.

When the first draft was finished, I asked Dennis Lee what he thought of it. He sent me eight pages of suggestions. Bill Percy, another friend, did the same. Eurithe also read the manuscript, suggested changes and proof-read for mistakes and repetitions. When the novel was accepted at McClelland & Stewart, another year went by before publication. Ellen Seligman, my editor there, worked me harder than anyone else; and I was a somewhat unwilling horse. But it was fun.

1991, another award, in memory of Milton Acorn in Charlottetown, PEI. I have only one really salient memory of the province's tiny capital city. Of a 19th century building on the main drag, a couple of blocks from the harbour. Brick, with a street frontage of fifty or sixty feet only. Surmounting the roof and overlooking the street, a large stone bust looked down. This bust was three or four feet in height, of an elderly man brooding down on his potato city. Not at all like Ozymandias, King of Kings; it was dirty and soot-covered from decades of sitting up there watching pedestrians.

I was curious, went into a stationary store across the street and asked about the stone watcher. The clerk told me; "It's the man who owned the building." He'd been some kind of merchant, of course, and was long dead. The name sounded like Taylor.

It seems to me the only reason a man would have a bust of himself installed atop his own building is that he wanted to be remembered. Which brings to mind Herostratus, in ancient Ionia, who burned down one of the Seven Wonders of the World, the Temple of Diana in Ephesus. Why? He wanted to be remembered, he wanted fame. And I think: who in Charlottetown will be remembered longest, Herostratus, Milton Acorn, Taylor, or the potato? I hope Acorn, but really believe it will be the Great Potato.

Some writers—and I think of Irving Layon especially—yearn to have their work live on into the future. That kind of immortality, which probably amounts to fifty or a hundred years at most, is not attractive to me. I shall not be around then to enjoy such possible fame. Now is my time, today and not tomorrow. I suppose it is theoretically possible to write for all time; but now is when the blood runs quick, the heart beats and your feet touch the earth. And those things are what I want to write about. My name is not Herostratus.

Awards and prizes are fine; I accept all of them with thanks, and I'm pleased to have the money if there is any. They are recognition that some people think you wrote well at one time in your life; I don't think they help you write any better, in some cases perhaps worse. There's the story that the ultimate award, the Nobel Prize, has resulted in some writers failing miserably to write anything worthwhile afterwards.

The things people say about you are often flattering, and generally exaggerated. Prizes and flattery don't have much effect on me, or so I think. In fact, sometimes a flowery opinion of your own work can be embarrassing, since it doesn't match the poems or correspond to how you feel about them yourself. And how *do* I feel about them?

Apart from that instant of communication between two people, generally male and female, in which vistas and landscapes are opened up and limitless—there is simply nothing at all like writing what you believe to be a good poem. It is an incandescence in your head, coruscation in your guts. Writing a good one is a twenty-four-hour high, and reading it again much later produces a strong echo of that original elation. The memory of that feeling does not fade.

. . . . .

They held an "Al Purdy Day" in Trenton, my hometown, on November 12th, 1990. My novel, *A Splinter in the Heart*, was set in Trenton, and McClelland & Stewart's publicist suggested this idea to the Trenton mayor and council.

There was a reception at the city library, a short reading by me, beer and sandwiches afterwards. I was presented with a key to the city and a placard that informed the cops I had free parking there to the end of my mortal days. During my reading I told the forty or fifty people present that I'd never read in my hometown before. But John Melady (who was present in the audience) had been teaching at Trenton High School some fifteen years before. He'd arranged a Purdy reading at the time. Then a member of the school board phoned Melady and asked if he'd arranged a Purdy reading. John said yes, he had. At which the school board member said, "How do you like your job?" Meaningfully. And that was that, no reading.

I asked Melady's permission before I told this story, which evoked some amusement in the audience. Apparently the reason I've never read in my hometown before 1990 was the general impression that I use four-letter words habitually. Now this is gross calumny and criminal libel, not to mention it's a fuckin lie.

Kerrigan Almey (the Trenton publisher of my *Quest for Ouzo*) later told me a gripping true story about that free parking ticket for life. He said the mayor of Trenton had originally instructed that the free parking should be for one year only. But Kerrigan, when he printed the parking placard, made it without limit. Then he grabbed a bag of nickels, rushed into the mayor's office and splashed them down on hizzoner's desk: "How long you think Purdy's gonna live anyway? Here, you cheap bastard, this oughta pay for Purdy's parking until he dies." Then he rushed back to his printing press.

I can't say much about Kerrigan's feelings at that point, but I do say thank you. And I am overwhelmed with burning curiosity: How many nickels did he give the Trenton mayor?

. . . . .

I read reviews to find out what's wrong with my writing; I read them for flattery and for truth, two opposite things. I regard myself as an odd kind of mainstream poet, and much closer to the style of mainstream American writers than British. And "mainstream" may be regarded here, in my case, as eccentric-conventional. I write to be understood, which means principally to be understood by myself. Paradoxically, while I write more like Canadian and US poets in style and diction, I like the slightly older British poets much better than the American ones.

A reviewer will sometimes say something that sticks in my mind. I remember well one Cary Fagan's remarks about *The Woman on the Shore* in the *Toronto Star*, that my poems "meander pointlessly and sound a bit too self-aggrandizing." But what puzzles me most is this passage: "Whether or not the reader likes these poems will partly depend on his or her reaction to Purdy's decidedly masculine voice."

I think he wants me to have a sex-change operation and make a gift of both testicles to Fagan. He needs them more than me.

One of the nicest publishers I've met, Marty Gervais, also doubles as book editor for the *Windsor Star*. In fact the nice people (although I hate the word "nice") far outnumber the pricks. Ken Adachi, who died a couple years ago after a kerfuffle about plagiarism, was one of the best and most lyrical of our book reviewers in the *TorStar*. Ken actually *loved* books; I felt badly about his death. Publisher Jack McClelland: someone I was always wary of, searching the nuances of his voice and facial movements for clues to what he thought about me. Perhaps he felt exactly the same. And both of us approached the other wearing full suits of psychic and businessman armour. And those cold, cold eyes . . .

This next one gets a bit difficult. I met Mordecai Richler a few years ago in the pub of the Ritz Carlton Hotel in Montreal. I think we liked each other, although one can never be sure about such things. Later Richler wrote a denigrating letter about George Woodcock that appeared in *Saturday Night* magazine. Now Woodcock is a friend of mine; I felt I had to defend him, despite liking Richler. I wrote my own letter for *Saturday Night*, denigrating Richler, which had the effect of shutting off any subsequent relations. In such instances, there's no way out: you're wrong no matter what you do. But I've always felt like apologizing to Richler privately. Here I do so semi-privately.

There will always be climbers who want to take shortcuts, people who hang onto your coat-tails because they think you're good and the condition will be magically transposed to them. They believe you can help them get published and become Atwood-famous. No names, but in any walk of life the climbers are identifiable (as apart from those who genuinely deserve help). And there will always be bureaucrats, who think the best way to get attention is to be president or secretary of a writer's union. As well, there are the writer-do-gooders who actually do good. But they must sometimes be a little uneasy about themselves.

Even in the small world of Canadian writing there are men and women of character and goodness, (among whom I do not number myself). Sure, George Woodcock. Alice Munro (why not). The worthy citizens like Fred Cogswell, without much talent. And the incorruptible ones: George Whalley, much too hidebound by what he thought he was; Bronwen Wallace, the recently dead lady from Kingston, whose integrity I discovered when judging at the CBC competition a couple of years ago; Dennis Lee, for whom gratefulness may distort my judgment; Ray Souster (I just wish he'd unearth some words of more than two syllables); dead Gabrielle Roy, sadly vanished Rod Haig-Brown; Sam Solecki, Casanova in a sport shirt; and mad one-track Milton Acorn. All my friends . . .

And more of them. Bob Weaver at the CBC, who said when I needed money: "Send me some new poems and I'll send you some money. In fact, I'll send the money before you send the poems." And we both did. However, those lunches with Bob at the Four Seasons across Jarvis Street (martinis with beer chasers) almost did for me.

Those sudden inexplicable affections you occasionally have for someone just met. Marc Pinchevsky, a translator of English to Russian in the Soviet Union, whose capacity for brandy much exceeds mine: may his booze glass always be full, and those silk stocking we gave his wife never wear out. Imantz Ziedonis of Riga, Latvia: how shall we remember what was never words and has no handle?

. . . . .

I should talk about writing, writers who influenced me, stuff like that. And dammit, I will, if it doesn't kill them or me. It's just that writers write, and critics talk. It goes rather like this: in the beginning was the word, after that came explanation and imitation. My reason for writing at an early age (thirteen) were (a) ego (ain't I wonderful maw?), and (b) fascination with words and their manipulation. Not a thought in my head about Truth or Beauty or immortal poesy.

A man named Padraig O'Broin said something about this in an early review of my stuff in the late fifties (probably then). O'Broin was a middle-sized, middle-aged balding Irishman who must've gotten romantic about words and poetry at an early age. He came to Canada late and died early, though not before he published a small magazine called *Teen Jedoir*, whose name I have undoubtedly misspelled. I was impressed by O'Broin and his love of "The Muse." He said things about me that had not been said before, which I hadn't thought of myself. And died shortly after. I suppose he will not be remembered, except in such transitory paragraphs as this one.

O'Broin made me more self-conscious about myself, about Carman, Chesterton, Stevenson, Gogarty—whose work I was imitating, as I earlier imitated Thomas in Vancouver. But I thought it ridiculous and pretentious to dismiss such feelings completely. In it boldest terms, the Muse is that idea of excellence we all must have somewhere in our minds, whether the excellence be of the craftsman making furniture or the pick and shovel labourer digging a grave. One must do whatever it is well. If not, the gift of life is boring and wasted.

But excellence is not just stringing words together, making sounds chime with other sounds; nor is it rhyme or euphony or alliteration, although it may include all of those things. But to say a thing in such a way that it goes bang in the mind when you're asleep or awake; and may replace truth or actually become truth, for I believe poetry is anything you believe it is, the word that slanders death.

It's very easy to say all of the above is crap. Of course it is. But also my kind of truth, which is proximate only, and each of us ought to have a different Muse. Hosts of these idealized figures of the Muse swarming around poets like locusts . . .

So I memorized and memorized at school, much of it lost in the mind's overflow. I immersed myself in Carman, Carman, Carman. And Byron:

> So we'll go no more a-roving
> So late into the night
> Though the heart be still as loving
> And the moon be still as bright.

And Browning, although I can't remember the last lines of "Home Thoughts" any longer. And Tennyson:

> And I dipped into the future
> As far as the human eye could see
> Saw a vision of the world
> And all the wonder that would be.

And good ol Anonymous:

> From the hag and hungry goblin
> That into rags would rend ye
> And the spirit that stands by the naked man
> In the book of moons defend ye
> That of your five sound senses
> Ye never be forsaken
> Nor wander from yourselves with Tom
> Abroad to beg you bacon.

(I am not, incidentally, consulting the book version of these poems
to ensure accuracy.)

And Chesterton, whom I love dearly still:

> Before the Roman came to Rye or down to Severn strode
> The rolling English drunkard made the rolling English road . . .

Who could resist Chesterton, as Hilaire Belloc said about him, and
said for himself: "Do you remember an inn, Miranda / Do you remember an inn?" (What a mystical phrase!) And Gogarty, who was Joyce's
and Yeats' friend, and gifted the Liffey River with five swans after it
saved him from a gunman's bullets:

> I will live in Ringsend
> With a red-headed whore
> And the fanlight gone in
> Where it lights the hall door
> And listen each night
> For her querulous shout
> As at last she steals in
> And the pubs empty out.

Remember, remember. And leave all the mistakes of quotation
where they belong, uncorrected: and the lines glow like fireflies in the
memory.

All those dead poets I mention belong back in schooldays, those and
many more. It's not that I had a really great memory: it was just part of
the school curriculum to memorize in those years. Between sex frus-
tration and poetry and playing football, I was bemused and not-much-
with-it a lot of the time. I snapped out of that lost soul condition in the

air force during the war years; and found new prosodic mentors in Vancouver in 1950. Dylan Thomas, of course, was the foremost of these.

I learned much from Layton in Montreal during my stint there in 1956 and later. And then I think I was overwhelmed by my own discoveries of new writers. It was wonderful to roll and tumble in the loose and magnificent rhythms of Yeats, the stern and sometimes puzzling disciplines of Auden, and most of all to be fascinated and enthralled by Lawrence. I don't say Lawrence is the best of those three, but he's the writer I learned most from, and whose own life was equally fascinating to me.

What did I learn from Lawrence? To let your mind go, allow it to move in any and all directions, where there are no road signs nor indications of altitude and planetary stop lights. It's like free fall in spaceships, no gravity there. Forget what you've learned of language and grammar and "creative writing." Other people too, they're no help at all. And judging other writers yourself, no matter what their reputations. Lawrence said he tried to write "poetry of the present," and I interpret that for my own uses. I think there is some sense in which the present is eternal.

Reasons for writing at all: to make a discovery, of yourself and something outside yourself. Something that will stand up, that means something—even as it disappears in a flash of evanescence (sic). Doors opening in your mind, other doors closing, beyond all distances and barriers on the edge of things.

Of course the end is death, which is defeat. Well—I think of a popular folksinger's song-poem lines:

> From the rockin of the cradle
> To the rollin of the hearse
> The goin up is worth the comin down—

Since the folksinger, a young man, had not then experienced the "comin down" and I'm just beginning to, I don't know if the sentiment he expressed is true or not. I suspect not. But the voyage of discovery and baffled non-discovery has been fascinating. The questions I can't answer, that no one can really answer, the space and time questions, and others about causality and deity—those annoy the hell out of me because I think they're unanswerable. And my own mental powers are annoying to me, since they're so limited and futile.

What comforts me: I have an almost unlimited capacity for boredom. If I didn't sometimes disguise this condition and habitual feeling in the everyday transactions of life, some people would look on me with extreme distaste (a few do anyway). Somebody once said that what we want out of life is "continual slight novelty"? Actually no, I think most people want to be carried away, outside themselves, by something larger than they are. Another aspect of human discontent is: people are rarely able to affect or influence the large things, governments and the like. And they'd like to. But as Auden said in a slightly different context, "poetry makes nothing happen."

My views on Canadian poets are fairly conventional. Klein, Atwood, Birney, Acorn, and Layton are best in my opinion, but not necessarily in that sequence. However, we have several others who could rank highly. And I'm tempted to place Leonard Cohen among the above-named to make a sextet. His first two books are "young man's poems," although he was a very singular young man. That would make the best of CanPo 50% Jewish.

I'm sorry to offend the traditionalists by not including at least one of the early people, like Lampman, or a romantic extract from the army of triple-named women. I find the early poets boring, despite an adolescent attraction to Carman. Only two 19th century Can. poems am I able to admire wholeheartedly. One, "The Ahkoond of Swat," by George Lanigan, was written in the US; the author was a Canadian, which might tell us something. The other by that great poet, Anonymous, entitled "Cholera." I have to quote its second verse, because I know my own critics are liable to shout, "Aha! He wrote it himself!" About cholera:

> We shut him out with a girdle of ships,
> And a guarded quarantine;
> What ho! Now which of your watches slept?
> The Cholera's past your line!

However, despite my strictures, I think CanPo stands up well in a world context. There are no *great* poets in this era, but many who are excellent. Despite abiding pessimism, I think Housman and Jeffers came close with their large vision just slightly before our time. But no one stands out now, however they might seem to for a moment or a day. And it's a world that has, in any but very narrow terms, abandoned poetry in favour of popular songs and prose that sounds "poetic."

The consensus of world opinion has always been fascinated by power, often attributing to that power other qualities that disguise the brute face of force. And there's the historian's tag line that history is written by the winners. The winner writes many things besides history. Literature, for instance. It is not invariable that the big world powers with large populations have most of the world's great writers, or that they dictate a few in other countries whom they prefer in that role. Such selections are probably made without conscious volition. But the USA, for instance, has a huge concentration of the world's media and information apparatus to make its least whim exceedingly powerful.

If Margaret Atwood or Robertson Davies, for instance, were to be selected by the requisite agencies and media outlets in the US for, say, the Swedish Nobel prize, for whatever reasons besides sheer merit, I think Atwood and Davies would have an excellent chance at the prize. It's easy to cite various writers in small countries to refute this idea, Neruda in Chile, the Aussie novelist Patrick White, or even William Golding in the lesser present-day England.

T.S. Eliot received the Nobel more for his "influence" on literature than the actual merit of his own work. On the basis of translation only, it's hard for me to believe that Neruda deserved this accolade. The Russian poet and novelist (Pasternak and Solzhenitsyn) who took the prize, did so mostly because the judges were anti-Communist. Only Yeats, whose work could not be refuted on any grounds whatever, was full value as best in the world.

· · · · · ·

Well, writing? My own writing is like myself. I am both brainless and also shatteringly intelligent, as well as somewhere in-between like most people. (And that foregoing sentence sounds exactly like the most refined and expensive bullshit!) I mistrust almost entirely "methods" and "schools" of writing—those who act like "I am the truth and the light," the critic who knows best. Writing is instinct and intuition, and a modicum of intelligence. Of course craftsman-ship rescues brains, and brains sometimes retrieve craft from mean-ingless structures of form.

If human beings ever know fully all their own meanings and motives and hidden-to-themselves feelings, it would be a sad day. That would kill impulse, inspiration and sudden generosity. I am personally much too self-conscious about all my actions to want an increase in the self-awareness. And writing to me is still a happy discovery of word and thought that sends me back to being a simple child finding a new toy. Or a man far in the future, delighted to discover he is able to be in love forever.

. . . . .

My home town is Canada, but Vancouver Island is one of the suburbs. I live there now. The landscape is green and lush. The climate is generally mild, and the bugs are not nearly as pervasive as in Ontario. Easterners move there by the plane-load. And the mountains soar and lift into the sky as if earth were aspiring to heaven. The lushness makes me slightly uncomfortable. I hate to completely abandon the areas where I grew up, and began to realize how awful and wonderful life can be. I am a stranger in the west, to some extent. But then, I will probably always be a stranger wherever I am.

My own life in some essential way has been writing poems. And the only thing that equals writing what you think is a good poem, is to write another just as good. It is like coming home after long absence, and knowing trees and water and land are yours, are your land; or waking with the woman you have known all your life and knowing she is your life; to feel the boundaries of yourself widen and expand in the sober drunkenness of your brain, to feel words and thought coalesce in the imagined reality of the thing itself . . .

You may take all the other arts from painting to musical composition; you may be an athlete breaking records, heart bursting with joy in yourself; researcher finding the formulas to cure cancer and bridge space.. You may but I don't. One more poem, that's what I say; or two if the gods are generous. Look in the mirror and say there ain't much more time. Look in the mirror and say:

> An aged man is but a paltry thing,
> A tattered coat upon a stick, unless
> Soul clap its hands and sing, and louder sing
> For every tatter in its mortal dress . . .

Yes, I'll take that.

I was altered in the placenta
by the dead brother before me
who built a place in the womb
knowing I was coming:
he wrote words on the walls of flesh
painting a woman inside a woman
whispering a faint lullaby
that sings in my blind heart still

The others were lumberjacks
backwoods wrestlers and farmers
their women were meek and mild
nothing of them survives
but an image inside an image
of a cookstove and the kettle boiling
—how else explain myself to myself
where does the song come from?

Now on my wanderings:
at the Alhambra's lyric dazzle
where the Moors built stone poems
a wan white face peering out
—and the shadow in Plato's cave
remembers the small dead one
—at Samarkand in pale blue light
the words came slowly from him
—I recall the music of blood
on the Street of the Silversmiths

Sleep softly spirit of earth
as the days and nights join hands
when everything becomes one thing
wait softly brother
but do not expect it to happen
that great whoop announcing resurrection
expect only a small whisper
of birds nesting and green things growing
and a brief saying of them
and know where the words came from

—*The Dead Poet* (1981)

Index